# BEYOND THE TAIGA
## Memoirs of the Survivor

*I dedicate this book
to the memory of my wife*

*The author with Yanek*
*at Saddlecombe 1995*

K. COLONNA-CZOSNOWSKI

# BEYOND THE TAIGA
## Memoirs of a Survivor

CALDRA HOUSE 1998

ISBN 1 872286 28 3

Printed by Caldra House Limited,
23 Coleridge Street, Hove, Sussex BN3 5AB England

# CONTENTS

# ACKNOWLEDGEMENT

I am deeply indebted to my counsin Felix Wentworth for his generous help in editing, producing and promoting this book and to his son Marc for sharing with me some of his impressive knowledge of computers.

I am grateful to Mrs Hanna Kępińska for her encouragement and advice.

My heartfelt thanks are due to Lt. Col. Władysław Sypel for supplying me with facts, dates and names from Regimental records and for sending me photographic material.

Thanks are also due to Mrs. Madeleine Maxwell-Arnot and to Mrs. Irma Stypułkowska for their valuable suggestions in connection with the choice of a publisher.

I am obliged to Miss Christine Somkowicz for her constructive observations.

Finally, I would like to acknowledge the help given me by my secretary, Mrs. Lesley Mead, who has sacrificed many hours of her own free time in the preperation of this work.

Saddlecombe Stud,                                                    K.C.C.
Headley, Surrey                                                   May 1998

# Chapter 1

# 'CUIR DE RUSSIE'

"ATTENTION, Attention – Approaching!!" – To Poles of my generation these words have a special meaning. Every one of us who remembers the early days of the war will recall this warning. It brings back memories of gloom, a feeling of foreboding, a fear of impending disaster. For me it is inevitably linked with that catastrophic chapter of our history. Frequently, in the course of the so-called September Campaign the Polish National Radio transmissions would be interrupted and a sombre, harsh, unfamiliar voice would utter this ambiguous threat. We didn't know what it meant. We guessed that it was some kind of air-raid alert, but for whom? No-one knew for certain. We all longed for news of the war, for guidance, for orders. We heard rumours that our armies were retreating, but we didn't know why. We suspected treachery, feared spies everywhere, and searched desperately for hard, reliable information. Instead, all we heard through the headphones of our primitive "crystal' radio sets was just: "Attention, attention, approaching..."

I was 18 when World War II broke out. Having just completed my middle school, I was spending my summer holidays on my family's country estate in Eastern Poland.

The Germans invaded Poland on 1st September 1939. By the middle of the month they controlled more than half the country. Their brand-new strategy, known as *Blitzkrieg* (or lightning war), never in that form tried before, was being used against us to great effect. This method, which only a few months later was to bring France, the greatest military power in Europe, to its knees, was being tested out on us. No amount of bravery or determination could stop the German advance. Horses against tanks proved a one-sided affair.

Then, on 17th September, at the height of the crisis, while the Poles were desperately trying to re-group in the East, the Soviet Union made its own move. We didn't know at the time that in a secret addendum to the recently concluded Ribbentrop-Molotov treaty it had all been spelled out in detail, and plans for yet another partition of Poland had been mapped out. We had never trusted the Soviets. Russia, to us, had always been a danger but we were not expecting this. We did, after all, have a valid non-aggression treaty with them. What was more, the Soviets moved into Poland without any official explanation; they even spread rumours that they were coming to help us fight the Germans. It wasn't long before their true purpose became clear: they were helping themselves to the Eastern provinces and leaving the Western ones to the Germans. The massive Soviet war machine was on the move. Endless columns of infantry, tanks and artillery started pouring across the border, day and night.

My parents' land lay right on the Soviet border. In fact a substantial part of the family's estate had been lost to the Soviet Union after the First World War. Ever since 1920 we had had just one Eastern neighbour: the USSR. The boundary dividing us from them was less than a mile away, and yet it was more than a week before we saw any Soviet soldiers. We smelled them much earlier, though. The unmistakable 'Red Army Smell' filled the air, aggravated by the warm weather. Poorly tanned leather is credited with producing this unique aroma.

There is nothing quite like it. I was told that the Russian Imperial army smelled just as strongly. Some humorist even suggested that this explained their singular lack of success in the First War, as it severely reduced the element of surprise.

My father was absent from our country home when the Soviet advance began. My mother, my sister and I were the only ones present. We tried to carry on as best we could. Soon the difficulties started piling up. Servants and farm workers started disappearing by the minute, taking horses and cattle with them. Most were local Ruthenian peasants, so they just vanished into the countryside without trace. The Polish staff remained, of course, faithful as always, but they were all women, their sons and husbands having been called up months before. It felt very strange. The Soviet border, so fiercely guarded by both our troops and the Russians for as long as I could remember, was no longer there. This formidable barrier, dividing us from the Soviet Empire, had gone overnight. Between us and, say, Vladivostok there were no frontiers...The cold draught from the dreaded East was creeping up on us. The sound of tanks in the distance, the drone of heavy bombers overhead and... the smell surrounded us all the time. The Russians were everywhere, but we were yet to meet them.

One warm moonless night I was returning on horseback rather late from a neighbouring farm. A mile or so from home I heard strange noises from the direction of the home farm. Immediately my pulse started racing: I knew at once that the Russians had arrived. The lights, the noise and the smell confirmed this beyond doubt.

I could not say I was surprised. After all we had been expecting them for more than a week. Yet somehow one had always hoped that the unavoidable could be avoided. Now I knew the time had come and, I hated to admit it, I was scared. Unquestionably, in our eyes, the Bolsheviks, as we called them, were the most barbaric force in Europe. Only 19 years previously they had invaded Poland, burning, killing and looting everything in sight. Although the 1920 war, when all this had happened, was just before my time, I was fully aware of their methods. Landowners and their families were fair game to them. "Put them up against the wall, Vanya" were the last words many of my compatriots heard before dying. 'Is history about to repeat itself? Am I going to end up with a bullet in my head? Will it be tonight? Is my fate already sealed, or am I allowed to influence it somehow? But how?' These and similar questions were racing through my head.

I longed to be brave, not stupid. To turn back now, which would it be? I envied the soldiers; they were told what to do. I felt green, confused, useless. Throughout my childhood I had heard many accounts of bold, clever escapes from near-certain death. I admired those heroes who unfailingly knew what to do and lived to tell the story. They always seemed to outsmart the Bolsheviks. I longed to be like them but didn't know how to do it...

While this conflict was raging in my brain my horse continued to walk boldly towards home, in total ignorance of my dilemma. He was going back to his stable, his hay net, his evening feed. The same danger was awaiting him too but he didn't know it. What bliss, I thought, not to know, not to have to choose.

In the end I did nothing. I let fate take over, after all it was stronger that me.

A shrill "Stoy" stopped us dead some distance from the gate. I heard the metallic click of the rifle. 'This is it' – I froze and shut my eyes waiting for the shot. Silence. I drew some air into my lungs and yelled with all my might.

Instead of the intended roar I produced a miserable squeal. I tried again.

This time it sounded better. "To moy dom" – (or this is my home). I knew that these words sounded almost the same in Russian as in Polish. The guard shouted back something, but his voice sounded less frantic. Presently a second man with a torch joined him and they signalled me to advance. I was instructed to dismount and raise my hands right up. Two more men appeared and a thorough body search followed. Its extent was incredible: they stripped me naked and examined every part of my body and every bit of clothing. They repeated the procedure twice, for good measure. I was left wondering who was more afraid of whom.

When I was allowed to put my clothes back on, a man in a leather jacket appeared. From his behaviour and that of the others I concluded that he was more important than the rest. He listened briefly to their report and then asked me to follow him in the direction of the house. We were stopped repeatedly by other sentries before we reached the front door. The Soviet smell was overwhelming here.

The house was swarming with soldiers. Leather Jacket knocked at the dining room door and then pushed me in. I hardly recognised the place. The room was packed and the air thick with smoke. A dozen men sat round the table and some more in every conceivable corner. It was really hot in there and yet they all had their hats on. A huge samovar was adding steam to the already oppressive atmosphere and tea glasses were everywhere. A short dark man with a pale face and Semitic features invited me to sit down. A chair was vacated for me. In a low voice he asked me if I spoke Russian. I said I did not. Did I speak Ukrainian, he enquired. I said I did.

"Are you the owner of this place?" he asked, having observed me for a while. I said my father was. He then asked me for the whereabouts of my father. He also wanted to know the reason for my coming home so late. His questions were straightforward, and so were my replies. I felt that he was not trying to trip me up. He seemed to accept my explanations and when he had finished he asked the others if they wanted to question me. Nobody did. My interviewer relaxed somewhat, pushed his hat back slightly and took a sip of tea. "Nice place you've got here, eh?" he said looking round. I agreed with him reluctantly, still worried that he would try to catch me out. This produced a roar of laughter from most of those present. The men started to crowd round me in almost friendly curiosity.

The pale man was getting into his act. My problem was that I was not sure if he was pulling my leg or was being serious. To be on the safe side, I assumed the latter.

"Where have you hidden your throne? he said suddenly, when the laughter subsided. I couldn't think what he meant, so I asked him to repeat the question. "Don't tell me you don't know what I mean, the t h r o n e..." he repeated very slowly, "the chair on which your father sits while your poor peasants are given their weekly thrashing". I looked at the others for a clue, but found no help there. I must have appeared genuinely puzzled, so he decided to re-phrase it all: "You said you were the son of the owner of this estate?" "Yes" I admitted. "And you want me to believe that you have never seen your peasants being beaten by your father's servants?" He looked round his audience for approval. Their eager nodding confirmed that they were with him. This could be a trap, I thought, I must deal with it decisively, or it could lead to disaster. I assured him, most categorically, that nothing like that had ever taken place either here, or anywhere else. "Do you live here with your parents?" he asked. I said I spent most of the year at school, but came here for my holidays. "So for the best part of the year you are not here. How can you vouch for what happens here when you are elsewhere?" He looked round his audience again. I repeated my previous assurances, with renewed emphasis. He said nothing and just sat there smiling.

It wasn't until years later that I came across a Soviet children's book, featuring a sadistic villain called Polski Pan, meaning Polish Lord. Polski Pan amused himself by watching his servants beating his serfs while he sat on a throne. I have a strong suspicion that 'pale face' was sharing an 'in-joke' with his comrades at my expense.

This kind of questioning continued for some time. He seemed to be playing an odd sort of game, blowing hot and cold, keeping me worried only to turn it into a joke later. For my part, I was trying not to get too confused and not to allow myself to be fooled. At intervals he delivered funny little sermons on the superiority of the Soviet system, almost tongue in cheek. He looked stern at times, and at other times friendly. At one point he even offered me a cigarette. He himself smoked a most remarkable cigar-like object that he rolled himself, by putting chopped tobacco stems into a piece of ordinary newspaper. It produced the most revolting smell, but he assured me it was more satisfying than a normal cigarette. His colleagues obviously shared his taste as they all smoked similar 'cigars'.

Mercifully my inquisitor then changed the subject. "You probably want to know where your mother and sister are," he said. "Don't worry, they are all right, you will see them when we finish with you presently". Then, in a louder voice, as if he were addressing a meeting he added, "In the Soviet Union everyone is given a chance to correct his misdeeds, even landowners like your family. Unlike the capitalists, we don't kill people without trial!"

I didn't mind his sermon: the main thing was that Mama and Krystyna were all right!

After some time they let me go. The only condition he made was that I must not leave the house.

As I was dashing upstairs to find my mother and sister I felt that, on the whole, things had gone rather well. I was generally pleased with myself.

In my stupidity I did not realise that it had nothing to do with what I had said during the interview. A single 'denunciation' or even a few uncorroborated complaints from any of the neighbouring villages, or even from someone with a grudge, would have been enough to result in our immediate execution. Only a few weeks later I learnt of several such cases.

Once at the top of the stairs I turned to my mother's bedroom. I knocked.

Silence. I opened the door and went in quietly. The room was pitch dark: the curtains were drawn. I called to my mother softly but received no response. I started to feel my way to the bedside table to find some matches. I heard some movement on the bed. "Mother," I said, "I'm back". "My God!!! Who is it?" a strange woman's voice cried in Russian. The woman jumped out of bed and ran to the far end of the room. "Grisha! Grisha!!! Help!!!" she screamed, while I was edging my way back to the door in darkness, muttering apologies in Polish. Then I heard someone running up the stairs. The door crashed open and an officer with a torch rushed into the room. He pointed the beam of his torch at me and then at the woman and... burst out laughing.

The light revealed the figure in the corner. The woman wore only a very short man's shirt, which covered her only down to the waist, leaving the rest in full view. The officer still roaring with laughter gave her a lusty smack on the buttocks and said: "Go to bed, silly thing. He thinks you are his mother" and unceremoniously pushed her towards the bed. He then turned to me and explained politely that my mother and sister had been moved elsewhere and that I should find them in the servants' quarters.

He was right. Soon afterwards I did find them in another room. They were well and very happy to see me.

Next day the Russians left. The smell remained, though. That unforgettable smell of badly tanned leather.

Years later I learned that after the First World War a well-known Parisian perfumer created a fragrance called 'Cuir de Russie' (Russian Leather).

It was based on that revolting Russian smell and was reportedly a commercial success. I am glad I didn't know anyone who used it. I don't think I would have liked it.

Incidentally, I never found anybody who knew for certain the real significance of the words: 'Attention, Attention, Approaching'...

# Chapter 2

# LYING LOW

We managed, somehow, to remain in Obory, our country home, until the beginning of November 1939, when the local Communist Committee decided that enough was enough. For several weeks prior to this, increasing pressure was being exerted on us. Frequent house searches, conducted in the middle of the night, were one of their favourite ways. My mother, who had a wonderful way with peasants, was at first highly amused by these futile exercises and regarded them as nothing more than a little harmless fun. The more respectable villagers started to come to her, though, advising strongly that we should leave. The trust between village and manor was still strong. It was something that had existed for generations and my mother respected the views of the village elders. They warned her that the Committee planned to alert Soviet Army Intelligence of our continued presence. Should that happen, of course, we would be doomed. The situation was far too serious. We had already extended our stay much longer than was prudent and to extend it any further would be suicidal. We had no choice.

One evening, in great secrecy, I dug a hole in the orchard, close to an old pear-tree. I worked flat out so as to finish before the inevitable nightly visit from the Committee. We wrapped selected objects individually in paper, packed them into wooden boxes and stowed these neatly in the hole. I wouldn't be surprised if our hidden treasure were still there today.

The following morning we departed. Our transport was provided by a trusted peasant (a smallholding owner) who agreed to take us to the county town, called Krzemieniec. We took with us very little. We had at our disposal only one small vehicle, drawn by one horse. The roads were dangerous at that time and a number of attacks were known to have occurred in our region on those who were too ambitious. The idea was to lie low, and await developments.

The choice of the county town as our place of refuge could be regarded, on the face of it, as rather bizarre. If our object were to disappear from view, so to speak, it would not seem the best place to achieve it in. There were only few landed families in our county, so for us, in Krzemieniec, anonymity was almost unthinkable. My mother was an optimist by nature and most of her decisions reflected her optimistic disposition. She was seldom wrong, though. Arrived at by processes that had little to do with cool logic, or even basic prudence, in the long run, most of her decisions proved not only right but lucky too. This time was no exception. By sheer fluke the choice of our place of exile could not have been better. As it turned out Krzemieniec was the only place in the whole of eastern Poland where the KGB (or more accurately the NKVD at that time), left all landed families relatively unharmed.

Why the landed families were left alone, I was never able to discover. Otherwise nobody else was spared. All lawyers, doctors, policemen, civil servants, government officials and such like were, eventually, rounded up and arrested, deported or even shot. My mother told me, after the war, that, according to one theory, the NKVD chief responsible for our district was himself of noble ancestry and had a soft spot for members of his old class. This unnamed official, allegedly, argued with his superiors that landowners were so completely insignificant as to make them harmless and not even worth arresting or deporting. This explanation of course, whilst possible, seemed to me most improbable. We all remembered that Felix Dzierzynski, the dreaded chief of Cheka, the forerunner of the NKVD, was himself a Polish nobleman. This, however, did not inhibit him from torturing and executing anybody, least of all the members of his own class. Whatever the explanation, the fact remained that ours was the only county, under Soviet occupation, which, to my knowledge, did not imprison or deport all its nobility, as a matter of normal routine.

All this, however, was something that we could not know in November 1939. As we set out, with Olexa, from Obory early one morning, on the 40-kilometre trip, in his one-horse wagon, we did not feel that, for us, it was a particularly historic moment, nor that after nearly 300 years of uninterrupted presence in that land, our family was out for good. Historic moments, I fear, do tend to be overlooked on such occasions, as one is usually far too preoccupied with more mundane, practical considerations.

Our lodgings in Krzemieniec were by no means palatial. We had at our disposal two rooms and a tiny space, which was, grandly, called the kitchen. My mother and sister were to share the bigger room and I took the smaller one. Our rooms were on the ground floor, while the owners, an elderly couple, moved to the first floor. There was no bathroom of any kind, so we had to use the kitchen for our ablutions and go outdoors for anything else. The immediate problem was the cold. Despite all our efforts, we failed to light any fires. Both the kitchen range and the stove obstinately refused to oblige. We spent the best part of the night trying various ways to make them work, but to no avail. In the end we gave up, exhausted. We put on all our warmest clothes and went to sleep, shivering in the damp and cold. Even this did not seem to upset Mamma. She told us that the best way was to try and imagine that we were on some sort of expedition or safari, and that it was all part of some fascinating adventure.

Joking and laughing, we went to sleep and, surprisingly, slept relatively well.

The following day, early, I went in search of some dry wood for our fires.

It took me a long time. At last I was directed to a nice little villa, belonging to a local notary. There I found two young fellows cutting logs who, someone suggested, might help me. This is how I met Dolek and Stach. Not only were they able to sell me some excellent dry logs, but also on hearing of our heating problems, offered to come over and give us a crash course in lighting fires. I learned that they were the sons of a local doctor. Dolek was 27 and Stach 23. They, too, were trying to keep a low profile. I was told that they had developed a lucrative business supplying logs, mostly to their parents' professional friends. As a result of this meeting, not only did I learn how a stove worked but I also made some nice new friends

It is amazing what a little warmth can do. It transformed our dungeon into a perfectly habitable place and our morale rose accordingly. Now that we had a good fire going in the kitchen, we felt we could attempt to cook something hot to eat. We were forgetting, however, that between the three of us not one had the foggiest idea of how it was done. After prolonged deliberations we decided to attempt an omelette. Even this, when ready, did not taste right. Fortunately, we knew how to make tea and that was excellent. During the weeks that followed my mother made valiant attempts to vary our diet and tried to cook other dishes, but in the end we consumed more omelettes than we had in all the preceding years put together. It seems incredible, today, that we were so utterly helpless in looking after ourselves. Even the simplest thing seemed a problem. My mother was not worried. She maintained her charming, light-hearted, attitude and did not allow the little things to influence her natural optimism. Humour was her answer in dealing with the petty discomforts. At her instigation we played games. We invented elaborate French names for very ordinary, rather tasteless, dishes and served them with great pomp, in a very formal manner. I usually impersonated a very dignified butler and my sister, Krystyna, took the role of a footman. Our culinary deficiencies were sometimes redressed by Tania, the daughter of Olexa, the smallholder. She was a charming peasant girl. When she came she cooked for us the most delicious country meals, which we all enjoyed immensely. After each of her visits we had sufficient food to last us for days. All we had to do was to warm it up.

Within a few weeks after our arrival we ran out of cash. The Soviets introduced their Rouble, by exchanging a limited amount for the old Polish currency. Although we lived very modestly, in a relatively short time we were broke. I decided to talk to Dolek and Stach, to see if they would take me on as a third member of their team. To my surprise, they seemed reluctant. Dolek, who was more of a diplomat, wouldn't come clean. No such problem with Stach.

His reply was clear and direct, but not what I wanted to hear: He turned to Dolek, first: "I think that Karol deserves a straight answer. I am sure he will understand."

Then he addressed me: "We have nothing against you, personally. On the contrary, we find you a very nice chap. But we both feel that you are not prepared for this kind of work. This job is very hard and with your background, we fear, it will be too much for you" He looked me straight in the eye. I felt rather hurt. What did he mean by my "background"? He was obviously treating me as some sort of aristocratic wimp!

"Thank you, Stach," I replied, "at least I know where I stand. I don't blame you for not wanting someone totally untried who may slow you down and impair your efficiency. I understand that very well. But this is easily resolved, in my view. Would you be prepared to accept me on a trial basis, say, for a week, without pay? A week should be sufficient for you to assess me as a potential apprentice. What do you say?"

"No, that wouldn't be fair," Stach replied, "if we took you on, you would be paid the same as us, provided you produced the same. As to the trial period, that is a different matter. We would have to discuss this between us. But this is not the main point. We have grave doubts about your ability to work. You are 18, you are tall and thin, you have never worked like this before. You come from a different background. Riding horses and playing tennis is no preparation for this sort of job".

"All right, I don't want to force myself on you", I replied. "Think about it for a day or two and let me know. I am not desperate; not yet. This is more a matter of pride with me, than anything else, so if you could see your way to giving me a try, I am confident you would not regret it. I have done a lot of sport at school. I was on the school decathlon team and, as you know, this requires a hell of a lot of stamina."

They did take me on, and within less than a week I was accepted as a permanent member of the team. I was delighted. The work was hard, but most enjoyable. They were both very competitive and, when they realised that I was not going to be a passenger, their own output went up considerably, presumably so as to prove to the junior that he was a junior.. After a while even this levelled itself out and we became just a good, well balanced team. They would tease me mercilessly though, but in a fairly harmless way. The slightest reference to my life before the war, either at home, or even at school, could provoke sarcastic remarks which at first worried me slightly, but later I learnt to accept them for what they were: a perfectly harmless leg-pull.

In addition to the satisfaction of being in partnership with two grown men, I experienced the luxury of financial independence and the pleasure of providing for my mother and sister. With lots of red Rouble notes in my pocket and plenty of new friends, mostly the sons and daughters of our clients, my social life was extremely active.

When we finished work, at about 5 p.m. we would go home to wash and change. We would then meet again, at an appointed place, usually, the house of a wealthy solicitor or doctor.

This was, of course, before the NKVD began arresting and deporting them all. It was, to me, a new world and I found it very interesting. The underlying mood of these gatherings was very strange. We all felt a sense of impending danger. We knew that the lull could not last long. We were therefore in a hurry to cram as much as we possibly could into what we knew could only be a short time, before that "something" took it all away again. Although I, personally, had never liked drinking, there was a lot of it going on. We drank rather superior "moonshine", produced by the local Jews and available at a very cheap price. We spent the evenings dancing to the music of a gramophone, the kind that one wound up with a handle at the end of every record. While I was not too keen on drinking I did love dancing. I would have gladly spent the whole night dancing to the few, rather scratchy records, were it not for the fact that I had to do well at work the following day.

Krzemieniec was a small town of some 20,000 inhabitants. It lay in a valley dominated by a huge hill, on top of which stood the ruins of an old castle built by Queen Bona in the 16th century, and called Mount Bona. The other feature was the Lyceum. It was a colossal school, founded at the very beginning of the 19th century by a philanthropist named Tadeusz Czacki. Almost from day one, after it opened, it became the centre of education in eastern Poland and included, among its graduates, some famous men. Juliusz Slowacki, the great romantic poet, was among them. As it epitomised the spirit of Polish learning, the Russians closed it, as a reprisal for the 1830 uprising. It was re-opened only in 1920, when Poland re-gained her independence. In the 1930s, justly or unjustly, it acquired a reputation for slightly "leftist" tendencies and consequently lost the support of the local gentry. It was no longer the place where they would automatically consider sending their sons to. Nevertheless it was impossible not to feel impressed by the sheer size of the place. Like Mount Bona, it dominated the town completely. Otherwise Krzemieniec was a pretty ordinary town. In winter it was covered in a thin blanket of bluish smoke that smelled of peat, the fuel used by the majority of inhabitants for heating and cooking. The population was mixed, with Jews possibly outnumbering the Ukrainians, who in turn outnumbered the Poles. It also boasted a railway station, our only link with the outside world.

On the corner, where our street joined the High Street, the NKVD made its headquarters. We watched it grow under our very noses. I can't remember what the place looked like before the war, but its new image was certainly sinister. The whole compound was surrounded by an immensely tall, wooden fence, some five or six meters high. The gates were manned by a heavily armed guard. Day and night, round the clock, the place was a hive of activity. At night powerful lights illuminated, not only the windows, but also the whole surrounding compound. This block never slept.

A constant flow of uniformed men moved in and out of the gates. They were unmistakable. They wore the usual Soviet khaki uniform, but their collars were very pale blue with matching pale blue bands round their hats. The combination looked horrid and, even today, it gives me "the creeps". These were members of the NKVD, or the Political Arm of the Soviet Forces. The faces of the men wearing them were also characteristic. They were usually pale and often flabby. It went with the job and their style of living: the sleepless nights and chain smoking. Theirs was certainly not a healthy life. The NKVD block glared in our midst, menacingly. Behind that fence, behind those permanently lit windows, hundreds of men worked overtime. They were preparing endless lists, collecting countless names. The fate of thousands was being decided by those pale men, slaving away, day and night. The malevolent spider was spinning its web. One day, soon, it would make its move.

* * *

It may sound strange but, I honestly feel that I gained something very precious as a result of the Soviet occupation, which maybe I would not have experienced otherwise: I got to know my own mother.

Previously, she had been to me just a distant image. A beautiful, glamorous, graceful image. But I did not know the person behind it. I loved her, of course. Who wouldn't love such a mother; but I couldn't say I knew her. When we were small, my sister and I were in the constant care of nannies or governesses. They lived with us, groomed us, and prepared us for the moments when we met our parents. We were conditioned mentally and physically. We were admonished to be extra good for these meetings, which would occur, mostly, once a day, in the early afternoon. Sometimes guests would be present and we were subjected to the intimidating attention of those strangers, ladies usually, who would drool over us, in simulated affection, while Mamma would look on and smile her lovely, mysterious smile. In my earliest recollections, the most precious were the occasional visits that mother made, "unofficially", to the nursery. She would be dressed for the evening and smelled heavenly. The fashions of the twenties suited her type of beauty. Even the "flower pot" hats and the very low waistlines gave her a certain elegance, which even a sleepy boy could appreciate. She was warm and motherly and I was so happy that she was my mother. We lived in Lwow then, and my parents led a very social life. They would often have people to dinner, which delighted me, as on those occasions, with a little bit of luck, I could hear my mother sing. The timing was my main problem, as we were supposed to be asleep by 8pm. Fortunately, in town, we lived in a flat and the nursery was not too far away from the drawing room, so the sounds of the piano gave me the signal that my favourite concert was about to begin.

She had a very special repertoire, which consisted mainly of Ukrainian peasant songs; a repertoire which one would not normally expect to hear in a drawing room. She made this style her very own and was greatly admired, not only for its originality but principally for the natural charm of its execution.

I would stand behind the drawing room doors for hours, shivering in my night shirt, motionless, fascinated, enchanted, a secret, adoring, invisible fan. Her voice was not great or powerful, but its delicacy and melodic quality were adorable. Her piano technique was not that of a concert pianist, but it was just the right backing for her repertoire.

The end of the 1920s saw the end of our carefree childhood. First, the economic climate changed. The Great Recession spread rapidly. It affected all aspects of the economy, including agriculture. Prices of agricultural produce, which had climbed steadily through the decade, suddenly took a nosedive. My father spent most of his time in the country, personally supervising his affairs – and we saw him rarely, a few days at a time. My mother looked pensive and different, perhaps worried.

One day she called me to her – I must have been nine at the

time. She looked sad. It did not seem, somehow, like a normal routine visit. She kissed me and hugged me for a while and then, suddenly, said: "If I were to die tomorrow, your father would want to re-marry. You would have a new mother." I was struck by panic. She must be ill, I thought, terminally ill, and was preparing me for this. I could not say a word, I was speechless. Fighting back my tears desperately, I knew that if I opened my mouth I would break down in sobs. So – I waited. She started to explain: No – she was not going to die, she was not ill. She didn't know quite how to say this to me, but she thought that I was old enough to be told. There was somebody else, whom my father had met recently, and liked very much.

I was so relieved! Mamma was well, she was not going to die... that was the main thing. I tried to concentrate on this. The rest didn't matter. The rest would have to sort itself out by itself. It was a matter for grown-ups. I was unable to understand it. It was all beyond me.

A few months later we changed apartments. We moved into a much smaller one. I was no longer taught at home. I started attending a day school in town. Our French governess was no longer living with us. She just came to teach us for a few hours a week. A year later my mother, with my sister, moved to the country, and I was sent to boarding school.

\* \* \*

Christmas 1939 was not a very joyous occasion. The NKVD had already started arresting people. At first, there seemed no pattern to it. Random arrests occurred, mostly of people whom we didn't know.

Soon, however, the real pattern emerged: several families, well known to my friends, were deported. We knew that the danger was edging closer.

My social life was much less active now. I simply did not feel like dancing. It was no longer a question of "whether" but rather "when" one would be taken. I spent more and more evenings at home. We talked a lot.

My mother spoke of the past, the distant past: the world of plenty, the world of elegance, lost in the days before the First War. Memories of old Vienna, of fabulous balls, of liveried servants, of glittering chandeliers. A fairytale world, unreal, remote, but which still lived in her with the reality of yesterday. It seemed like a tonic to us, in our present predicament.

We also did something we had never done before: we spoke about my father. She felt no bitterness about it, not a grain. Her unbelievable optimism was unshakeable. She was sure that all would be well in the end, that one day, they would be reunited. Even in this she was right and her instinct did not fail her, but it took six years before it happened.

"Never run away from a problem, or from danger", she would say, "face it head-on. The more faith you put into it, the quicker it will go. Goodness always conquers evil. It is much, much more powerful, but you must give it a chance. Fear makes one weak and vulnerable. Once, I met a tiger tamer", she remembered, "in Vienna, years ago. He was a very interesting man. I asked him if he was ever afraid. He said that, if he were, even for a split second, he would at once be killed. It was his supreme courage and confidence which kept him alive. It is the same with everything else in life!"

She told us many stories, which dramatically illustrated her philosophy. One such story I remember well. It took place during the First War, but at what stage of it I am not sure. My mother, who was still unmarried then, was staying with her sister, my Aunt Isabella. Aunt Isa, as we called her, and her husband lived in an old castle, perched high up on a picturesque hill. On that occasion her husband was absent but her mother, my grandmother, was with them. A detachment of murderous Cossacks was reported to be in the vicinity. They were roaming through neighbouring villages, terrorising the population. The three ladies were sitting in the drawing room, working or reading when the butler announced that some Cossacks were at the main door threatening to break it down if they were not immediately admitted. He suggested that there was still time for the ladies and children to make their getaway through a concealed passage under one of the towers. The sisters looked at one another – and smiled.

"On the contrary," said my aunt, "go the front door and invite them in. Only the officers, of course, and bring them right here."

The sisters got up together, and without a word, together sat at the piano. They started playing and singing their favourite Cossack ballad.

When the butler brought in the Cossack colonel and his staff, the concert was well under way.

My grandmother, a formidable old lady, who in bearing resembled Queen Mary, the wife of George V of England, was sitting in her characteristically erect pose, in the corner.

She placed her index finger to her lips, and glared at the Cossacks severely, so as to ensure silence and respect for the occasion.

They tiptoed their way to the piano, slipping clumsily on the parquet floor in their heavy army boots, and then just stood there, in awe, listening enchanted. The music, their own music, the serenity, the beauty of this experience was stronger than the evil in their hearts. "So, you see," my mother would conclude, "it is a bit like the tiger tamer. They didn't touch a thing. On the contrary, they left us a flask of kerosene for our lamps."

She never had any trace of malice in her, and was infinitely generous. I often used to go to see my father during my school holidays, before the war. I knew that sometimes I would stay longer with him than with her. "Of course you must see him," she would say. "He is a very lonely man. It is good for him and it is good for you." "Yes – but is it good for you, that's what I want to know?" I demanded. "Oh – I am fine, don't worry. It will all come right in the end," she assured me.

When my father was living in his cottage, during the last years before the war, I used to go to him and stay for days, sometimes weeks. A good part of my holidays was spent there. I enjoyed these long, uneventful visits. We had a lot in common, he and I. I shared his passion for horses. He was a successful breeder of Anglo-Arabs, and in his youth had been a good and knowledgeable rider. He had hunted with most packs in the country and told me a lot about foxhunting in England and Ireland. This he had never experienced himself, but had many friends who had. He always said that perhaps I would one day be able to fulfil his great ambition. He was a lonely man. Divorce was non-existent at that time, and even separation was a rare occurrence. He was ostracised by his uncles and cousins and did not have many friends. His isolation was largely self-inflicted. At heart, he was a true Victorian and had a streak of Puritanism in him. His isolation seemed to be a strange form of retribution. He was a complicated man: an old-style country gentleman and yet with strong intellectual interests. He wrote a lot, almost compulsively, largely for himself as little of his work had been published. Only his short articles and essays occasionally appeared in print.

We never spoke about his unfortunate sentimental attachment. The lady at the root of it all was also never mentioned, as though she did not exist. I hinted rather strongly, at the very beginning, that this was the only way I could feel comfortable with him, and he adhered to this unspoken arrangement meticulously.

During the Soviet occupation my father took a room, also in Krzemieniec, but at some distance from where we lived. I continued to visit him, very much with my mother's knowledge and blessing.

\* \* \*

Shortly after Christmas 1939, Olexa, the smallholder, Tania's father, began to visit us, slightly more often than before.

He brought with him food and milk, refusing any money for it, on the grounds that anyway it came from our property. This seemed fair enough, except that it was not consistent with his earlier behaviour. My mother, who could read the peasant mind, was sure that we should soon find out what lay at the bottom of this sudden surge of altruism.

One evening he came, as usual. He brought us a large piece of meat and for me my own pair of ski boots, which I had forgotten to take when leaving Obory. My mother looked me in the eye and smiled. She seemed to imply, with her expression, that she thought the moment of 'denouement' had arrived and that presently all would be revealed. It was indeed revealed, but not quite in the way we expected.

Olexa asked if he and I could go for a walk together. He wanted to talk to me, man to man. I knew that my mother was highly amused at this, but this time she kept a straight face. We stepped out into the dark. The night was cold but fine. Olexa walked in front of me rolling from side to side, the typical peasant walk. Then he stopped, turned round and said: "I have been wanting to talk to you for some time. You know that I own some land. Not many acres but, technically, I am a landowner. In this respect I am nearly as vulnerable as you are, according to Soviet laws. They call them 'Kulaks', you know?" "Yes, I know," I replied, wondering where this was all leading to. He smelled of tobacco and manure and other peasant smells. A man of nature; if I ever saw one. Physically wholesome, mentally a little slow but cunning, deferential, but a little suspicious. I waited for him to continue. "I can read and write," he said, suddenly - as if to shock me. "Not very well, but I read a whole page of one of your books the other day. I do go to the house, sometimes, to keep an eye on things," he added in case I thought he was helping himself to some of my books.

"You see, I have been thinking," he continued, rather hesitantly. "Yes... I have been thinking... In many ways we are equal – now – you and I. We weren't until now, but now we are, as far as the Soviets are concerned, at least."

"In the eyes of God, we were always equal," I said, unoriginally, just to say something.

"They don't believe in God. You know that?" he said, rather anxiously. "Yes, I know that, too," I assured him, "please go on".

"So, as I was saying, since you and I are equal – now – do you think you could... teach me to be a gentleman like you?" he looked at me anxiously. "Not necessarily a great gentleman, but maybe ... a small gentleman. They wouldn't know the difference, being peasants themselves; now would they?"

I was trying to keep a straight face. I was thinking of what my mother's reaction would be when she heard all this. Still I had to say something. I wanted to be honest, certainly not flippant. "Olexa, this does not make any sense to me at all. Why do you want to get yourself into deeper trouble? This new system is the 'dictatorship of the proletariat', they say. As you are now, you have a reasonable chance of passing for a proletarian. If you became a gentleman, you would have no chance. What's the point?" I asked.

"*Slava!*... That is the point. I want to have slava I want to feel that, maybe, even for a short time I would be somebody *vazhny*," he replied. Slava is a difficult word to translate: it combines glory, fame and triumph, while "vazhny" means important, authoritative.

This seemed to me crazy and totally unexpected. I knew, in my heart, that I could not agree to this. Even if I did, it could never succeed.

"Let me speak to my mother and see what she says," I said, at last.

"Oh, no, no. You must not. This is confidential, as I said: man to man," he protested.

"I am sorry, Olexa, unless I can consult with my mother, I cannot agree to anything. I am straight out of school, I am inexperienced, and I have never done anything like that before. Don't worry, she will know what is best".

In the end he agreed that I should speak to my mother, and that I would then tell him what she said. He was anxious that she might not take him seriously.

"Oh, do tell us what it was all about," my mother was all eager and excited, when I returned. "Olexa wants me to teach him how-to-be-a-gentleman," I rattled, in a flat voice. My mother said nothing, for quite some time.

"Oh, my dear, this could be serious. Did he say why?"

I explained his reasoning, as best, as I could: "He prefers to go down in a blaze of glory, of Slava, as a "vazhny" gentleman, rather than stagnate as a second-rate proletarian," I summed up.

"Amazing," said my mother, "amazing and rather wonderful. But we must save him from this, of course. He must come and talk to me, at once".

"He doesn't want to talk to you. We agreed, that I should tell him what you said," I said, knowing, that she would not let go.

"What nonsense, of course, he must talk to me. Tell him that I want to see him about Tania. He will come, you'll see," she said with complete conviction.

My mother was right. Olexa did come, the very next day. I watched him anxiously. He stood by the door, his fur hat in his hand, in the attitude which peasants had adopted for centuries under similar circumstances.

"What is it, Olexa, what do you want my son to do for you. Something about giving you lessons," she started rather severely.

"Yes, milady," he said, looking uneasy, "Surely, there is no harm in that?"

"There could be if, in the process, you pervert the course of nature," her voice was kind and soft, now. "You see, we must all improve ourselves. It is not only our right, but our duty. This is what God wants us to do. But this improvement must start from within us, not from the outside. Applying polish to the surface is not enough. If you take an old pair of boots, you can make them shine, from the outside, but they will not change. They will still be the same old boots, with a bit of shine on them."

She looked at him with all the kindness, she was capable of. She spoke from conviction, absolute conviction.

"You must be what – 45 perhaps? It is too late for you to change and certainly not like that. By all means, try to improve yourself, do something positive, improve your reading and writing, or learn to speak more correctly, but don't taunt nature by playing a comedy, by pretending to be someone you are not."

Olexa stood there. There was no expression on his coarse, weather-beaten, face. Was he resentful? I couldn't tell.

"I told Master Karol, that I wanted to talk to you. It is about Tania." When she said that he looked up, awakened, as it were, from his heavy sulk.

"Yes, I do. I want to tell you that I like her very much. She has a charming personality and she has talent. Now, she could easily improve herself, with a little bit of help".

"Oh – milady!!" said Olexa and his face lit up. It was different, all of a sudden, radiant. "Oh, milady! would you agree to help her, teach her. Could you make her into a great lady, like you, perhaps? That would be such a joy for me."

"I can promise you nothing. I can but try," said my mother, "the rest is up to her".

I walked Olexa, back to the shed, where he had left his horse and sleigh. He was a different man. "Oh, Master Karol," he touched my sleeve with his hand. "She is a great lady, your mother, a real lady." His happiness was all over his face. His happiness and ... relief.

\* \* \*

New Year's day 1940 was rather sad.

We celebrated it quietly, hoping against hope that during this new year our problems would not increase. Any more ambitious hope, we knew, would be tempting Providence. The main thing was that, unlike many others, we were still free. We had watched the NKVD spreading its reign of fear wider and wider. It was unrealistic to hope that they would have forgotten us. The lights behind that close-boarded fence blazed as brightly as ever. The railway station was filling with people, entire families, waiting in the cold for the arrival of cattle trucks, which were to take them to Semipalatinsk, in Eastern Kazakhstan. Grandmothers, grandfathers, mothers and children, big and small, babes in arms some of them – all destined for deportation, as punishment for their crime. The crime of being alive.

January passed – nothing, February – also nothing. We carried on with our log-cutting work, but our customer base was shrinking. Many of our clients vanished, without trace, either into the faceless crowds at the railway station or, worse, behind that tall fence of the NKVD block.

In early March, a rumour spread that the Soviets were planning to call up young men into the Red Army, even from among the Poles, who were not Soviet citizens. That for us was the last straw: Dolek, Stach and I decided that we had to run for it. To serve in the Red Army would be a fate worse than death, we concluded. As Easter that year was exceptionally early, 24th March if I am not mistaken, we decided to leave soon afterwards.

A rather sketchy plan was drawn up. As we wanted to join the Polish Army in the West we could either escape via the Southern route, crossing the Romanian or Hungarian border, or via the Northern route through Lithuania. We chose the Northern option, although the Southern one was more usual. That had by then become rather risky and difficult to cross. So instead of France as the final destination, we opted for England via Lithuania and Sweden. Lithuania was not, as yet, occupied by the Soviets and the Lithuanian government meanwhile, profiting from the confusion, had annexed the north-eastern part of Poland, including Wilno.

There was a suggestion that this newly established Lithuanian border might be less well guarded and could, therefore, offer a better chance for a successful crossing. My father favoured this plan, because it involved England. Despite the war he was still convinced that it offered a much better range of opportunities.

Half jokingly he argued, that it would not be entirely impossible for me to meet and marry in England some well bred, rich, English rose, who would not only make me a good wife, but also provide me with the opportunity of owning some good Irish hunters and of riding to hounds.

In this plan, cousin Cecilia was to play a key role. She was the daughter of my father's cousin and the wife of the Polish ambassador to the Court of St. James's. It was assumed that this remarkable, and as yet unknown to me, lady was possessed of limitless possibilities and of an inexhaustible willingness to promote all my father's hopes and ambitions. All I had to do was just... to get to England.

When eventually, years later, we finally met, she and I had a good laugh about it. I told her of my father's secret designs on her diplomacy and of the task allotted to her. She assured me that I was not alone. She had discovered many more relations, whose existence she had never even suspected, who had very similar ideas, with the additional complication that they were, actually, physically present in London at the material time, whereas to her considerable relief, I was not. She told me that she had, in the meantime, developed a pretty effective technique for disposing of their ambitions, without any inconvenience to herself.

We had a good three weeks to get ready. Dolek, Stach and I were to leave Krzemieniec by train, to a place called Oszmiana, which was as near to the intended point of crossing as we could safely hope to reach without arousing too much suspicion. From there we would go forward on foot and... play it by ear. Despite my complete greenness, this struck me as a very ill-conceived plan. We had no contacts, no intelligence of any sort and no experience. I told myself, though, that my doubts had to be unjustified, that my companions were so much older and consequently wiser. But still, deep down, the doubts persisted. We obtained the necessary travel documents and fixed 9.30 am on 31st March 1940, as zero hour. We also acquired some gold coins, which proved remarkably easy to obtain, in exchange for Roubles. Gold, we learnt, was the only currency acceptable to guides whose business it was to help illegal emigrants.

I spent the night prior to our departure in the house of my companions. My mother was to join us there in the morning for the final farewells. I was dreading this, although I knew that it was part of the whole drama and had to be faced.

Very early that morning, at about 6 a.m., I went to say goodbye to my father, who lived a short distance from the doctor's house. Despite the early hour he was fully dressed and shaven and was sitting at his desk, writing. There was a half-full glass of very strong milkless tea on the table, in a familiar silver holder. A cigarette was burning, unattended, in an amber cigarette holder. The air was thick with smoke and the sweet smell of oriental tobacco was very strong. He hadn't slept much that night – that was clear.

"Oh – Karol – so your train leaves at half-past-nine?" he asked, without expecting a reply. "Here, I have something which I have decided you should have. It belonged to your grandfather.

As he was also named Karol, the initials are more suitable for you." He handed me a huge gold pocket watch, a Patek Phillip, a collector's item, no doubt, but the last thing I needed on a journey like this. It was heavy, and was decorated with a coat of arms, coronet and all. I thanked him and prayed that I was not about to receive any other similarly impractical item.

"Remember me to your cousin Cecilia. I was close friends with her father. She was a small girl, at the time.

She must know a lot of people in England, an ambassador's wife, and all that. She could introduce you to some hunting people there. I was never able to hunt in England. The Quorn, Dachowski told me a lot about it. Oh – if only I were younger, I would love to come with you ! .

I had in front of me an old, tired, lonely man, a hermit-like figure. What was the force that was holding him back, preventing him from living a normal family life? I knew that I loved him and I so much wanted to help him, to give him that last decisive push in the direction in which, I felt, he now was ready to go. But there was no time, I was irrevocably committed.

We embraced – and I left. I had a huge lump in my throat. Did I feel then, that I would never see him again?

Predictably, the scene at the doctor's house was dramatic. The doctor's wife was in a bad way. She was crying uncontrollably. My mother was there, too, and was doing her best to help her. My sister was not there. Wisely, she had decided to stay clear of all this. For my mother, who was an outsider, it must have been very difficult. I could not even exchange a word with her at first. Finally, I took her away to another room and we spoke briefly; the useless, harried talk before departure. She was very calm and – quite magnificent. Her self-control was superb. One could see in her eyes the sadness and worry which she felt, but absolutely no tears; not one drop. Oh, I was so proud of her! She held me for a while, made a sign of cross on my forehead – and we parted.

I looked back briefly. The doctor's wife was raving and crying, while my mother just stood there smiling her lovely, sad, mysterious smile.

When we had turned the corner, on our way to the station, Stach turned to me. "Does your mother ever cry?" he asked. "What do you mean?" I said, rather shocked. "Oh – never mind," he shrugged his shoulders. I gave him a long, hard look. He didn't understand, did he? To him, my mother's self- control was something bizarre, inhuman almost. The loud crying and wailing was, for him, standard behaviour for a loving mother. I was so glad my mother was different. The memory of those lovely, sad, tearless eyes, gave me all the courage I would need so badly in the difficult years that lay ahead.

We reached the station and boarded the train. It was relatively empty and we found a free compartment. We sat down and waited.

When the long train started pulling away from the station, I looked through the half-frozen windows. I saw Mount Bona, towering over us. That ruined castle had seen wars, invasions, and disasters. Cossacks, Tartars, even Turks had passed this way; all with unfriendly intentions, and of course – the Russians, many, many Russians. One invasion more, or less...one disaster more, or less... On the time-scale of centuries – did it really matter ?

On the other side stood the great mass of the Lyceum, lurking in the distance, the symbol of national pride, of historic identity, of lofty aspirations. It stood empty, lifeless. Once again the Russians had closed it down.

Meanwhile, the train was gaining speed. It was taking me – to my destiny. Again, I felt helpless in its grip. Will it be England, the Allied Forces and – who knows – even a bit of foxhunting – or a dismal Russian jail or, maybe even, a bloodstained wall, facing an execution squad?

How could I know that I was to experience all of this – the lot – but in a different, totally unexpected sequence...

# Chapter 3

# INTO CAPTIVITY

I was arrested together with my two companions, Dolek and Stach, by a Soviet border patrol while trying to escape over the Lithuanian frontier in the early hours of 6th April 1940. As we learnt afterwards we were, at the time of our arrest, only a few hundred metres short of our intended goal.

Our failure was principally due to the choice of guide who, although recommended by an innkeeper in the local market town, proved disastrously unreliable. The deal we made with him was that for 20 Imperial Gold Rouble pieces, payable half down, half on completion, he would escort us to the other side of the border.

We met as arranged at 10 pm on 5th April and started on our five-hour march through the snow, aiming due North. We avoided roads and walked across country, over fields and through woods. The night was cold, there was no moon and hardly any wind. My companions and I had rucksacks on our backs. Although we were not on skis, we were dressed as for skiing which, in those days, meant a woolly hat, a short sheepskin coat, plus-fours, thick woollen stockings and heavy leather ski boots with strong metal buckles. Our guide wore a full-length sheepskin coat, a fur hat and long felt snow boots.

About four hours into the march, still some distance from the presumed Soviet border, in the middle of nowhere, the guide announced that he was going no further. He was not interested in the rest of the money he declared. He was going home! We were thunder-struck. We protested, we pleaded, we threatened, all to no avail. He would not give any reason. His cunning little eyes looked at us expressionless. He kept on repeating that he would not go any further. Stach pointed out to him that he must obey. "There are three of us, we can make you go," he said.'You can kill me," he answered "but I won't go". On hearing this Stach jumped on him like a tiger, pulled him to the ground and drew his hunting knife. "We will kill you," he hissed, "we can't let you go, you fool. You gave us your word. You took our money. I am not joking." It was evident he was not. I looked down at the guide. He was staring straight at Stach, unflinching, unafraid. "Go on, cut my throat I am not moving" he said in a croaky voice.

At first I was sure I was dreaming. Reality could not be as absurd as this. If I made a real effort I would shake myself out of this nightmare, I thought. I strained every nerve in my body trying to wake up. Alas...it was not a dream... This was reality and – what was worse – we were trapped. Things were getting out of hand. I was horrified. I looked at Dolek. Dolek looked uncertain. I felt I had to intervene. I grabbed him by the sleeve and pulled him to one side. "Is Stach bluffing, or does he mean it?" I asked him in a whisper. "Look Karol, we have no choice, surely you must see that. How can we be certain this worm will not alert the border guards?" He sounded apologetic. "But we will have murder on our consciences. Can you live with that?" I asked. "This is not murder, this is self-defence," he replied. But I felt there was doubt in his voice.

"If the border is not far away and we make a dash for it, we will get across it before he is able to alert anyone. The odds are in our favour. Do we know how far we've got?" I persisted.

Dolek gave me a long look. He turned to Stach: "Wait Stach. Karol may have a point. Let this Judas pay us back the ten gold pieces and let's take one of his snow boots off to slow him down, and let's go without him." We both looked at Stach, who was still lying on top on the guide with his Finnish hunting knife resting against the guide's jugular vein. The guide lay, unprotesting, motionless, pinned down to the snow by Stach. He did not seem to care. "Do you agree with Karol, then?" asked Stach. "Well, yes and no. I see his point of view," said Dolek, true to form. "Say yes or no, for heaven's sake. Make up your mind man for once in your life. We are losing valuable time. Do I kill him, or let him be – yes or no? – quickly!" Stach insisted.

We did let him be. He did not pay us back anything, either. He said he had left the money at home. We even let him keep both his snow boots. We just ripped open the seams round the soles, so as to make walking more difficult and left him where he was, sitting in the snow. He looked expressionless, unmoved, as before. I wondered if, at heart, he was grateful. Was he capable of such a noble feeling?

36

After consulting our compass we moved off quickly due North. The border could not be more than a mile away, we concluded. The snow was deep and the night cold. Still, with a little bit of luck we should be safe within an hour.

I looked back once or twice to see if our treacherous friend was making his way home, but I couldn't see him. Even against the white background, at 50 metres, you could see nothing. This gave me a good feeling. If we couldn't see the guide at such a short range, who could spot us, particularly not knowing where to look?

There was practically no wind. The snow was very deep, up to our knees in places and we were walking with difficulty. Still, we felt quite confident, the nasty episode with the guide almost forgotten.

I don't know who heard it first, but all three of us stopped dead in our tracks, and held our breaths. From our right, from the East, we could hear very, very faint voices – singing. "Could it be we have crossed the border already, without noticing – could this be Lithuania?" asked Dolek in a whisper.

"I can't tell you who is singing," said Stach, "you know I am tone deaf. Ask Karol. He is our musical expert". I listened, but couldn't tell either, so we decided to press on, still aiming due North.

It was some minutes later that it hit me: "Katiusha..." I whispered, "I'm sure it's Katiusha..." Both my companions looked at me in horror. "They must be heading this way". (Katiusha was then a popular Russian marching song.)

As we listened in dismay, the tune was getting progressively clearer. What were we to do? We had no idea how far from safety we were. Equally we could only guess the way the patrol would be taking.

We speeded up as much as we could, talking hurriedly, in short, breathless, whispers. It all depended on where our trails would intersect we decided. If the Russians were to pass through the gap between us and the border, they would not see our tracks in the snow – and all would be well. In that eventuality we should lie low and wait until they passed ahead of us. But, if as it seemed more likely, we were further north than the line they were taking, they would see our footprints and would give chase. What should we do? Without hesitation we decided, unanimously, to press on. It couldn't be too far now... We lengthened our strides and our pulse rate increased accordingly. We were still sure we could make it.

We were wrong, quite hopelessly wrong.

As it turned out, within half an hour from first hearing the singing, we were running for our lives, blinded by flares and being shot at, from a very uncomfortable range. The Russian ski patrol had intersected our tracks only 300 metres to the South of us and immediately went into action. We felt like sitting ducks. We were running in the deep snow, at the end of a long, snowy trek, trapped, heavy-limbed, unable to move any quicker. I often relive this scene in my nightmares. I can still feel the pain in my muscles, in my lungs... and the fear, the impotence....

I did not see Stach fall. I was a few paces in front of him. I only heard Dolek shout for me to stop. I obeyed before I knew what had happened. I looked round and saw that Stach was lying, curled up, clutching his right leg below the knee. As another flare floated down, its blinding light made Stach's figure look very dark, black almost, against the contrasting whiteness of the snow. I had difficulty in focusing properly. Dark spots were dancing before my eyes, spots of exhaustion. I couldn't see if there was blood on the snow. The patrol was closing fast, shouting orders. Dolek suggested that we had better raise our hands. Obviously the race was lost. My body was glad, my soul sick with fury.

What happened next was a muddle of frantic activity, screams, intimidating gestures. We submitted meekly. Our world was at an end. There was no point in resisting. Even the worry about Stach faded into the helplessness that was taking over. The time of decision had gone. From now on we were on the receiving end of orders. We would be at the mercy of these screaming strangers who would decide everything.

Despair... I experienced my first taste of despair!

\* \* \*

Anybody who has spent any length of time in a Soviet prison will know that it's the initial shock which is the most difficult to absorb.

After a while, with a little bit of luck one gets used to the appalling squalor and particularly to the overcrowding – provided, of course, that the interrogations are not too harsh.

I found the first shock quite devastating. I still remember the feeling when I was first taken to my cell; when the door opened and revealed some 30 men lying on the floor, packed tight like sardines, into a space not much bigger than an average room. I was pushed in and there was not enough room for me to stand on, let alone sit down. It was then that I was seized by barely controllable fear, almost panic. I stood for a long time, petrified. But eventually someone shifted just a few inches and pushed someone else, and before long I was sitting on the floor – next to the bucket (which, I soon discovered, was in considerable demand, day and night). An hour or so later I saw another arrival. I was able, even then, to watch the horror on his face and recognise the same feelings I had felt only a short time earlier. It made me feel better. It was my turn to give some of my space to this miserable being and maybe a word of encouragement. He would occupy my space from now on, next to the bucket ,and I would move away by a few inches, until someone else arrived. And so it went on.

As I progressed away from the bucket, I started discovering a new world, a 'prison world', a totally different environment from anything that I could have imagined. It was governed by its own internal laws, its own sense of justice, of fairness. Almost immediately one learnt to accept and respect it . One learnt to adjust one's own ideas, to evaluate human behaviour according to prison standards. One began to recognise good and bad on a different scale of values. Above all, one accepted the prison ways of sharing things. In this respect the prison world seems better than the other, normal world. Things are divided in accordance with very strict rules, which are self imposed and self-regulated, and any cheating is nipped in the bud. This was demonstrated to me almost immediately after my arrival, when our bread rations were pushed into the cell. The loaves were uncut, and I watched how much trouble was taken by those of my new colleagues in charge of such things, to divide the bread into identical portions, without as much as a knife to assist in the process. One man picked up a small piece of crust which fell-off. He was made to give it back at once and very severely reprimanded.

After a few weeks I was only a few feet away from the window, a far cry from the humble beginnings and my unfashionable 'bucket-slot'. Although the window was boarded-up and all one could see was a little bit of sky, I started feeling that, perhaps, things weren't so bad after all. Even when I discovered that I was supporting a sizeable colony of lice on my person and had to learn to deal with them, even then I did not feel as alarmed as all that. Everybody had lice – so had I. There was no point in getting too upset.

Right from the start I got separated from Dolek and Stach.

Just before that happened we agreed that we should all pretend that we were trying to cross into the Soviet territory from Lithuania, and not vice versa. We felt that, like this, we might be treated less severely. This proved to be a mistake. Stach's injury did not look serious. His ski-boot saved him or, more accurately, the heavy metal buckle on it. The bullet had ricocheted off it, and all that remained was a very nasty bruise. When we parted he was able to put some weight onto his right foot and hobble about without too much discomfort.

To begin with, my interrogation was not too bad. The officers in charge seemed young and inexperienced and they tended to ask the same questions over and over, every day, and wrote down the same answers, in very laborious longhand. It took hours. They seemed to have all the time in the world. So had I.

One slightly humorous incident occurred when my personal belongings were being listed. I had on me, at the time of my capture, my grandfather's heavy gold pocket watch that my father had insisted I should take with me to England. I was very worried about it, as it was engraved on the outside cover with our family crest, coronet and all. I could not think of any plausible way of explaining my having such a compromising item. It proved to be no problem at all. My inquisitor accepted without difficulty my flimsy tale that my grandfather was a small-time watch repairer and this watch had belonged to some rich nobleman, who died and his family never claimed it as they had to flee the country. No further questions were ever asked of me, and this item vanished and was not included on any subsequent list of my belongings. As it was a Patek Phillip, I am sure that it is still keeping perfect time for its present owner, perhaps an heir of that young KGB lieutenant.

I was repeatedly transferred from prison to prison. Each time I started next to the bucket and gradually progressed away from it. It no longer seemed such a terrible thing. My powers of adjustment were being developed rapidly, and I was now able to take most of it in my stride. There was only one nasty moment at this stage of my captivity: the news of the fall of France. The date was

22nd June 1940. I was, again, in relative proximity of the boarded window and the warm summer air was coming to me in delightful puffs. Outside, the loudspeakers were playing the 'regulation' Soviet popular music which, to tell the truth, I rather liked. I had a pleasant feeling that things were not too bad. Suddenly, the music stopped and the voice of the announcer could be heard: "We interrupt this programme for an important message : Germany, our glorious allies, have accepted the capitulation of France"... To me, and to most in my cell, this was unbelievable. It was a catastrophe. We were all counting on France which, with its Maginot Line, its most advanced, most famous army, would be able to teach Hitler a real lesson, something which had been impossible for us a few moths earlier. Now, all our hopes were dead, life was not worth living.... I mourned the fall of France for a long time.

Shortly afterwards I was transferred to Polotsk, a town situated on the Soviet side of the old Polish border. This time we were not housed in a prison but in a church. Several hundred, or perhaps a thousand, men were locked up in this most unsuitable of buildings. No attempt had been made even to adapt it to its new function. It looked like a normal church. In fact it was a nice Roman Catholic church in typical Polish baroque style, still relatively clean and with its lofty ceilings, in the middle of summer, a very pleasant change from the airless atmosphere of our previous premises. I chose the altar of St. Anthony, one of my patron saints, and established myself there, right on the altar steps. I felt safe under the watchful eyes of this familiar statue.

Although we were kept there against our will, it was, for most of us, difficult to forget where we were. The majority of my fellow prisoners were Poles and, like me, Roman Catholics. Despite considerable opposition from prison guards, we managed to obtain from them a 'symbolic concession' that, in deference to the 'holy place' in which we were, we would be permitted to put the many buckets which had to be dotted round the church inside the confessionals, so that they would be hidden from view of the numerous statues of holy men and women, presumably not yet conditioned to such indecorous sights. A nice little touch of patriotism and, in our eyes, a small victory over Communist godlessness.

Up to that point my stay in Polotsk was fairly uneventful. In fact, of all the prisons I have been to, this was the best. In the middle of summer it was cool, there was plenty of air and, in addition, I met a lot of interesting people.

My nightly sessions with the KGB followed more or less the same pattern as before.

The same questions were asked, the same answers given, and these were laboriously noted in my file. This was already getting quite thick, but although it contained many sheets of paper there was little to distinguish one sheet from another. One evening I noticed that my interviewing officer, a young lieutenant, a rather unintelligent individual, had great difficulty in writing. His right hand was heavily bandaged and he was obviously uncomfortable. He told me that he had to go to hospital to have his hand seen to, and that he would be handing over my file to one of his senior colleagues. He added that my case was almost complete and in a few days, he hoped, it would be ready to go to the Central Prosecution Office for their final consideration.

He anticipated a sentence of three years, without trial (this was standard procedure under Soviet law). Three years was the shortest I could expect. I was, by now, fully resigned to this and did not worry, unduly. I certainly did not expect that, at this late stage, things were to undergo a dramatic change.

My next interview was the following night and it took place much later.

Instead of the usual 10 or 11 pm I was not called until about 3 am.

I was shown to a much larger room, furnished much more elaborately and was confronted by a very strange-looking man. The first thing I noticed were his eyes. They were deep-set and very black, and glowed with great intensity. His forehead was very square, protruding at the top and forming two little bumps above the temples. His hair was dark, receding on top, but so arranged as to cover these bumps. This in fact rather tended to emphasise them. His features were regular and could almost be perceived as handsome, except for his mouth. It was the mouth of a woman. Red lips, curved and with a rather voluptuous expression – definitely out of place in an otherwise austere setting.

From the very outset I felt uncomfortable in his presence. Those glowing eyes looked at me and straight through me, half bored, half inquiring. I noticed a volume of poetry lying on top of his desk, Alexander Pushkin's "Gypsies". He spotted that immediately, and smiled. The smile made me feel guilty. I looked away, trying to conceal my indiscretion. He lifted the volume from the desk and said, sounding as if we had been conversing for hours, "My favourite – I love his early poems. They are so fresh, so pure. I know them all by heart, of course. You do too, I shouldn't wonder". I did not know if it was a question or a statement, so I said nothing, but felt even more uneasy.

It wasn't long before my worst fears were confirmed. Very soon he saw through my flimsy evidence and discarded it out of hand as "All lies, and very poor lies at that". He told me very early on that my case was so pathetic and bored him to such a degree that he had to try and make it into something more amusing, more fitting of his investigative skills. He sounded as if he were convinced that I shared his opinion, such seemed to be his style, and that I would join in his little charade willingly, since otherwise he would have to use other methods which, frankly, also bored him to tears. "But anything would be preferable to this," here he pointed to the file on his desk. "This is beneath contempt!" He knew, he said, that at heart I agreed with him. "The calibre of our young officers nowadays is very poor. You see here weeks, even months, of government time spent on producing waste paper. No wonder our prisons today are like holiday camps. When the great Felix Dzierzhinsky was alive – a fellow country man of yours, if I am not mistaken – ah! then it was a different story. We had a really good team going. Those were the days..." He pushed his chair away from the table and looking at the ceiling, started reciting a poem. I listened in confusion, totally bewildered by this extraordinary behaviour. The man was mad. Dangerously mad. He carried on with the poem, now looking at me, now at the window, and then again at the ceiling. I was not in a particularly receptive mood for poetry, but I had to admit it was beautiful, and beautifully delivered. He must have gone on for some time, perhaps for half an hour when, suddenly, he stopped and pressed the bell on his desk. A guard came in and he ordered that I should be escorted back to the church.

I crawled back, over the sleeping bodies of my friends to my place at the foot of St. Anthony's altar, totally exhausted, but above all petrified.

It was dawning already and I desperately wanted to sleep, but was afraid to. I started to pray to St. Anthony, who looked at me serenely from above, to get me out of this unbelievable nightmare. I carried on praying even in my sleep. I woke up very tired. I desperately needed to speak to somebody about my predicament, but could not think whom to turn to. Eventually, I confided in a middle-aged gentleman, a local landowner with whom, I discovered, we had certain distant family ties. He listened very attentively and said: "You seem to have met Lucifer personified. Whatever you do, do not agree to anything he suggests. He will try to break you down. He will then offer you a 'way out' by getting you to sign a statement, admitting to some crime you have not committed. This is an old trick of theirs. You plead guilty to crossing the border. That is all. Stick to it whatever happens. This is your only 'crime', nothing else. Good luck!"

Lucifer did offer me a way out and it was as my adviser had described, except that he did it almost at once. After a particularly prolonged session involving a heavy helping of Pushkin and Lermontov, he outlined his proposal: if I admitted to having spied for the British he would see to it personally that I was treated leniently on account of my young age. He would prepare a short statement for me to sign. We might have to include some sketchy details concerning my instruction from, say, Neville Chamberlain, but this need not be terribly accurate and two intelligent men like he and I could easily produce this in one or two sessions.

"What do you say?" he asked cheerfully. I took a deep breath, winding myself up to reject it forcefully, when his hand went up "Stop! Say nothing that you may regret later. Have one of these," he said, offering me a cigarette, "and go to your cell and think it over." He pushed the button and ordered the guard to escort me back to my place.

From then on he stepped up the pressure. He used two powerful tools: fear and sleep deprivation. He didn't use any physical violence, didn't have to. He said, "I believe in the power of words. A whole philosophy, the Christian philosophy, is based on One Word. 'In the beginning there was The Word. The Word was with God. The Word was God.' It will surprise you, no doubt, but I agree with this, my god is the word: the poet's word, the thinker's word, MY word!! I believe that people who have a way with words can do anything they wish, move mountains. Our faith, the Communist faith, is also based on words – possibly more than one," he added and smiled.

He knew that in me he had a good guinea pig. I was responsive and receptive to the words of poetry and to his own words. He knew he could make me shiver with fear. Poetry and torture to him were the same, the utilisation of words, by putting them into the service of Art – or of power, Communist power. The power of his words was stupendous. His great facility with poetry, his enormous arsenal of linguistic knowledge, his literary skill, could be used in the service of political science. His 'creed' was being serviced by his art – the art of manipulating words.

He would draw his chair close to mine and would terrorise me with words. He knew I was fascinated, mesmerised and that I was responding. The actor in him was assured of his audience – his captive audience. His voice would flood me, choke me, and fascinate me. He would evoke hideous pictures, which would make me shiver. He soon found that I had a horror of mental illness and of going mad. He used this to great effect. He painted terrible images of lunatic asylums. He described horrendous scenes. He put me right inside these ghastly places and forced me to imagine that I was mad. He told me of drugs that could be used to induce terrible images, voices, visions, and apparitions. He described those visions in the minutest detail, in the most unbelievably frightening way. And – he would not let me sleep. When utterly exhausted, I snatched a few moments, I could not rest. I began to have some of those visions.

Ten days later we were still at it. The psychological pressure was colossal. I was sure I was going mad. Which would be preferable, I agonised, to go mad or to be shot for spying? The latter began to appear to me to be more and more tempting. Some residual grain of obstinacy in me still refused to yield. But even this was wearing very thin.

One evening I was sitting dozing on the steps of my altar when the guard came to escort me for interrogation. He told me to take my things with me. I knew this was bad. While I was packing I whispered to my immediate neighbour asking him to tell my 'noble friend', that I was being taken away, this time for good. He himself noticed me leave, and when I signalled to him that I had my things with me, he smiled and made a reassuring gesture. He looked worried though.

I was told to deposit my things in the corridor and was pushed into Lucifer's office. He was standing up already, looking at me with his most satanic expression. He started speaking immediately. He said that, as I had refused to co-operate with him and did not trust him to help me out of this unholy mess, he had decided that he had enough evidence to have me shot without delay unless, of course, I was prepared to agree to his terms here and now.

At this moment something unbelievable happened to me. I felt most vividly that a part of me detached itself from my body and from now on I saw myself and my oppressor from above. I still knew that I was below, standing in front of him and that Lucifer was drilling me with his eyes, but I was also some six feet above – suspended in the air – viewing the scene as a spectator, while still retaining a close identity with the figure below. It felt as if I was looking through a periscope. I was still "I" and yet – I was able to observe the whole scene from another perspective. I did not find it strange at the time and it wasn't until some time later that it occurred to me that something very odd had happened to me.

With the benefit of my 'periscopic' vision I observed the scene. I looked with detachment, but without indifference. On the other hand I still seemed to retain, somehow, a certain amount of awareness in my 'earthly' capacity. I was aware, for instance, that I had just refused Lucifer's final offer.

As I watched – through my periscope:– two guards came in and I was led out of the room and marched down the stairs into a small courtyard. I saw that it was surrounded by a high wall. "So," I concluded, "this is where I am to die." I thought this without panic – just as a matter of logical fact.

A part of me started to pray, but prayer was not coming somehow. The other part, my 'terrestrial self', smelt the night, the cool summer air and felt a mild feeling of regret, of sadness. If, before, there had perhaps been, somewhere, a mild feeling of fear, there was no trace of it now. I was just sad, sad to have to die this way, sad that my mother would not know where or how I had died.

But at least, had she known, I was sure that she would have approved.

"I must remember to face the firing squad with a defiant expression and above all refuse the blindfold. This is how, she had always said, she would have liked to die".

No-one offered me a blindfold, so I could not realise my 'last ambition'.

I was pushed against the highest part of the wall. I felt the brick-work with the tips of my fingers. I desperately tried to pray, but couldn't. Instead I looked at the sky. The stars were shining at me from above. "Where shall I be in a minute or two?" I took a lung-ful of air and waited. My heart was beating in me, like a fright-ened bird, but I did not feel frightened – I was just very, very sad. I waited for the shot.

* * *

The next thing I remember is that I was standing in a very con-fined space, in complete darkness, propped against a wall. I felt very stiff, and my back hurt. I tried to straighten up but couldn't, the ceiling was too low. I felt around me and found that I was in a very small cubicle the size of a wall cupboard. I tried to ascer-tain if I was injured, but concluded that I was not. For the life of me, I couldn't remember where I was or why.

After a while I heard someone outside. I called. The key was turned in the lock and the door opened. A KGB guard stood out-side with a piece of bread and a can of water. "Where am I, what happened?... " "Ty v karobkie," was his reply, which means, "You are in the box," in prison jargon, a punishment cell. So that's where I am I thought as I drank avidly from the can. "How long have I got?" I asked him through the door. "As long as it takes," was his reply.

I had a bite of bread, but did not feel hungry. A bad sign in prison. I'll have it later, I thought, making a real effort to remem-ber what had happened.

My brain refused to deliver. "Mustn't push it," was my conclu-sion, "It will come back, in dribs and drabs perhaps, but come back it will".

It did come back to me eventually, but it took quite some time. It felt like doing a jigsaw puzzle with bits scattered all over the place. I kept finding pieces that didn't fit anywhere. Eventually, a picture emerged but by no means complete. Lucifer, it seemed, had let me stand in front of his improvised 'firing squad' and watched me for a while. He then asked me if I was going to co-operate. I remembered myself screaming that I was NOT. He then lost all interest and ordered me into a "Karobka". After that I remembered nothing. So, – I concluded – I was alive, but how long for? Meanwhile, I concentrated on finding some way of relieving the pressure on my back, and not lean so hard against the wall. It took a lot of effort. It was not easy to squeeze my six-foot frame into a sitting position and give my back some rest as well. The floor was wet, slimy and smelly but as it was still warm, I could sit, but not for long. Oh! how I longed to be able to stretch out... After some considerable time they came and escorted me to the latrine. This was real luxury, but I found that my legs felt very wobbly. I asked the guard how often was I allowed out and he said that once in the morning and once at night, for three minutes each outing. Good, I thought, at least this would help me to measure the time. Otherwise, without a watch, or a window, how could one tell? Being able to know the passage of time seemed to help.

Still this dreadful lack of space was getting to me. I was feeling pretty low. There must be something I could think about. But what? It had to be a subject that would last me for some time, for "as long as it takes" if that was the duration of my punishment, according to the guard. After a long process of elimination I decided that I was going to build myself, in my mind, the most elaborate dressing room. I shall plan it in the minutest detail, I resolved. Every cupboard, every hanger, every mirror, will be placed with the greatest precision. It will be built to the highest specification to accommodate all that a young sportsman would ever require, including plenty of space for riding boots. Particularly lofty ceilings would be a feature of this exclusive design. On this I went to sleep.

I was released from my cubicle as suddenly and inexplicably as I got into it. How long I spent there I cannot tell. Feeling very weak, I could barely walk. All this time I had lived on bread and water, and my legs felt particularly wobbly.

I did not return to the church. They took me straight to the station or, more accurately, to a kind of warehouse a short distance away from the station. There I met several men from the church. Not my noble friend, unfortunately. He was left behind. Could it be that Lucifer had his eye on him, now that he had given me up as a dead loss.? For his sake, I hoped not.

Within a week we were on our way. They loaded us into specially adapted cattle trucks. Each truck accommodated 40 men. We lived on wooden bunks, arranged on two levels. There was a primitive stove used only in winter and – the inevitable bucket.

It took us about a month to reach Kotlas. The truck had no windows, only a huge sliding door, permanently shut, secured with a padlock. The only way we could see anything was through ventilation slits, placed high up on the side walls. By watching the position of the sun, we tried to guess which way we were heading. Most of the time we were pointing North.

There was one personality that dominated this long journey. His name was Dziekonski. Whether this was his real name or a pseudonym, I cannot tell, but he was a most remarkable character. He was a natural storyteller. For one or two hours each evening, he would have us spellbound, telling us stories. They were romantic thrillers, which he delivered, keeping his eyes shut, in an even, melodious voice, exactly as if he were reading a book. He never hesitated, never stopped for thought. The words just flowed in a steady stream until he came to the end of a 'chapter'. He then opened his eyes and looked round to see if his audience wanted to ask any questions. We would invariably beg him to go on – which he either agreed to, or not, depending on his mood. All his 'novels' took place in England. The plots were complicated, and involved a great number of characters who often re-appeared in his subsequent stories. At the beginning of each session he would give a short summary of previous instalments, then allowed the audience to ask questions, and when everybody was quite ready he would begin the instalment programmed for the evening.

Dziekonski, as a man, was a total mystery. He never talked about himself. No-one knew who he was or what he was by profession. He was short, rotund and friendly-looking, and on the surface easy-going, until you asked him a personal question. Then he would immediately change the subject or retort, "I am not asking you anything, please do not ask me". He was very touchy in that way.

Our truck was a mixed bag. There were Poles, Bielorussians and Jews. They all spoke Polish, of course, so they all enjoyed immensely Dziekonski's literary evenings. There was one old Orthodox Jew who was very ill, suffering from dysentery. He knew he was dying, but he insisted that he couldn't possibly go before the end of Mr. Dziekonski's story. He said that he wasn't sure if Abraham, in heaven, understood enough Polish to tell him properly, how the story ended. He died the following night in his

49

sleep, although there were still three instalments left. He was a nice man, with a pleasant sense of humour. We prayed for him and hoped that, in heaven, he had found some Polish-speaking rabbi with sufficient literary talent to reproduce for him, faithfully, the bits he had missed.

Kotlas was a huge transit camp which served as the main 'distribution centre' for the Northern camp system of European Russia. From there we went partly by train, partly by barge, still further North.

Before we arrived in Kotlas, I was given my sentence: I signed acceptance of the findings of the Central Prosecutor's Office, namely that I was guilty of "unlawfully crossing the border." In prison jargon I was a Tourist. I signed gladly. I felt happy that my spell in prison was over. Somehow the fact that I had been sentenced to five years' hard labour did not seem to bother me. Anything was better than my experiences in Polotsk, the horror sessions with Lucifer, or the stretch in the box.

From Kotlas we went by train to Ukhta, where we boarded a barge. There. for the first time I saw the real Taiga, the endless stretches of pine forests, criss-crossed by the most majestic rivers. I was enchanted with what I saw, so much so that when we were boarding the barge and I was waiting in the queue to descend into the hold with the rest of the political prisoners, I seized the first opportunity to remain on deck, to be able to watch the magnificent scenery. This was the luckiest reflex I ever followed.

It was like this: as I was waiting my turn to go down a long slippery ladder to the bottom of the hold, a young Russian criminal approached me. He saw my ski boots and offered to buy them off me. On the spur of the moment I replied, "You can have these for nothing if you arrange for me to remain on deck with you and your mates, and if you promise to supplement my food rations for the duration of this trip". He looked at me and smiled, "Your little kettle is cooking all right" which roughly translated means, "You are not so daft, are you!" and then he added, "Who, in his right senses, would want to go down there?" We shook hands on the deal, he found me a good place between him and his mates and looked after me very well for the remainder of the journey.

It was only a few days into the trip that I realised how lucky I was. Down below in that hold it was pure hell. There was no air to breathe, all the food that was dropped down by the guards was

50

stolen by gangs of petty crooks, and they had no water to wash, or even to drink. People were dying by the dozen. I am sure I would not have survived, weak as I was, had I not struck that deal, which I did for a totally different reason.

Instead, I arrived at the transit camp much refreshed. I felt really well, ready for anything. I was confident that I would be able to adjust to the new conditions, to the hard work. Five years was a long time but, as all the criminals I met on the boat had served a lot longer than that and survived, I was sure I would be all right too.

We had now reached the northern regions of the Taiga. Five or six hundred miles further North was the country where white bears lived. In fact the Russians refer to this whole region as 'the white bear country'. To send someone "to the white bears" or "na bieliye miedviedie" means to be banished to the far North. All this sounded most exciting.

In my childish optimism I did not realise that my young age, my resilience and my good physical condition were no match against the combined powers of the climate and the Soviet labour-camp system. Nor that, unless I was exceptionally lucky I would not last a year – let alone five. It is such a blessing that we cannot see what fate awaits us...

Chapter 4

# THE LAW OF THE TAIGA

After some seven days, still well to the South of Pechora, we were ordered to disembark. Those of us who had travelled on deck and had thereby avoided the hell below it, got off first without difficulty and were told to wait on shore at a good distance from the gangway. Armed guards with bayonets fixed made sure we did not move from there.

From where we stood we could barely see the dreadful sight of the remaining travellers emerging from their pit of death. I preferred not to look. I couldn't help, though, hearing the high-pitched shrieks of the guards who were supervising the operation. *Davai, davai, bistrey*! they were yelling in a frenzy, urging the poor wretches to move faster... It sounded awful.

As I waited with the group of Russian criminals, in whose company I had travelled, I thanked my Guardian Angel for inspiring me to conclude my boot deal, and thus avoid the fate of those who had had to travel below deck.

The march to the nearest transit camp was also ghastly. Those unfortunate stragglers who were weak and walked with difficulty were placed at the tail end of our column, surrounded by more than a dozen malevolent-looking guards, all armed to the teeth, complete with those long pointed bayonets manifestly ready for use on the slightest provocation whilst we, who were at the head of the column, had only four guards to watch over us.

The camp we were aiming for, my criminal companions told me, was some seven kilometres from the river jetty, a long distance for any unfit person, impossible for those who were in a bad way. As the screams of the guards at the rear became more frantic, I knew that before long we were bound to hear the ominous sound of a shot. 'Shot while trying to escape' would say the official report in the victim's personal file. One more lie to add to the billions on which Communism fed its subjects, one more death to add to the millions that had paved the way of Stalin's road to true socialism. 'Shot while unable to move' would have been the honest truth.

I can't remember how many shots I heard during this macabre procession, but quite a few. Each time I heard one I shivered. I tried to console myself that at least that victim would be spared the long, slow lingering agony which would otherwise have awaited him. The groundless feeling of optimism that I had briefly experienced on the boat was evaporating fast...

It took us the best part of the day to complete this relatively short march. The weather was warm but humid and the ground was very wet. We were, it seemed, on some sort of a swamp. My legs felt very tired, despite my relatively comfortable boat trip. I couldn't imagine what it must be like for those who had had a bad journey. The mosquitoes and humidity added to our discomfort..

On arrival at the camp, we spent a long time being counted. Counting was a never ending process in the Gulag. One was counted in the morning, before leaving for work, and on return in the evening. One was often counted several times during the day if anything had occurred that aroused the suspicion of the guards.

That particular evening there seemed no end to it. Innumerable times we had to form five abreast and each row was told to advance three paces, while several worried-looking NKVD officers would call aloud "*Odin, dva, try...*" and laboriously write down each number onto their large clip-boards. Presumably the numbers of those alive, added to the numbers of those who had been shot en route, did not produce the expected total. The NKVD did not worry, it seemed, how many people had been killed, as long as the overall numbers tallied.

Then we were segregated. The Russian criminals went their way. We, the political prisoners, all ex-Polish citizens, were put behind an impressive wall of barbed wire, under the watchful eyes of observation towers. We were then further segregated according to our physical fitness, most of the sick and the weak being squeezed into a separate barrack.

I found myself in a small barrack of some fifty men who, by Gulag standards, were considered physically fit.

The following morning, first thing, after a normal prison breakfast, a man arrived.

He introduced himself as the Deputy Manager of the transit camp. He came, he said, to give us our orders for the day, which was to be a full working day. We were going to 'lay a carpet', he explained, a wooden carpet on the swamp to facilitate the progress of the motor vehicles. "It's an easy job" he said "just right for your state of fitness. It shouldn't take more than a couple of days, three at the very outside. I need twenty five men. Any volunteers?"

I was a little surprised at the informality of this invitation, but decided to try. "Might as well start with an easy one first," I thought. Evidently I was not alone. Three dozen men raised their hands at the same moment.

"All right," said the Deputy, "we have more than enough volunteers, so the next job for me is to select a brigadier. Who is the best Russian speaker among you?"

After a little hesitation, some people pointed to me.

He turned and looked me in the face . That was when noticed the squint. It was a terrible squint, most disturbing. "Can you read and write Russian?" he asked. "Not really," I replied, still struggling to compose myself. "Can you read this?" He took out from a pocket a visiting card. "Mihailov, Andrei Vasilievich," I read with difficulty, "Deputy Manager". I was anything but fluent, I knew. "OK, that will do," he said. "From now on you are the Brigadier, responsible to me for this group of men." "Oh, I don't know," I protested, "this may be difficult. I am probably the youngest in this group; it could be awkward..." "Anyone against?" asked Mihailov, squinting round the audience, a well-known trick used at Soviet meetings, in order rapidly to achieve a semblance of democratic unanimity and usually met with dead silence. This time, however, to my embarrassment, I could hear something resembling a subdued cheer.

"Yes, yes," friendly Polish voices whispered to me, "Yes, Brigadier, you take it. We won't let you down!"

I was surprised by this sign of confidence, bowled over would be more accurate. Even Mihailov seemed taken aback. He sounded a little hesitant, when he said: "It seems you are popular. I should be careful about that, if I were you...Too much popularity is not appreciated around here." Then regaining his previous attitude, he asked: "What do they call you?" "They call me Karol. Karol Czosnowski" I replied.

"Karol, Karol, there is no such name in Russian. Karol means 'king'. We certainly don't want any kings here" he smiled. "I shall call you Kiryl, that sounds near enough. OK? Kiryl then, I want you now to select twenty five men from this lot and have them standing outside the barrack in ten minutes' time".

Although I was flattered by this demonstration of confidence, deep inside me I felt uncomfortable. I had the unpleasant feeling that events had taken over, that I had not been given time for a considered decision of my own. To crown it all, from that moment on, everybody started calling me 'Pan Brigadier' or Mr. Brigadier.

When Mihailov left us, everybody started to speak at once and I sensed a feeling of enthusiasm in the air, which was totally unjustified. I clapped my hands. This resulted in a moment of silence. "Those of you who volunteered" I said loudly "line up against this wall. I want to have a look at you" Their immediate and eager compliance gave me a good feeling. Nearly all the fifty men, who were in the barrack, lined up looking at me eagerly. That's ridiculous, I thought, this is more than before, they all want to take part. Some sort of herd instinct, no doubt.

It took me longer than I thought to select my 25-man team. Those left behind looked cheated. They pleaded to be included. In the depths of my mind I wondered who was going to be sorry in the end. During my selection I tried in vain to find some young peasant types. Those I knew would serve me best, being used to physical effort. There were some peasants in our group but most were too old and not all that fit. So I went for those aged between thirty and forty who seemed in good shape. Unfortunately they were mostly of the town-dwelling kind, minor functionaries or railwaymen, who constituted the large majority.

When we eventually lined up outside the barrack Mihailov appeared with another man who looked like a clerk. He said that he himself would not be going with us to the site, but that "Kolya here will go with you and show you what to do".

Kolya was a type, as I established later, frequently encountered in Soviet offices. Small, pale, rather frightened looking, probably a junior accountant in his pre-prison life who, by some miracle, had found his way to the Gulag administration and remained there for the rest of his term. In conformity with his kind, he was bearded, bespectacled, rather shy and very polite. I found later that most of them survived by treachery. They reported everything they had heard and seen to their bosses including, if necessary, the most damning secrets of their best friends. On the whole, a dangerous type.

The guards, true to form, took a long time counting us before departure.

Twenty five plus two seemed a very difficult computation, but eventually we got going. My brigade was marching behind me cheerfully. Somebody even tried to whistle a swinging marching tune, but was cut short by the nearest guard who, pointing his gun at the offender, demanded dead silence. In less than an hour we reached the spot.

Kolya explained the task before us. "All you have to do is to pick up these logs from those piles on the side" he pointed with his beard in the direction of stacks of light timber placed at intervals by a line of pegs in the ground "and lay them tightly across the driveway, following the line of these pegs".

"What is the approximate length of this new driveway?" I asked. "Oh, I don't know" he said in a frightened voice "I don't know. You must measure it yourself. It will be from there, to there," and he pointed to two fairly distant invisible points. "But Citizen Mihailov told us that it would be a two-day job." I said. "This looks to me more like a week's work in the best circumstances". "Oh, I wouldn't know that either. You must ask him. All I was told was to show you what you had to do." "Will Citizen Mihailov be there this evening so that I can discuss it with him in more detail?" I asked. "Oh, no," said Kolya cheerfully, "he has gone to the district office and will not be back for three days".

Kolya departed eagerly, as if desperate to escape my questions. He was useless. I viewed the task facing us. It seemed utterly hopeless. All we had in the form of tools were some very tired looking spades, three rusty pick axes, and one cross-saw. The ground was boggy, uneven and covered with a layer of very thick moss, the wood-stacks looked uneven and knotty and, at a glance, the distance between the two points indicated by Kolya not less than 700 metres.

I divided my brigade into five gangs of five men each and appointed one leader to each gang. I suggested that we should try a formation of two plus two plus one, so that two men in each gang would be levelling the surface, two more carrying and laying the timber and one tightening the timber, so that the logs did not separate but locked into a tight wooden carpet, as Mihailov called it. I left it to the individual teams to decide if they preferred to work in this formation continuously or change round, so that each one had a go at each separate task. I spaced them some 20 metres apart.

I myself planned to walk from gang to gang and help out if necessary, but before anything, I decided to pace out the distance and make sure that the pegs were in a straight line.

I signalled to a guard for permission to move away from my group, but at first he wouldn't let me. It took me sometime before I could make him see that this was essential. One guard came with me, nervously pointing his bayonet at my back, his index finger resting on the trigger. I hoped that he would not trip up on some root and accidentally put a bullet into my posterior.

My inspection revealed all sorts of problems. First the pegs were not in a straight line. Secondly, even if they had been straight, somewhere round the half way mark there was a hollow which we would either have to fill in or else change the direction of the roadway so as to miss the un-evenness of the land. What should I do? I asked the guard. He wouldn't even talk to me. He just screamed at me nervously each time I came near to him.

I went back to the main body of my men and asked the head guard. His answer was that we should start working immediately otherwise he would report us for sabotage. He did not specify what precisely this involved but, something pretty unpleasant, I was sure.

So I decided to follow the general line pegged out, hoping that someone would help us before we reached the hollow.

After the usual preliminaries and inevitable delays, the work started well.

In fact my men were so eager to prove themselves that before long I became worried that they were using up too much energy in the process. I was longing for the kind of steadying influence a few experienced middle-aged peasants would have exerted and shown them how it should be done. By the end of the day (we were supposed to work a twelve-hour day) we had done quite a bit more than I had expected.

On returning to barracks I went to look for Kolya. When I finally found him, he proved as useless as before. He didn't know anything. He kept repeating that he had told me all he knew already and there was nothing more he could do. I asked him for the commandant. The commandant didn't live here, he assured me, he lived in another camp but, anyway, he had also gone to the District Command and would only return in three days, by which time Andrei Vasilievich himself should be back. Finally he said he could not talk to me any longer, as he had work to do. He shuffled away in a terrible hurry.

I returned to my barrack very worried. I called a council of war with the section leaders. They weren't much help. They all seemed too tired to think. All they wanted to do was rest. I was now sure that the initial flame of enthusiasm had already burnt up their meagre energy reserves, which was bound to affect their future performance.

The next morning my gloomiest predictions were exceeded a hundredfold. Most of my brigade were complete wrecks. They could hardly walk. They were all stiff and achy and their joints refused to bend. Our output was pathetic. We laid a third of what we had planned. The problem of the dip seemed insignificant compared with our miserable performance. I knew that it was serious. We would not be able to show anything like the output which was expected.

I was trying to help as much as I could. I tried to be everywhere at once, offering both encouragement and physical assistance but, to be absolutely honest, I was feeling pretty tired myself.

The third day proved a little better, but not much. To add to my already profound depression, Kolya appeared around midday. "Oh dear, oh dear..." he started moaning, even before I had time to greet him. "Oh dear, oh dear... There will be trouble... Much trouble when Andrei Vasilievich sees this! You are not even halfway, are you?" He was right, we weren't. But when I started explaining that the men were tired, that we had no tools and that the terrain was very unlevel, he didn't want to listen. He kept on repeating "There will be trouble. A lot of trouble, I can see that..."

That same evening, at about nine o'clock, I was summoned to face my ordeal. Mihailov was sitting behind a small desk in his tiny office. He looked very cross. His face was red and his squint quite terrifying.

His opening words were ominous: "Do you know the Russian word SABOTAGE?" he asked in a sinister whisper. I nodded unhappily. "And do you know what happens to those who are found guilty of sabotage?" I nodded again, hoping to avoid Mihailov's description which, I knew, would be pretty nauseating.

From that moment onwards he was roaring at me in a most ferocious way. Communism educates its followers in this procedure and therefore they are very good at it. So was Mihailov. He mixed threats with accusation, in a way done the world over by superiors to torment their inferiors, but his version sounded more personal. It gave me the impression that he himself felt hurt. Phrases like: "You have betrayed me. You have abused my trust," sounded like a friend reproaching a friend. He even said,"Kolya told me that, on the first day, your performance was passable but from then on, as soon as you realised that there would be no immediate supervision, you stopped trying. You just went to sleep. Why did you do this to me? To me who trusted you!"

He continued in this way for some time. I stood there and waited. After a while I did not hear his words. I was watching his face instead. The handsome half of it. I discovered that, if I concentrated on it and blocked-out from my mind the ugly half it looked almost friendly - worried but friendly. It was the other side of his face that was terrifying.

As a result of this mental form of 'editing' I could almost feel friendly towards him, I could even like him. And what was more significant still, I did not feel afraid of him.

When finally he ran out of puff, I looked straight into his good eye and said: "I am sorry Citizen Deputy. I know this has created a problem for you. But I can assure you, most categorically, that it was not intentional . My men are weak and unfit, they are straight from prison, they have endured a very bad barge trip, and a long and tiring march. They simply cannot do more. But I am sure that in a week our output will improve substantially".

"You don't get it!" he screamed. "You didn't listen to a single word I said. In a week you will all be in chains waiting for the verdict of 'guilty on a charge of SABOTAGE'. His voice faltered. He seemed short of breath, like those who suffer from asthma. He started wheezing too.

Then he gave me a long look and said. "You are young, and you are new, so I am going to give you one more chance to prove yourself to me. I give you tomorrow. If you can get your men to give me a normal day's output tomorrow, I will not denounce you".

"Thank you, Citizen Deputy, for you generous offer," I replied "but I am afraid that I cannot accept. It would be dishonest of me to promise you something which I know I cannot deliver. Tomorrow is still too early. My men will not be able to improve their performance sufficiently as yet. Could you see your way to giving me a week, or five days at the very least, and then I hope we shall be able to work more normally?"

"You are forgetting where you are," he raised his voice again, but with some difficulty, "you are not in a position to bargain with me. You are in the taiga in a forced labour camp. If you want to survive in the taiga you must be tough, ruthless. If you have men working for you, make them work until they die and that way you protect yourself. I have given you this job because I wanted to help you. I liked you and now you are repaying me like this."

He hesitated and in a different, calmer voice he continued. "In this God forsaken place you must learn to look after number one, nobody else. If men under you refuse to work you beat it out of them. If that doesn't do the trick you call in the guards and they will do it for you... It is either them or you. If you are kind to them, you die. They die too, of course, but this should be nothing to you. The only thing that concerns you, is that you yourself should live. To hell with anybody else. That is the law of the taiga."

He looked at me again. Momentarily, I glanced at the ugly side of his face.

I saw there the confirmation of his dreadful philosophy. I knew that he was capable of doing just what he had said. Killing somebody to save himself. I knew that I could not.

"If these are the rules of survival," I said in a very low voice, "I am afraid I cannot do it. I am not able to do what you tell me to. If it is any good to you I offer my resignation. I am no good to you as a Brigadier under such conditions."

The strange thing was that I was aware that, by saying what I just had I could, in effect, be signing my own death warrant. But as I said, Mihailov somehow did not scare me. Unlike Lucifer, my interrogator in Polock, he failed to instil in me the deadly brand of terror which only true evil can do.

Incredibly, despite everything he had said, I could not feel that he was really evil.

"Resign!" Mihailov was now laughing, a painful, ugly sort of laughter, mixed with an asthmatic cough. "Resign? This is incredible. How stupid can you get? Who are you, where have you grown up? This is not a gentlemen's club, or the Corps of Pages or something. You don't resign in the Taiga. You either obey and live, after a fashion, or you die."

Here he gave me another strange look. He started wheezing

again and became very short of breath. Then he composed himself and said: "I lived in the taiga as a prisoner, you know. For twelve years. Six of them in the mines of Vokuta..." He paused for breath looking at me intensely, as if to see if he was getting through to me. He certainly was. I looked at him in amazement.

I knew that it was not unusual for minor administrative jobs to be given to certain ex-prisoners in the Gulag service, but I had never met one until now. I wondered if he would open up some more.

After a while, still with difficulty, he continued. "I was about your age when they arrested me. My father and mother were arrested too. 'Dangerous element', you know, the usual charge. After a while I ended up in Vorkuta, in the coal mines. 500 grams of bread a day, that was our lot. My mate and I spent twelve hours every day underground, with nothing but a pick-axe each. A pick-axe and bare hands, those were our tools. Then one day there was an explosion. A part of the tunnel collapsed. My mate and I were buried, trapped, the two of us. After some time it became clear that we were suffocating. We were going to die together. It wasn't to be a hard death. I knew that you just go to sleep. I was ready. I didn't mind. Then suddenly, I received a blow, here on the temple" he pointed to a spot just behind his bad eye. "I thought that something had fallen on me from the ceiling. And then I realised that it was my mate. He hit me. It was he who decided to kill me, so that he could have a better chance of surviving himself. Just like that...

He was weak and he couldn't kill me with one blow. It was enough to disfigure me for life though. But I killed him instead. First, I strangled him with my bare hands and then I hit him again and again with all the rocks I could find until his head was like pulp. I collapsed myself. They found me some hours later still breathing. I spent four weeks in hospital. They didn't do a good job of my eye, but I can see a little." He smiled apologetically.

For a moment I forgot my own problems. I was really moved by this horrible story. What a world...

"I told you this to illustrate to you the laws of the taiga. As I said: It is either them or you. The average is one winter. That is all you've got. Millions don't even get that far. To survive your term you must be tough. You must have no pity, no compassion and if necessary, you must kill."

"When they were building the railway line to the North of Kotlas," he continued "They used to say: 'God doesn't go any further. He gets off at Kotlas. From there on to the North, is the Devil's country.' The Devil's country and the Devil's laws. The laws of the taiga..."

"Go, I have no further use for you," he suddenly turned to me harshly.

My interview was finished.

Before leaving I looked at him and, quite spontaneously, I said, "I am sorry. It must have been awful. You must have suffered..."

He smiled bitterly. "Not any more. It is the law of the taiga, like I told you."

The following morning a guard came in. He called my name and I was told to pack my things. I was ordered to join a group of prisoners destined for another camp. I was worried. I didn't know what the purpose of this transfer would be. Sabotage... death... or just a plain transfer.

After a third move I began to think that maybe Mihailov had let me off the hook. With each move I became more hopeful until, eventually, I relaxed.

For a long time afterwards I was intensely puzzled by Mihailov's behaviour. Strangely, it was not the fact that he had let me go. This, somehow, I had half expected.

What I found inexplicable then, was that he had taken so many risks in the process. That he had chosen to be so frank, that he had revealed, to a total stranger, his Gulag past and confessed to have murdered his own best friend. Above all, that he had made such damning comments about the System. This, if overheard or even reported by me, could have caused him a great deal of trouble.

Today, I know that he was trying to help me, that in his own strange way he was trying to spare me the tragedy that he had experienced himself. In short, that he was motivated by goodness.

Today I believe most passionately that in everybody, even in the most hardened criminal, there is an element of goodness which, if activated, can produce extraordinary and unexpected acts of generosity. The problem is in finding the key.

By the sheerest coincidence, I had found his key. His half-distorted features helped me in this. They seemed to reflect the image of his soul.

I have no doubt that the following day he would have adopted his other mode, that of Deputy Manager of a forced labour camp, and would have reverted to being as ruthless and cruel as the job demanded. But the fact that he had had enough goodness and generosity left in him to let me go was proof that, despite it all, at heart he was still a good man.

I shall certainly remember him as such.

# Chapter 5

# SASHA

My own working life in the camps started at the top. Almost immediately I became a lumberjack. It was an exceptional distinction as, for most people, it took a long time to reach those dizzy heights. Lumberjacks were regarded in the camps as a race apart, supermen, the equivalent of the top footballers or pop stars of today. They had the best food and the best clothes, and they were looked up to by their mates and even by the camp authorities. Like most other important events in my life, this one also happened by pure chance.

From the main transit camp in Kotlas, I was sent, in quick succession, to a number of smaller transit units. Here, in the heart of the Taiga, we were subjected to further selection, after which, we were told, we would travel to our ultimate destination.

I was feeling better. The long journey on the barge, fresh air, better rations, all started restoring my energy which I had feared I had lost for ever in the foul confinement of the prisons. I was young and athletic and was beginning to feel that, just maybe, I was not a total write-off; not yet.

One evening some of my younger companions and I were playing silly games in the barrack. Each one of us was showing off. When my turn came, I decided to risk it, and try my old 'piece de resistance', a slow handstand, balancing on the edge of a heavy table. There was one in the middle of the passage-way. It looked more difficult than it really was. The slower one did it, the better it seemed. In the final phase, I would end up almost vertically, balanced on my forearms. When I discovered that I could still do it, I was delighted. I also got a round of applause. My companions tried it, one by one, but they all failed.

I noticed a young Russian watching our horse-play, with an air of superior indifference. When all calmed down and everyone had retired exhausted, he slowly approached me.

"Hello", he said. " "Hello", I replied. "Where are you from?" he asked.

"I am on my way from Kotlas. They haven't told me where they are going send me yet". "A good trick you've got there", he said cautiously. "Oh, that, it's nothing," I said modestly. "It's not bad. You need a pretty strong back to do it that slowly, I suppose," he said. "Maybe, I wouldn't know", I said.

Suddenly, he lifted his arm, and with the palm of his hand brushed the side of his head, as if to smooth down his hair, flicking into view a heavy, golden bracelet on his wrist which made a rattling noise. This was followed by another flick, this time to pull down his shirt sleeve. The whole manoeuvre looked exaggerated and artificial, almost convulsive. It must be a nervous tic, I thought.

He offered me some tobacco with a friendly "Pokurim", or, "have a smoke". I accepted.

As he was rolling his cigarette, I took a good look at him. He was of medium height with light brown hair, very expressive dark blue eyes with thick dark eyelashes. His face was handsome, but showed nervous tension. He wore a tweed jacket either bought or stolen from one of my compatriots, a Russian-style blue shirt, light blue trousers and brown, cowboy-type boots. He gave an impression of neatness, almost elegance. Unlike many of his type, he did not smell of violets which was a great help. His hair was quite something. It was short at the sides and at the back, it was shaven at the edges so as to form a perfectly straight, horizontal, line on the neck and, instead of sideburns, the hairline formed two sharp points just in front of each ear. It looked as if he were wearing a wig. This style was very fashionable with the Red Army. I called it the Guillotine style as it looked purpose-made for that macabre instrument. His figure looked strong and athletic. He moved lightly and gracefully. Despite his strange mannerisms and dandified looks, he radiated manly strength.

"I am Karl Efstafievich Czosnowski", I introduced myself. "They call me Karlusha here." "And I am Alexander Grigorovich Krafchenko, but you can call me Sasha," he obliged.

This was followed immediately by his bracelet-rattling flick. He cleared his throat. "What is your speciality?" he asked. This is Russian for "What is your trade, or profession?" "I was at school when the war started. I have no speciality" I replied. "Have you done much sport while at school?", he continued. I said that I liked to ski in the winter and ride in the summer, that I played ice hockey and tennis and volley ball, and was on the school decathlon team, where running and jumping was my forte. I asked him what sports he liked best, but he did not answer. Instead, he continued to look at me, like someone about to buy a horse.

"Would you like to be a lumberjack?" he asked suddenly.

"Is that what you are?" I asked, in total surprise.

"Yes. I could teach you. If you have stamina, it could suit you, you know".

"I am very unfit now," I said, I am straight from prison. Six months is a long time!"

"Oh, that is nothing. If you start now, when there is no snow, you will be fit enough for when the real hard work begins. Snow and hard frost, you know," he added by way of explanation.

Now this was a tempting proposal. Lumberjack... the elite... head and shoulders above everybody... very tempting, I thought. Better food, better everything. "Povalshchiki" they were called, the heroes of the North...

"Are you sure I could make the grade?" I asked hesitantly.

"I am sure of nothing," he said, in a half-irritated voice, "It's just an idea."

"Could I stay near you, do you think, so that I could see how it's done?" I was trying to be cautious, at the risk of annoying him further.

"You would be with me all the time. I would take you as my partner, for a trial period at first, naturally," he explained patiently. "I lost my partner last week in an accident. Such a pity, he was a good man. It is better to work in pairs at this job, although I have been working alone all last week and still maintained results – averaging 120 percent - not bad after seven years," he said proudly.

"So you are a stakhanovite," I said. "This is fantastic! How come you are here, with us, in this camp?"

"It's a long story," said Sasha.

"Are you a political prisoner? We are all political here, I thought," I continued, being inquisitive.

"Political? Not on your Nelly! – robbery with violence, "he said proudly, "1935, ten years, with three years' "dobavka" (or addition) for unruly behaviour".

I calculated rapidly: He must be 26 now, another eight years to go. He will be 34 when he leaves – that is, if he does not earn another dobavka.

"What are you here for?" he asked.

"Illegal border crossing, five years to go."

"Child's play. Not worth talking about. So you are a tourist," he teased me, amicably.

"That's right," I agreed.

"Will you think about it then?" he insisted, "and let me know tomorrow. I am due to move North anyway. If you agree, I will talk to the planning officer. He knows I am in need of a mate. I could arrange everything. For a month's trial only, of course," he added.

"Of course," I repeated.

"So, will you think it over, sleep on it, as they say. I'll see you in the morning."

I was about to walk away, but I turned round quickly.

"I am very honoured and very tempted to accept your offer. You are an experienced and successful Povalshchik I can tell, but I am worried that I could let you down."

"I know," he said, "You are a proud man. You don't want to be a failure. But you have a month's trial. If you don't like it, I shan't keep you. You will not lose face. I understand. It cuts both ways. Goodnight."

"Goodnight, Sasha, and thank you," I said pensively, knowing I would not sleep much that night.

Next morning, I accepted. Sasha fixed everything with the management, and in the afternoon we were off, some 70 kilometres due North. We travelled in an open wagon. It was September and still very warm. The problem was the mosquitoes which made the journey less than agreeable. There were four of us in the wagon: the driver, Sasha, myself and an armed guard, for my benefit. Sasha was incredibly rude to the guard. I thought he was silly but, somehow, he seemed to get away with it. When I asked him some time later why he was taking such unnecessary risks, he told me the guards were afraid of him. He said that his three-year dobavka was for beating up a guard who had previously struck him. He had taken his rifle from him, had dumped it into a river and had taught the guard such a lesson that he ended up in hospital. I still couldn't understand. In my experience, men were shot for much less than that. Sasha, however, assured me that a stakhanovite Povalshchik was not subject to the same rules. The camp commandants were too preoccupied about meeting their targets to shoot valuable workers. Dobavka was the way they solved their dilemma, which apparently did not worry Sasha. Somehow I could not believe it, but his attitude was the same to all those who were supposed to guard us.

It took us two days to reach our destination. The camp was small, with only two large barracks and two or three smaller buildings. There was only one observation tower and a relatively low fence, circular in shape. "Krug" was the name of this camp which, in Russian, means circle. The total labour force was 80 men, nearly all involved with timber felling.

Timber felling comprised three main functions: the lumberjacks, the drivers and the stackers. The lumberjacks' job was to fell the trees, cut them into six-metre lengths, cut off all the branches and burn them on the spot. The drivers, or "vozhchiki", had a short sleigh and one horse. The sleigh was used both in summer and winter and the driver would lift the thick end of the log onto his sleigh, secure it with a rope and, leaving the thin end of the log on the ground, drag it to the stacking area, where the stackers would build huge piles, preferably on a bank of a river or by the side of a road. The timber would be transported mostly on water or, occasionally, by truck to the industrial centres for processing.

Each of the three groups had to fulfil a daily quota called the norm. If you fulfilled the norm, all was well. If you consistently under-performed, you would get into considerable trouble: in addition to being subjected to constant bullying by the "bouncers", your food rations would be reduced in proportion. On the other hand, if you were fortunate enough to over-fulfil your norm, you would have privileges: better and more plentiful food, better clothes and the glory of being a stakhanovite. At the end of each shift a surveyor would measure your output and often, after some heated argument, would record your performance. If men worked in pairs, or groups, the performance of that team would be assessed and the allocation of individual credits within the group would be made on the recommendation of its leader, who usually got the highest score, and the rest would be shared out pro-rata, in accordance with some simple formula agreed within the team.

Sasha was a very good teacher. He was strict but fair and above all, very patient. First he helped me to select my tools which consisted of a narrow-bladed lightweight arch-saw and an axe. The saw was a delicate instrument. The frame was made of wood and the blade was kept taut by twisting a string. By adjusting its tension, one could regulate the tension of the blade. A well-set, well-maintained saw was, to a Povalshchik, what a Stradivarius violin is to a concert violinist – irreplaceable. After a while people could become sentimental about their luchkovkas. There were even several songs in praise of this unique piece of equipment.

The main feature of the axe was its long handle and a fairly light head. It was well balanced and, in expert hands, capable of fantastic results. Sasha showed me how to use the tools correctly. The luchkovka was a solo instrument. You placed your left knee against the trunk of the tree, bent the other knee slightly, and placed the blade of the saw some 12 inches above ground level so that the cut would come towards you. Holding the frame in both hands you would move your arms, pendulum fashion, without exerting any pressure on the blade. A well-tuned luchkovka was a very efficient tool, capable of cutting softwood trunks, say 18 inches thick, in under 10 minutes. Your back took a lot of strain as you were bent right down with extended arms.

I found the axe more difficult to use at first. The action was reminiscent of a golfer's swing with the leading arm held straight except that the direction of the movement was more horizontal. When done expertly it was a graceful sight. It was difficult to achieve accuracy and to begin with Sasha was doing the all axe work, while I concentrated on the sawing.

It took us about three weeks to get our act together. After this we were a reasonably credible team. Our results were good. We averaged 230%, of which Sasha took 128% and I, 102%. I thought it was very generous of him, as I don't think I produced more than 90%, but he seemed happy and I was delighted. We worked nicely through October and the first week of November. It was getting cold, but there was no snow. Sasha was warning me that snow would make a big difference and that the job would be more demanding.

It came in the second week of November. The first fall was not too heavy, but soon digging was getting us down. I was coming back really exhausted and was worried that I had overestimated my stamina. I slept badly. I was too tired. I felt we were wasting too much effort shifting the snow, and that there should be a better way of dealing with it. I suggested to Sasha that instead of digging, we should use a kind of snow plough and pull the snow away, instead of lifting it. I improvised a wooden gadget with a little harness and some rope. One of us would pull like a horse and the other would manoeuvre the 'plough'. I suggested that we cleared all the snow first, before starting any cutting, thus profiting from it being still fresh and soft. Falling trees tended to compact the snow which slowed us down considerably.

Within a few days the system was working well and we were back on top.

A number of other teams started to use our little invention and it worked well for them too. My prestige was much enhanced and Sasha was delighted.

My relations with him couldn't have been better. He was a nice man, kind and generous. One had to be very careful, though, not to upset him as he was also a bundle of nerves. He was insanely touchy and could get aggressive, even violent, when provoked. He was intensely proud. We used to discuss it and he admitted that he was aware of it and that it worried him a lot. "I cannot stand pity. I would rather die that feel that someone was pitying me," he used to say. I reassured him that he needn't worry. Who could possibly want to pity him? He was a successful man, after all.

The atmosphere in our camp was fairly good. All the inmates were in the stakhanovite class. The authorities were quite relaxed and there was little trouble.

Sasha slept on a wooden bunk above me and spent most of his evenings setting and sharpening our tools and – preening himself. He had a small, round pocket mirror framed in something like imitation ivory, previously owned, no doubt, by his girlfriend or sister. He would spend hours adjusting his pointed sideburns, setting his hair and pulling faces. I was surprised that a proud man like him did not feel ridiculous. "Far from it," he used to say, "this is what keeps me from ending it all, you know... As long as one is neat and tidy, one feels superior to these filthy animals." He looked around him with disdain.

In complete contrast to his mirror sessions, he liked to win arm wrestling competitions. He was unbeatable. He would take on everybody and – invariably – win. This accomplished, he would have a 'quickie' in front of his mirror to make sure that perfection was not disturbed. In a strange way, he was feeding his insane, obsessive, pride. Both his looks and his strength were, obviously, necessary to maintain his fragile 'normality'. I was sometimes worried that, one day, someone was going to beat him and there would be no telling what the consequences would be.

That "someone" came in the shape of a Tiger. Not a real tiger, but a man nicknamed Tiger. Unlike the big cat whose name he assumed, this individual was most unprepossessing. He had a small head, large trunk, short arms and legs and short, stubby fingers. Impossible to imagine how he got his nickname. He was neither aggressive nor friendly, spoke little and spent most of his free time near the stove, playing "droomla", a Russian version of a 'Jew's Harp', which one placed in the mouth and activated with one finger. The tune was obtained by altering the shape of one's mouth. Not a nice sound and, certainly, not a nice sight!

Somebody came to Sasha and suggested that he should challenge Tiger to a match. Sasha was at a delicate stage of shaving the hair around his ears and brusquely sent the man away. I knew that the situation could not remain like this for long. Sasha would not be Sasha. Sure enough, in his own time, he walked slowly to where Tiger was sitting playing his droomla, stood in front of him for a while, flicking his bracelet as usual. Tiger stopped playing and looked up. Words were exchanged and the familiar preparations got under way. A small crowd gathered around passively to watch another Sasha victory. The result did not seem in doubt, only the speed and the style would be at issue.

As soon as they got to grips I knew that something was wrong. Sasha started moving his feet under the table, a movement which I had never observed before. I looked at their faces. They were calm enough. A look of grim concentration, nothing unusual. Tiger's legs were steady as a rock, Sasha's were not. It was taking a long time. I was standing more or less facing Sasha and although his arm had not shifted from the vertical, I knew he was beaten. He gave me one short, desperate look. His pride was being assassinated, I thought. What would happen now – my God – poor Sasha.

Soon afterwards his arm collapsed with a thump. It was over... he had lost.

I thought that Tiger behaved well. He got up, gave Sasha a friendly pat on the shoulder and said something like, "It was a very close thing". There was no sign of triumph in his attitude, if anything, a little embarrassment. Sasha got up without a word, did not even look at Tiger and – not bothering to wash – climbed up to his bunk, covered his head with a "bushlat" (a sort of overcoat), and I did not see him until the morning.

The next day he seemed normal enough, but I knew he had not slept well. His eyes, usually so bright, were dull and red. He looked older. It went on like this for about a week and I thought that he was getting over it, until one day Tiger and his team were allocated a line of trees next to us. This was the best part of the forest, where the trees were old and tall and, in proportion, one spent less time digging the snow than cutting the timber.

When Sasha realised what was happening I thought the devil had possessed him. He went berserk. The speed and fury with which he attacked his work was insane. He was beside himself. He was shouting at me, something quite new, even if I stopped to wipe my nose. He himself was everywhere. I never saw such a performance. In about an hour we were well ahead of Tiger's team. In fact, we moved in front of their felling line and were thus exposed to the danger of their falling timber. When I pointed this out to Sasha, he cursed me in a most unfriendly fashion.

In his rage he seemed determined to hurt me. He said things that I had never heard him say before, that if I wanted to work with someone else he could soon arrange it, or that if it were not for him I would be dead already, lying in some mortuary instead of being a stakhanovite; that I was not pulling my weight and that he had to work harder to make up my shortfall, etc. etc. "Leave me alone, I don't want to see you. Go and burn those branches at the back – go! – go!" he shouted at the top of his voice.

I obeyed miserably, knowing that there was no argument. Meanwhile Sasha was leaping about like a squirrel, from one fallen tree to the next.

When the accident happened, I did not see it. The smoke temporarily obscured my view. One second Sasha was perched on a felled tree cutting off branches by deadly accurate swings of the axe – the next he was lying in the snow, a shapeless heap.

When I got to him, he had his face in full view. He had a horrible, deep gash on his left cheek and his left ear lobe was hanging, like a grotesque earring, oozing blood. He looked at me helplessly. The same look as during the Tiger match, I thought. A bandage was soon improvised and rescue got under way. I was looking at him, lying there. A shapeless, helpless bundle. A makeshift stretcher was quickly constructed and we loaded him on a sleigh. He would have to travel at least 20 miles to get some expert medical help.

Just before he was taken away he asked for me. His face was already very swollen and almost unrecognisable. It was a laughing face. His eyes were not laughing, though. I could not make out what he was saying. "Mirror – he wants you to take his mirror," someone interpreted. I looked at him. His tragic, laughing face said, "Yes". Clumsily, I started, searching in his pockets. His eyes helped me to locate it. I took it out and held it up. "Shall I look after it for you until you come back?" I asked, my voice breaking badly. One of the crowd said, "You have it. He won't need it where he is going..."

I looked at him for a sign of confirmation. There was none. His eyes were not focused. They were looking in – not out.

Within six weeks he was out of hospital, we were told. They transferred him to an invalid camp miles away. His injured ear had to be cut off and his face was badly disfigured.

In January he was dead. He took his own life. He simply went out one night – and froze to death.

I kept his mirror for a long time. Somehow, I got used to it and it did not seem so horrid. It was finally stolen from me by a pick-pocket in Baghdad, when I was on my army leave.

# Chapter 6

## MARIA ALEXEYEVNA

From early childhood, I was made aware of the existence of Guardian Angels. My nanny, an authority on such matters, assured me that my own personal Angel was constantly with me. She taught me a little incantation which was meant to remind that celestial being of his obligations towards me:

> Morning, evening, day and night
> Keep me always in your sight.

I repeated after her. I still do, to this very day...

She was quite sure that Guardian Angels could assume many disguises: sometimes as men, sometimes as women, or even as dogs, or horses; they were not fussy. If my nanny were with me in Northern Russia in the winter of 1940/41, she would have readily recognised that my personal Guardian Angel temporarily assumed the name of Maria Alexeyevna Makarova, or simply Dr. Makarova.

*   *   *

So as to maintain some chronological continuity in my story, let me go back to the time when poor Sasha suffered his ghastly accident. A few days after he was taken away I was informed that I had to leave Krug. Was it because they were reducing the labour force there, or because they felt I would be no good without Sasha, I wasn't told. In fact, I think that possibly I could have stayed, since one of the members of the Tiger team had come to me a day or so earlier and made me a tentative offer to join them. But that was unthinkable, Sasha would never have forgiven me, so I refused. There was no other way, I had to go.

When I reached the new camp, I immediately knew that the change would not be for the better. The camp was huge, with seven 'stork's nests' (observation towers), security was fierce and so were the guards. Even the trees in the surrounding forest were thin and poor. How could one possibly hope to fulfil the norm, I wondered.

The following day I met my new mate. I didn't like him. He was a pale-faced young Armenian, called Vasily. He looked weak, flabby and effeminate. He had huge black eyes, but there was no honesty in his gaze. I couldn't work effectively with somebody like him, I was sure. I protested. In Krug, one would not be expected to team up with someone one did not like, but here, I was told to shut up and mind my own business.

It only took three weeks to confirm my worst fears. I was in deep trouble. My performance was poor, so was my reward. "He who doesn't work, doesn't eat, was the first commandment of the Gulag creed, irrespective of circumstances. So my food was cut. Every day I grew hungrier and weaker. I was also showing the first symptoms of tsinga.

Tsinga was the name of a particularly deadly form of scurvy, which is widespread in the Northern regions. First your legs begin to swell, then deep wounds open where the swelling is greatest. Finally infection sets in – and that, usually, is that. I have seen perfectly healthy men die of tsinga in less than a fortnight. It was not long before I couldn't put my boots on. Even the noisy "bouncers" stopped shouting at me. They knew what was happening. They allowed me to remain in the barrack while the rest went to work. My wounds were getting deeper and smellier. I could barely drag myself to the kitchen in the morning to get my breakfast. In the evening some good soul would fetch me my 500 grams of bread and my very thin soup. My life was rapidly draining away.

One dark morning a small group of officials appeared in our barrack. Three men and one woman walked slowly up the centre passage separating the rows of bunks. The barrack was deserted; only those seriously ill remained behind. The quartet stopped to talk briefly to each invalid and moved on. When they finally reached me I saw the men were all camp officials, including the Commandant and his clerk. The third was also local, but I couldn't place him. He held a large clip-board and was making notes. The woman was a total stranger. Under her overcoat she wore a white overall. She asked me a few questions, she made me to walk a few paces, she looked at my wounds. She thought a short moment and without a further word, left the barrack. The men followed. I was not surprised. Even medical personnel – and I assumed she was a doctor – could not help people with certain diseases. I knew that mine was such a disease. There was nothing that anyone could, or would, do. I just crawled into my bunk and went to sleep. I prayed not to have to wake up.

At about noon, one of the 'bouncers' shook me roughly. I was furious. Why didn't they leave me to die in peace? He told me to collect my things and be ready in ten minutes. He would help me to go to the secretariat to collect my pass, he said. "Where are you sending me?" I asked. "How should I know?" was the unhelpful reply.

I was ready. I managed to pull one boot on properly, the other only half way. I hobbled miserably as far as the door, when the bouncer offered me his arm. With difficulty we got to the secretariat. I was given my pass and was told to go to the main gate and wait for a guard. Still not a word as to where I was going.

It was only there that I learnt that I was being sent to the field hospital – San Gorodock. I was not sure if I should be pleased or worried. I was past caring by that time.

San Gorodock did not look imposing. From the outside it seemed a normal barrack, a little larger, maybe. The roof was steeper which gave it more character. It reminded me, in a way, of pictures of Swiss chalets.

Inside it was much nicer. It had clean, white walls, wooden, well scrubbed floors and wide double doors. It radiated simple comfort. I began to perk up at once. I was instructed to take off my clothes, which were immediately taken to be de-loused, shown to the shower and given a clean towel and a piece of blue speckled soap. A clean night-gown was provided. I asked about my wounds. They could be washed too, I was told. I felt distinctly better when, in my clean night-gown, I was shown to my bed. My legs were expertly dressed and bandaged and I was given a very "Ritzy" meal. For the first time in weeks I slept, literally, like a log.

It was about 10 o'clock the following morning, when I first met Maria Alexeyevna properly. I was brought to her consulting room. She was sitting behind a small desk, writing. I waited. When she had finished, she stood up and, without looking at me, went to check some bottles in the medicine chest. With her back to me, she told me to sit down. It was some minutes later when she finally came and faced me. "Ah!" she exclaimed, "the young man from camp 91 I saw yesterday. You come from Poland, I believe?"

"Yes," I replied. "Thank you for allowing me to come to this heavenly place."

"Oh," she shrugged her shoulders, "Don't thank me. In theory, I should have found you earlier, but we have no room. It's a doctor's nightmare. We are trained to save lives, but we are not given the means with which to do it..We take one and leave ten to die. I can't remember why I chose you. It could be your age, your blue eyes – or just your good luck. The other ten will be dead within a week. But let us talk about you, since you are here."

She smiled a most radiant smile and started unwinding my bandages. I observed her, as she was working. In her middle thirties, I thought, brown hair, big brown eyes, nice regular features, a small child-like mouth, white teeth, spoiled only by one gold tooth, just visible, when she laughed. Her skin was her greatest asset , peaches and cream I thought. Although not very tall and on the plump side, the general effect was pleasing, graceful and warm. I liked her at once.

She was quick and efficient in treating my wounds and, while she worked, she kept up a very pleasant and easy conversation. I noticed her voice. It was low, for a woman, but very soft and melodious. She laughed a lot. She asked me about Poland, my family, my school. At once, I replied frankly, without hiding anything. She was that kind of person. She teased me, when I told her that my father was a landowner. She said that, strictly speaking, she should have chosen a nice young proletarian and not a member of the upper classes, an enemy of the people. She laughed heartily, to make sure I did not take her joke the wrong way. I did not. Nothing she could do or say, would be taken the wrong way. She was perfection as far as I was concerned.

Our morning sessions continued for some ten days. Each day she found me better. My swellings were going down rapidly. The wounds looked less inflamed, but were still there.

She spent a lot of time on my treatment, and we talked. We covered an amazing range of subjects. She was obviously finding our little sessions amusing. I was over the moon. She became to me, at once, a member of my family , a young mother figure, or older sister , I could not tell which.

We talked about everything, including politics. I soon

discovered, to my amazement, that she was a devout Communist. She worshipped Lenin and his revolution. She told me that when she met him in person, she was only fifteen. She spoke of the enthusiasm, hope and good things which she thought the revolution was going to bring. The passion of her faith was unbelievable, particularly when I also learnt that , like me, she was a political prisoner. This did not make any sense, I told her. How could she worship a system that turned on its own true followers like her ? "But this is not important," she would argue, "our generation is nothing, our lives are finished. I will gladly sacrifice my life in the knowledge that future generations will benefit from what we have created."

When I protested that this did not make sense, she would say, "This is nature you know. A lot of the best things are brought about only through suffering. A woman giving birth suffers, but from her suffering a child is born. It's natural, do you know what I mean?" "But how long is this going to take?" I protested, "I have seen men who have helped to build the revolution, who believed in it, as you do, and they are locked up with us for crimes they have not committed. How can you accept a 'religion' like that?" She looked at me with curiosity: "You are religious, I suppose?" she asked. "Yes," I said, "and my religion makes much more sense to me, than yours. At least it tells me that if I have to suffer here in this world, I shall be rewarded in heaven. I, myself, personally, shall be compensated for my own suffering, not some anonymous "future generation". She looked at me again, with a mixture of curiosity and pity. "I am not – religious, I mean. I am a doctor and I know that we are just a chemical formula, and that a soul has no such formula, but I am not a militant atheist. I feel that people should choose what to believe. I was always getting into trouble for saying such things. "Loose talk, they call it – very naughty," ... she giggled like a schoolgirl.

Within a fortnight after my admission into San Gorodock, I was well enough to be discharged. My legs returned to their original shape, they were not swollen at all, only the wounds were still there. Maria Alexeyevna told me that, according to hospital rules, she would have to send me back to the camp. My wounds were under control and I could treat them myself.

I was very sad. I felt safe and would be at a loss without my Guardian Angel, I told her, and she laughed.

The following morning she was going to see me for the last time. I went to her consulting room as usual, at ten o'clock, but she was not in.

She was late. At half past ten she came, in a great rush. I was hoping for a nice, long session, our last, but she seemed in a tearing hurry.

"Karlusha!, what are you doing sitting here like an old man?" she said almost harshly. "Pull yourself together, you are no longer ill..." I was totally baffled. What's got into her? I wondered. Without any explanation she asked me to read labels on various medicine bottles which stood on the shelves. This was crazy, I thought, but obeyed. When we got to the last bottle she took out a book. It was a medical manual. At the end of it there was a long list of drugs. The book itself was written in Russian, but the list was in Latin. I read on. She looked pleased. "You will do," she said at last, half to herself and half to somebody, other than me. "You will do"...

She suddenly turned to me with her normal relaxed expression: "Karlusha, I think I have found a way, a way for you to remain here, at least for some months and help me and my staff. You can read Latin and it suddenly occurred to me this morning that we have a vacancy for an apprentice Lekpom (a sort of para-medic). You could work here and learn at the same time. I will teach you personally. What do you say?"

I couldn't believe my luck, but did not want to let her down. I asked her many questions and we discussed it at length. It really seemed to me that, with her help, I could do it. I accepted with joy, with gratitude, with all my heart.

* * *

It took only ten minutes for me to change roles, from that of a patient to a member of the hospital staff. I collected my things and was shown to a little room at the back of the building. I was to wear the hospital uniform – grey trousers and a white smock. I was not given any specific duties at first, just to obey my superiors which, in my case, was everybody else who worked in the place.

The staff was not numerous. In order of seniority it consisted of Maria Alexeyevna, Boris Ivanovich the administrator, a little man nicknamed Moskvich (meaning Muscovite, his city of origin) and a young man nicknamed Shovel who, like me, was a nurse. I was to share a room with Shovel. Boris Ivanovich and Moskvich each had a small separate room. Maria Alexeyevna didn't live in the building at all but was not very far away, as each morning she arrived on foot, even in the most dreadful weather.

My room-mate was a very strange individual. He was slow, but thorough, pedantic, one might say. Everything had to be done just so. He had big bony hands that looked distorted by some nasty disease, but he could thread a needle in a flash, his stitching was perfect and his bandages stayed forever. When he was working he would stop, from time to time, look around him slowly, rolling his eyes, as if to demand applause. He used to do it even if there was no-one about that he could see.

Outwardly, he seemed very calm, but somehow one felt that he was not, that inside he was disturbed. "Slightly cuckoo," Maria Alexeyevna would say, "in the nicest possible way," she would add. He was very friendly towards me and I learnt a lot from him. Sometimes he gave me the 'creeps'. A very poor sleeper, he could never stay in bed longer than an hour at a time. He would go out several times in the course of one night and on his return I would hear him say in a low voice, "All asleep..." At first I was sure that he was making inspection rounds of the wards. When I asked if I could assist, he would say nothing, rolling his eyes in his strange way and smiling darkly. One night I got up and followed him. I saw that he didn't go to the wards, but went out of the building. Naturally, I assumed he preferred the fresh air to the rather primitive staff bathroom. But I soon learnt that his nickname Shovel derived from the grave-digging duties which he performed in the Spring. All the dead were kept throughout the winter in a sizeable wooden hut. The bodies were frozen solid, so was the ground. Shovel was in charge of the hut, the mortuary, and went there frequently, often at night. I thought that he cared more for the dead than the living. Not to say that he was not the best possible nurse. Certainly very odd though...

Boris Ivanovich, by contrast, was a man of the world. He was good-looking and his manners were perfect, courtly, one might say. To Maria Alexeyevna he was reverent, a prime minister with his queen. She teased him a lot, because of that. He pretended to be amused but plainly, was not. With me, he was very nice. When he discovered that I knew the titles of a few operas and the names of their composers he immediately assumed that, in me, he had found a young fellow opera enthusiast and proceeded to share with me his impressive knowledge, although, at the time, my operatic education was actually very poor. Very soon, however, under his guidance I was able to sing to his satisfaction the Russian version of Italian grand operas. I learnt the great arias from Pagliacci, Tosca and Aida – which, I found, sounded just as dramatic in Russian as in Italian. Boris Ivanovich had a very good ear for music but no voice, and he used me as others use an instrument or a gramophone. He would 'conduct' his own opera while I was singing the Russian libretto. He was quite a character. His greatest problem, particularly for someone so elegant and courtly, was his surname which was totally unsuitable. To a Russian, Chlenov sounds, if not rude, certainly ridiculous and because of that we seldom used it. (It sounds uncomfortably similar to the non-abusive term for a male reproductive organ). On the rare occasions when we had to use it, we tried to pronounce it casually but it would invariably provoke a reaction ranging from a rude giggle to a more subdued "I see," or "You are not serious". I always wondered if it was not possible to change one's name, legally, in the Soviet Union.

It is very difficult to describe Moskvich, except to say that he was grey. His hair, his beard, his clothes, even his spectacle frames, they were all grey. Grey, grey everywhere – except for his eyes, which were yellow, or more accurately, such a light shade of brown that they looked bright yellow.

They resembled and, after a while, one could swear they were, a pair of fried eggs. This illusion was increased by very powerful spectacle lenses.

Neither friendly, nor hostile, the yellow yolks just glared from behind the well polished glasses without blinking. After a while it was difficult to remember what their true function was. Moskvich's function was also difficult to establish. No-one could tell me, precisely, what he was supposed to do. Naturally, rumour had it that he was a KGB snooper, which I seriously doubted. Maria Alexeyevna liked him and, whenever we said rude things about him behind his back, she would scold us. She said he had had a very hard time in prison and that he was accused of being a Trotskyist. Not the best recommendation for a KGB agent, unless it was just a cover. But I would trust Maria Alexeyevna's instinct in such matters. She was never wrong.

It was not very long before I found my own 'slot' in the hospital machinery. Shovel was very kind and allowed me to select my own level of involvement. I concentrated on the care of the patients, while he devoted a good part of his time to the upkeep of the hospital equipment, hygiene and such matters. He was also responsible for the intensive care section. A complete ward, comprising some 20 beds, became my main responsibility. In addition I helped Shovel in the intensive care section, which was about half as big. I soon mobilised the assistance of the 'walking wounded', mainly those with broken limbs, who were very useful in all the simple repetitive jobs, including the making of beds, preparation of laundry and so on, which gave me more time to concentrate on the nursing. As a result, all the early morning chores were finished well in time for when Maria Alexeyevna came for her daily inspection at 9 a.m. I would then take my patients individually to see her in her consulting room and stayed with them watching at first and, eventually, helping with the treatment. After a while I was allowed to perform most jobs under her supervision.

My relations with the patients were excellent. They all seemed to like and trust me and I was glad that Shovel did not appear to be envious. I had a feeling that all was going well.

The medical problems facing us could roughly be divided into three main groups: first there were the diseases caused by insufficiency of vitamins, principally Tsinga, or scurvy, in its various forms. This was by far the most widespread illness and caused the greatest number of fatalities. Next were the diseases of the digestive system, also resulting from poor diet. They, too, were devastating and in the main very difficult to treat. Usually, by the time the patient reached the hospital it was too late. The percentage of recovery was very low. The slow, relentless decline of a man afflicted with, say, pellagra, was most painful to watch. Innocent-looking at first, the disease would rapidly take hold and a normal-looking man when first admitted, able to help us with small jobs, would grow weaker and weaker. No matter what we gave them, their bodies would reject it. Very few survived. The whole process could take as little as a couple of weeks.

By contrast, the third group, the so-called mechanical problems such as wounds, fractures, frostbite and so on, offered us a good rate of success. Despite a total lack of antibiotics (penicillin was yet to be invented) and a great shortage of anaesthetics and even pain killers, most of our patients survived. I truly admired the courage of the men who endured prolonged 'torture', including amputations, performed 'live', with only occasional help from drugs. They groaned and cursed, but displayed superhuman self control. Quite, quite unbelievable.

Maria Alexeyevna was a superb teacher. She had infinite patience with me. She was seldom in a hurry. As we had so few drugs and practically no equipment, she taught me to concentrate on the psychological aspect of healing. She believed in the importance of helping the patient to help himself through his own defence mechanism, the 'treatment of the soul', she would call it, which I found rather amusing, coming from someone who emphatically denied the existence of the soul. She taught me how to compose myself when faced with the most horrible injuries, how to project calm and inspire hope in the most hopeless circumstances, while maintaining and transmitting compassion. She was the best example of 'drugless' medicine. She was fantastic. When I watch today some of the Western physicians, practising their skills, I often think of San Gorodock and of Maria Alexeyevna. How much could these modern pillars of medical science learn from the little Russian lady-doctor. If one could only combine her ability to treat 'the soul' with their techniques for treating the body, how much further forward we would be.

Maria Alexeyevna would say: "Our job is to heal, not to dispense pills," or "Hope is the most effective drug". Later, when I was working alone I found that I, too, was able to help my patients, even in the most hopeless circumstances.

I used to sit with the dying and felt that I was able to assist them in the transition from life to death, and although hope of life was no longer possible, another kind of hope appeared, so that in this strange process the soul could be 'nursed' from this world to the next. Death came with dignity and calm – as a reward, not as a punishment.

\* \* \*

Maria Alexeyevna used to go home, to wherever that was, at about 7 p.m. Quite often she would come back again at about nine o'clock to see a patient, or do some paper work, or simply to talk to us, relax or sing.

These were, for me, the happiest moments. We used to sit

together in the little pantry, on very uncomfortable wooden stools. Boris Ivanovich would bring his guitar, Moskvich his clipboard (which, inexplicably, he always placed face down), while Shovel brought the tea-making equipment and would make tea, which we drank in unbelievable quantities with amazing amounts of sugar, and we would sing.

Maria Alexeyevna had a lovely, rich, mezzo soprano voice and a most remarkable ear for harmony. She was slow to get going, but once started she never wanted to stop. Together we would sing very late into the night, in a state of total oblivion. Boris Ivanovich would accompany, skilfully and discreetly, on his guitar. I used to take the melody and she would move up and down, with her heavenly voice, in perfect harmony. Sometimes, she would get adventurous and her harmonic experiments would bring her so close to dissonance that the result sounded almost uncomfortable to my ear, but I learnt to stick to my melody regardless and, if I succeeded, the result was pleasing. "You must learn to trust me" she would say. "You are not used to our gypsy harmony but you will soon find that it's best suited to our songs. It's powerful, it tickles the soul..." Again, the poor non-existent soul, I smiled inwardly, while the music flowed on.

When all went well and to her complete satisfaction, she would let herself go. She seemed in a trance. Her face looked angelic, slightly arched eyebrows, eyes half shut, silky long lashes, head tilted to one side and, out of her childlike mouth came that incredible sound – straight from heaven. Our repertoire was increasing and improving. We both liked gypsy romances and Vertinsky ballads.* She taught me some very sad prison tunes and I introduced her to Italian and French songs, which was great fun because she couldn't learn the words. To disguise this she would make me sing normally, words and all, while she used to "fiddle around" as I called it, and do little hops and somersaults with her voice – in a sort of mini-coloratura.

Although I carried the melody, she retained total control of our little duet. We used to laugh that she conducted with her eyes. While the languid, slow tune flowed along she looked ecstatically indifferent but, when the tempo changed, her brown eyes would

* Vertinsku – an émigré Russian poet-composer, performing in Paris, was known and admired in the USSR.

flash like lighthouse beacons and she would impose the new rhythm, without moving a finger, slow and powerful at first, finishing in a controlled dash towards the end of each verse.

Boris Ivanovich was her most ardent admirer. He treated her with his elaborate reverence and paid her courtly and eloquent compliments which she accepted with grace, but without enthusiasm. She rewarded him from time to time by agreeing to sing a few arias from his beloved operas. She was at her best when she sang Carmen. Her voice was particularly suited to this type of music. She even managed to make very Spanish 'faces', with just a hint of arrogance and a suggestion of gypsy castanets. Boris Ivanovich was ecstatic. It was easy to imagine him in a different, more elegant world, say outside the stage door of the Moscow Opera, a bouquet of flowers in hand, greeting his favourite prima donna while his carriage waited discreetly round the corner. It made one forget the hard pantry stools.

There were also nights when we could not sing if, for example, someone was badly hurt or recovering after an operation. So we would talk instead.

She would then tell us stories, and soon would have us all in stitches. Her many talents included impersonations and mimicking. She was most amusing in her parodies of pompous officials.

Those were the happy times.

There were also times which were less happy, when she was moody. I dreaded the days when she was difficult and unreasonable. It often happened the morning after a particularly good night's singing. I thought she was 'picking' on me and it hurt. The moment she came through the door I could tell she was in one of her moods and I knew I was in for a rough ride. She would start by mocking me mercilessly – my Polish accent, my manner. The more careful and polite I tried to be the more annoyed she got. She would say things like "Why are you always so nice – nice," she would emphasise the word, as if she really meant "nasty, nasty." If I ever asked her to explain, she would get even more provoked: "You always want everything explained – explained. You are not stupid, so why don't you work it out for yourself, tell me why?" My sole defence was escape. I would leave her as soon as I could and run away to my ward, to my room – even to the mortuary, anywhere. I was hurt – my Angel, my idol, was cross with me – what could I do? Inevitably, I had to return, as duty called and things had to be done. Patients could not wait. In most cases she would say nothing and she might even smile. Just a hint of a smile, and immediately all was well with me – all was forgotten. I was her slave, I knew.

Of course I knew, too, that there were thousands of valid reasons for her moods. Her life was very sad. The long years in prisons and camps, the prospect of more years in this remote, god-forsaken region. For what she went through she was remarkably 'normal' and cheerful, all things considered. A relatively young and still very attractive woman – what a life for her....!

One morning I shall never forget, she came in and, at first, I thought a difficult one was about to begin. But after a while I looked again and saw that she was different. There was no aggression in her. I thought I saw a hint of a smile. She looked odd. An odd smile too. She did not say anything for quite a while and I was not going to say anything, either. But after some time she started, "I went to a party last night." I looked at her in silence, willing her to go on with her account. "Alexey Andreyevich's birthday, you know," she continued. I nodded. "They were talking about you, he and his friends," she smiled.

Alexey Andreyevich was the principal secretary in the regional headquarters, himself a political prisoner, but he enjoyed a great measure of freedom on account of his connections and administrative skills, and led an almost unrestricted life.

I saw him quite often when he called on us at the hospital for treatment. I thought him the nicest of Maria Alexeyevna's admirers and a very civilised man.

"In fact they were teasing me, quite mercilessly about you, you know," she continued. "Teasing – in what way?" I asked, astonished.

"Well, you wouldn't believe it. They said that you and I have a thing going between us. You a tall, good-looking young man, with me 12 years your senior. How wicked can people get?" she smiled again.

I could not believe it. I was incensed. How dared they. The dirty, dirty old men. Was there nothing that was holy for them, that was pure, that was good? They had to reduce everything down to their own level. Horrible, quite despicable!

I really let rip. The feeling of injustice and the power of my fury gripped me by the throat. How could people be so hateful, so stupid, so crude... I was truly, truly indignant. I loved Maria Alexeyevna, I conceded. I admired her, even worshipped her, but to me she was a saint, a mother, an Angel, my Guardian Angel.

I must have gone on for a long time without looking at her. I knew she was sitting there, under the avalanche of my words of indignation and wounded fury. When I looked up at her at last, I saw large tears rolling down her cheeks. She looked defenceless and weak, my teacher, my Angel had turned into a woman. In fact she looked far more like a girl. I went to her and kissed her hands. I begged her forgiveness. I was sure she knew how hurt and offended I was. She also knew that my love, my pure love for her, did not change as a result of all this. I declared that I would get a special permit and go and see Alexey Andreyevich and punch him on the nose, unless he apologised to her publicly. She smiled weakly and said that that would not be necessary. She was still sitting there and drying her tears. I could not believe that I was the cause of all this.

On the whole, Maria Alexeyevna enjoyed very good health. I seldom saw her unwell. Even when we were all sneezing and coughing she was unaffected. Only once, I recall, she developed a particularly nasty cough which she was unable to shake off. Day after day, she would sit behind her desk, or attend to her patients, coughing embarrassingly. "I really will have to do something about it," she would turn to me and say. "It is ridiculous for a physician to carry on like this. I may have to call on your medical skills, Karlusha, and ask you to rub my back with the camphor mixture. I suppose you are capable of treating a woman, as well as you are treating men". I assured her that it made no difference and was well within my capabilities. "Would it not upset you?" she looked at me, with mild anxiety. "Really?" "Really," I assured her, in my most professional manner. "Very well then, let us do it after evening surgery tonight".

"You are sure you are up to it?" she asked again. "Well up to it," I replied, feeling slightly offended that she could ever doubt it.

She left early that afternoon and returned at about six. She saw a couple of patients and, half an hour later she asked me again, in case I had changed my mind. I was quite fed up and told her not to be silly and go behind the screen and get ready while I prepared the treatment. She laughed and obeyed. I felt important . I felt in charge.

Coughs were mostly treated by rubbing patient's backs vigorously with a camphor based preparation. The result was to improve the blood supply to that area and, on the whole, the treatment worked well, despite its simplicity.

When Maria Alexeyevna emerged from behind the screen she wore only her skirt, and in front of her upper half held, firmly, a bath towel. She looked girlish, meek and quite charming. Suzannah in the bath came to my mind.

I assumed my most professional manner: "Lie face down on the couch, please", I said in a firm tone. It pleased me that she obeyed my command in total submission. I poured the fluid into the palm of my left hand and spread it gently over her back. I did the same with the other one and started to work.

Her back was white and smooth and firm. She draped her towel under her so as to obtain a maximum degree of propriety. Her face was half buried in the towel, but she was watching me with one eye. When she spoke her voice was muffled and she coughed gently from time to time. I got working, lightly at first, increasing the pressure gradually, for better results.

"Oh", she groaned "It's good. I feel better already. You have good hands. They are strong but gentle. They are a man's hands." "What else could they be, silly," I said quite naturally, surprising myself with my own courage.

"Do you know, what I am thinking?" she said, "I wonder what your good friend Alexey Andreyevich would say if he saw us like this," she giggled wickedly. "I don't give a damn," I replied, encouraged by my own boldness. "Now – don't giggle, be quiet and relax." I tapped her back to make my point.

She watched me with her one visible eye. "How are you Karlusha?" she asked in her muffled voice, " are you all right?" Of course, I am all right. My state of health in not at issue. It's yours, remember? 'How are you?' should be the question." "Oh, I am fine. I could go on like this forever. This is doing me a power of good." "Another three minutes," I looked at the clock on the wall, "we must not overdo it." "No, doctor," she said and laughed. "Oh, sorry, I am not allowed to laugh."

I knew that with every week that passed my time was running out. I also knew that I was supposed to sit an exam and that if I passed, I would be transferred elsewhere, where I could use my newly acquired skills.

No-one could tell me how difficult the exam would be. Maria Alexeyevna maintained that she was quite sure I could pass. I did not share her confidence. I was also not informed what would happen if I failed. Back to the forest and to my lumber-jacking, presumably.

When the time finally arrived, it proved a complete anti-climax. The medical panel took only one hour to reach a unanimous decision: that I was eminently qualified; and they rewarded me with a piece of paper which conferred on me the title of Lekpom, or medical assistant. I felt indignant and cheated. It seemed all wrong. I had prepared for this so diligently and they seemed so casual about it. The panel appeared more interested in my ability to read and write Latin than in my medical knowledge. They asked me several times at which university I was studying for my medical degree, and did not want to believe me when I assured them that such was not the case. They nodded gravely and looked puzzled. The whole thing was a farce, tailor-made for Maria Alexeyevna's 'take-the-mickey-out-of-the-clueless-official' act.

\* \* \*

It was only a matter of days after the examination that I had to leave San Gorodock. I got up much too early. I had an eternity to wait. I packed and re-packed my miserable possessions. I made several emotional goodbye trips round the wards, the consulting room, the pantry, the storeroom. I even called briefly at the hut where the frozen bodies of my patients remained awaiting the spring burial. I felt that it would not be right to leave without, at least, a short visit and a short prayer.

Maria Alexeyevna was busy all morning and I did not see her. She arrived late and shut herself in the consulting room with Boris Ivanovich. I was winding myself up to knock on her door some ten minutes before the appointed hour, when Boris Ivanovich appeared and announced that she would be out presently. He told me to wait in the hall. I heard the sleigh draw up at the front door – but still no Maria Alexeyevna. I was getting frantic...

Abruptly, she appeared. She looked most official. White overall, stethoscope, gloves showing from her pocket. Comrade-director of San Gorodock personified, I thought.

"So – Karlusha, you are off," she said in an indifferent tone.

"Your transport is waiting I see. So, it's goodbye at last?" "Yes," I said miserably.

"Karlusha," she repeated, more softly this time "Let me look at you. My Golden Boy. Life will make a man out of you.... one day."

What on earth did she mean, I wondered silently, she knows I shall be 21 next year. "Never mind" she went on, "you are a good boy. I hope you will remember your old Aunty Maria Alexeyevna sometimes."

"Oh! I will, I will" I repeated urgently. "I shall never forget you and all you have done for me..."

"Never say never, this is silly, I told you," she said severely. "Still, I must not boss you any more. You must establish your own authority," she added. "So, let me kiss you goodbye. May God bless you." She paused. "You will think you have converted me to your silly superstitions, but it is only a figure of speech, of course," she added.

"Of course..." I repeated. She kissed me on the cheek, ruffled my hair, and pushed me quite hard away towards the door. "Go. Go quickly, you must not keep them waiting."

I opened the door, my eyes full of tears. I resolved not to look back.

When I was at a safe distance, I did look back. She was standing in the open door. She looked small and frail and... old, somehow.

Even Angels have their 'off-days', I concluded, while stubborn tears kept rolling down my face.

\* \* \*

When I go back in my thoughts to those distant days of San Gorodock – to the few short months which represent such a small portion of my long life, they still seem close and vivid and fresh. Surprisingly, I can recall my companions, my patients, even myself – as I then was – on the threshold of my life, half boy, half man. Above all, I can recall Maria Alexeyevna. Frequently, through the ups and downs of the years I called on her in my thoughts. I thought of her. Did she survive the war, I wondered? Did she survive Stalin? Did she ever get back home, did she remember me – her devoted, clumsy young assistant, who annoyed her sometimes, amused her sometimes and who worshipped her with all his heart. Because he still remembers that he owes her... his life.

# Chapter 7

# FAIR DEAL

When we left San Gorodock the weather was good. The sky was grey as usual at this time of the year, not because of the clouds but on account of the position of the sun. It was just peeping over the horizon, and not giving much light. We were three in the sledge, the driver, the guard and myself. We had some 150 miles in front of us, which meant at least five days if the weather was favourable, otherwise it could take anything up to a fortnight if we had to shelter somewhere en route.

No-one was in the mood to talk. I was still trying to control my emotions and felt quite unable to speak. The guard did not talk, because guards just do not talk, and the driver was the strong, silent type, who only talked to his horses. These were a nicely matched pair of local ponies, slightly similar in type to the Norwegian Fjord, light chestnut in colour with a black stripe all the way down their backs. I knew the breed from my lumbering days as they were in great demand on account of their toughness and soundness. The snow was creaking crisply under the plain wooden runners of our sledge. It was not often that I had been allowed out of the camp, and it was even less often that I was able to observe, at leisure, the Taiga and the Arctic country in winter. So after a couple of hours of brooding I started to take some interest in my surroundings. In the poor light one could faintly see the silhouettes of trees lining our route. Endless, endless ... mostly pines and cedars showing dark grey against the light grey of the sky while everything else was white. The whiteness seemed more severe in the semi-darkness of the Arctic day, thus the predominant colours were shades of grey against the backdrop of stark whiteness. Occasionally, one could see a white squirrel or even a white fox crossing our path. Everything that lived seemed to be white in this zone.

The snow was deep but well settled and the horses were trotting quite comfortably for a mile or so at a time and then would be allowed to walk for a while. Little bells mounted on their harnesses jingled pleasantly. I was enjoying all this quite a bit, despite my sadness and despite the uncertainty which lay ahead, of which I was fully aware. I was about to take on my very first job and although looking forward to it, I had no illusions about the risks involved. For the first time in my life I was to be on my own with no-one to give me any support at all. No Maria Alexeyevna to guide me, no-one. The camp where I was going was an "All Criminals" unit and that was sure to involve nasty, violent men. Would I be able to cope, completely on my own?

At about three in the afternoon just as the last of the greyness of the day melted into the blackness of the night, we stopped to let the horses have a rest and a feed. Very quickly the driver lit a fire, put some snow into a metal bucket, melted it down over the flames and gave the horses a drink. Meanwhile the guard and I packed some more snow into another metal container and waited for it to boil. We then mixed some cereals for our own meal.

When eventually it was fully cooked and steaming invitingly, the guard took a bottle of vegetable oil, which he kept wrapped in a dirty rug under his seat, and ceremoniously poured out three measures into the dish and handed it to the driver to mix. The resulting delicacy was called "kasha" and as it consisted mostly of oats and had a good measure of vegetable oil in it, it was, by our standards, fairly nutritious. We all took out our own rations of bread which we sliced using a piece of string (we were not allowed to have knives). The guard, a free man, could possess a knife, but used his bayonet instead. His bread was white, while ours was black. While we were having our kasha and our bread the guard reached into the sledge for another metal container, also wrapped in some sort of cloth or towel. It contained a magnificent chunk of real, fresh lard, a kilo of it at least. Using his bayonet again, he cut a slice, half an inch thick, placed it on his superior bread and calmly proceeded to chew. We watched in awe, a free man having his meal.

We never expected to be offered anything, not even the skin, we were mere prisoners after all... Fat of any kind has always been in great demand in the North, but fresh lard was the stuff that dreams were made of.... The guard knew we were watching him and this added to his enjoyment. It consolidated his sense of superiority over us. This was, after all, the food of gods, and only gods could have it.

I couldn't tell if we were going to spend the night at this spot or not. I was watching for signs from my companions, but neither of them was doing anything in the way of preparations, so I waited. There was no wind and although the frost was hard, I was warm. The other two were sitting quietly by the fire, smoking, while the horses were munching their straw. No-one spoke. I did not dare to ask in case I betrayed my ignorance.

An hour or so later I understood what we were waiting for. From the East, from behind the trees I saw the moon rising. A huge silver disc shone magnificently through the tops of the trees. Its light was noticeably brighter than that of the Arctic sun. Reflected by the whiteness of the snow the trees were clearly visible now. They looked like black lace against the silver disc. Quickly we gathered our things, stowed them into the sledge, the driver adjusted the horses' harness while the guard and I put out the fire. Very soon we were on our way, trotting cheerfully through the Taiga and this endless, magnificent avenue which, at some distant point, was going to lead us to our destination.

My thoughts were different now. I felt hope in my heart for the first time in a month. These last few weeks in San Gorodock had been very unhappy. I had been dreading the future, it seemed dark and menacing. Why should I now be more confident, I mused, nothing had changed, nothing at all, and yet I felt quite relaxed. I sensed that, somehow, all was going to be all right.

At about midnight we pulled up in front of a wooden hut where, I assumed, we would be spending the rest of the night, and so it turned out.

We started early the following morning, having slept well in the warmth of our hut where, to my delight, we found a big iron stove and even some dry logs left behind by some previous inhabitant. The horses could shelter in a small annexe, big enough for the pair. Having eaten our kasha (no lard for the guard in the morning) we replaced the logs we had used, mucked out the stable and, in pitch darkness, hit the trail. We lit a small kerosene hurricane lamp and hooked it next to the driver. The light it gave was very poor; in fact it seemed more of a hindrance than a help, as it cast a long shadow right in front of the ponies' heads. But that did not seem to worry them and they trotted merrily into the blackness as if it were broad daylight.

A couple of miles into the drive we came to a shallow valley. By the shape of the terrain and especially by the line of the trees I could tell that we were driving on a frozen river. I knew that rivers in winter formed a very useful communication network, the best highways of the North. It felt warmer than the day before, which could mean that snow was on the way. I ventured a comment on this, the safest of subjects. The driver gave me a pitying look and did not reply. Immediately I regretted my boldness and resolved to shut up, regardless. After some time, however, he looked up and said almost politely, "It won't bother us, we are on the river." To which I nodded in reply, but could not work out what he meant until some time later, when it did begin to snow heavily. For the river banks formed natural guidelines which helped us maintain our course despite the blizzard.

The snow was falling steadily now, but our clever ponies maintained their pace, alternately trotting and walking. The driver checked the time with the guard, who had a watch, when we passed a particular landmark. We were doing well, despite the weather, he said.

We stopped for lunch in a sheltered spot where the river divided. The bank was high and formed an overhang. The fire was lit on a stone slab which protruded conveniently from the face of the bank and the usual routine ensued, including the oil measuring ceremony. The guard, in addition to his thick lard sandwich, also consumed a generous portion of kasha. We exchanged glances with the driver, who, of late, had seemed to grow a trifle less negative than hitherto.

Nothing of significance occurred that afternoon or evening. The snow seemed to ease somewhat, but the cloud cover denied us the benefit of the moon, so useful the night before. As we drove in darkness (not counting our miserable torch) I felt totally lost in time and space. We stopped for dinner at another natural shelter. This time it was on the bank of the river. We left the sleigh on the ice down below, unharnessed the horses and, all together, scaled the frozen bank. The place offered reasonable shelter so, I assumed this would be where we could spend the night.

After our evening meal we made ourselves as comfortable as we could by the open fire and, eventually, dozed off. How long I slept I cannot tell but when I woke up I didn't know where I was. Instead of the usual impenetrable darkness the whole world was alight. I could see everything around me for quite some distance, the river, the trees, the empty sleigh below, the sleeping men and the horses. I looked up and, to my amazement, it seemed that the sky was ablaze with the strangest sort of light. It was yellow-green in colour and was pulsating in an irregular rhythm. To tell the truth I was petrified. I couldn't make it out. It did not look like fire, it was not the moon and yet it was so bright. The ponies were also very disturbed; they too looked at the sky and fidgeted nervously.

I decided to wake the driver on the pretext that his horses were panicking. He woke up at once. Without a word he started to make preparations for immediate departure. I was too shy to ask him anything but I observed him closely, hoping for clues. His behaviour was having a calming effect on the ponies, who stopped fidgeting immediately and, I had to admit, also on me. He asked me to put the kettle on and to wake up the guard. He said: "This is bound to last a few hours, we might as well make use of it". Somehow the way he said it and the way he looked at the sky, in the way one looks at the sky for indications of the weather, gave me a clue. I was beginning to understand. What we saw in front of us was a particularly impressive example of Aurora Borealis or the Northern Lights. Now that I knew what it was, I started to enjoy the spectacle. While the driver and I were working together preparing for departure, I began to pump him for every bit of information his long experience in the North gave him. He didn't seem to mind. He was, for him, quite talkative now. He told me that this type of light could last for a while, hours sometimes, that it could change colour, that it produced shapes and waves and, sometimes, noise like thunder. The guard didn't say a word. He behaved strangely in fact. He did not seem to want to look at the sky. I asked the driver, when we were far enough away not to be overheard, why the guard was behaving so strangely. He shrugged and said "It takes people in various ways, just as it takes animals. You saw that the horses didn't like it. So some men don't like it either." "It doesn't seem to bother you," I said, as a sort of compliment. "I don't like the red ones," he replied, "that I don't. I know it's nasty, bad luck some people say. But this I don't mind, it can be quite useful at times – like today."

We only managed to have a sip of boiled water and a nibble of bread for breakfast, and we were off. We wanted to get the maximum use of the light. The guard was having a bad time. He was shaking all over as if in a fever. He kept his face buried in the collar of his greatcoat, and his slanting, Mongolian eyes had a vaguely insane look about them. I told him I was a medical assistant and asked him if I could take his pulse. He shook his head and told me to go to hell. I looked at the driver, but he pretended not to notice.

We were on our way. The ponies trotted gaily, all previous worries forgotten.

I wished the guard could get over his. Meanwhile I watched the magnificent display that nature was giving us. Now that I knew what it was, I was completely enchanted by it. Shapes started forming in the sky. From East to West an enormous arch appeared. It moved and waved like a huge curtain in the wind. But there was no wind. There was no moon either; it must already have set while we were asleep. One could just see some stars through the transparency of the curtain. The arch started sending orange beams of light upwards, into outer space and then, very gradually, the shape would change again. It was a curtain again, but this time long and low, stretching from one horizon to the other, its grand, majestic folds waving like some velvet drapery. The greenish orange glow began to darken, first at the fringes at the very bottom and then suddenly, all the way up to the top into infinity again. It was now quite red and getting redder.

I looked at the driver. He seemed all right, but rather tense. The curtain changed into an arch yet again, and again gigantic pulses of light shot up to the celestial darkness. It was getting redder too and the driver shuddered: "This bit I don't like" he said "this means blood." He said it in a flat, emotionless voice, but I saw that he was uncomfortable. He looked at the guard over his shoulder, as if to make sure that he was not listening. "It was like this during the troubles, when Yagoda was in charge, you remember?" I didn't, but I knew whom he meant. "Men were dying like flies then in all these camps". He was referring to the dreaded head of the KGB (or more accurately NKVD, as it was then called). "So how long have you been here?" I asked out of politeness. "Since 1931, ten years next September," he replied. I looked at him closely. He could not be more than 26, I decided. "So how old were you when they got you?" I asked. "Fifteen, that's all. And I got twenty years. A train job – robbery.. Would have been a real beauty had we not been denounced – by a mate, too!!." He looked over his shoulder again, just in case. A slow grin appeared on his face. I did not dare to look round to check why. The driver flicked his forefinger discreetly across his own throat and looked at me again with amusement. By a minute movement of his head he confirmed that this gesture referred to the guard. I smiled and looked round myself. Yes, no doubt about it : the guard was drunk. He was fast asleep, rolling gently with the movement of the sleigh. How and when this had occurred was still unclear, but the result was plain to see.

We carried on with our conversation as if we were alone. He told me of the bad days when he had had to work on the railway, building the Vorkuta-Krutaya line where the average was four men dead for each metre of track. They only got 600 grammes of bread a day and some soup, mostly water, and they were expected to work hard 12 hours a day in 40 below zero.

I had heard similar stories many times before. There was little new in this particular one. But no-one hearing it at first hand could expect to remain unmoved. The infinite human degradation, suffering and hopelessness came through every such account. No-one could escape the sense of indignation at the injustice and barbaric cruelty involved. And yet the driver, just like those before him, did not seem to resent the harm that had been done to him. On the contrary he seemed to recount his own version of 'the bad old days' with humour and with pride. "What you see here today seems like a holiday camp in comparison with the old days," was the phrase one frequently heard from the survivors of the Yagoda and Yezhov days.

Meanwhile our celestial fireworks display was burning itself out. It changed from the dark red to violet, back to yellow-green and then turned to a greyish glow in the sky without any definite shape or movement, but still bright enough to provide us with very useful visibility for navigation.

The guard was snoring away drunkenly, producing the most revolting gargling noises. The driver was chatting pleasantly, and the ponies were maintaining their normal walk and trot routine, but making good progress. Soon, it would be time for breakfast and a snooze, I hoped.

The driver and I had our usual breakfast. The guard had a monumental hangover and did not touch a thing. He went back to sleep and only revived in time for lunch. During lunch he had a little bit of kasha and then turned to his lard box. We were watching him, as always, mainly to see whether his hangover had spoiled his appetite. He had difficulties in undoing the string but eventually, with slightly shaky hands, got his precious delicacy out and cut a fairly thin slice with his bayonet.

The driver smiled a knowing smile as if to say: "Still feeling a little queasy?" but then, unbelievably, the guard stuck the slice onto the point of his bayonet and stretching his arm towards the driver held it there as if inviting him to take it. I could not believe my eyes. I was sure I was dreaming. The driver was surprised too but kept remarkably cool. For a long time nobody moved. I held my breath. "Take it," said the guard, invitingly shaking the lard in front of the driver's face. The driver looked at him steadily and did not answer for quite some while. "No, I am all right with my kasha," he said quite calmly, and resumed eating it. "Go on, take it," insisted the guard. Unbelievably, the driver did not seem interested. "No, I am not hungry." He sounded perfectly convincing, and yet I knew that he was dying to have it.

It was only when the guard asked him a third time that the driver accepted, still very slowly and with the dignity of a bishop. It suddenly dawned on me: of course – this was the old-fashioned peasant 'protocol', which I remembered observing at village functions in Eastern Poland. Correct behaviour demanded always that one should refuse twice if offered anything to eat or drink, and only accept on the third invitation. I was amazed this was still practised in the no-man's land of the northern Gulag. I felt the greatest possible admiration for the grace and poise of this amazing breed.

The peasant 'good manners' survived in this man despite impossible odds through prisons, labour camps, through cold and hunger. Neither Yagoda nor Yezhov or their NKVD were able to kill the old customs, and the old dignity that went with them. I was sure that even if I tried my hardest I could not convincingly have reproduced this amazing charade with anything like the dignified manner of this common criminal. I resolved to try, though, if for no other reason than to express my admiration for what I had just witnessed.

My own effort in producing two convincing refusals fell well short of the intended one. On the scale of one to ten it probably reached only two. But honour was satisfied, and while I was avidly inhaling the magnificent aroma of this divine nourishment, I had the pleasant feeling that my reputation was relatively intact.

The problem now was how to extend the pleasure to the maximum. On rare occasions such as these, the established method was to eat the indifferent bits first and to leave to the end the very best. I watched the driver. Deliberately he bit the skin off and chewed the hard, leathery stuff as slowly as possible, sucking out all the juices in the process. What was absolutely inedible he threw into his kasha and left it there for later. Only when this was fully completed did he start nibbling, very slowly, at the lard itself. I followed his example faithfully. After all, he had ten years' experience behind him and I was still in my first year.

Half way through this absorbing procedure he suddenly stopped eating and looked at the guard with a smile. It was a most engaging smile, slow and shy, but charming. It reminded me of Gary Cooper, then a well-known Hollywood star. "And what are we supposed to forget in consideration of this reward?" he pointed to the piece he was just eating. "What do you mean?" asked the guard in a hoarse voice. "You won't want me to believe that all this is just because of your generosity?" He still maintained his Gary Cooper grin. "It wouldn't have anything to do with the quarter of a litre of moonshine you were helping yourself to, while we were admiring the lights last night," he added after a pause. "What moonshine...I have no moonshine – you know we are not allowed to drink on duty," said the guard insincerely.

"Even for medicinal purposes?" suggested the driver still enjoying it hugely. "Maybe, but I think we need not go into this. The best thing would be to forget what happened last night altogether," and the guard winked confidentially.

"I suppose you couldn't spare a drop of it to wash down this lovely "zakuska"* the driver persisted, regardless. The guard became very annoyed. He grabbed the driver by his coat and pulled him close to his face, yelling : "Don't try this game on me, prisoner, or I will shoot you like a rabbit.!!!" He looked very convincing. I wished the driver would stop it and let us enjoy this moment in peace. He did eventually, but somehow, the enjoyment was gone.

---

* Zakuska – Russian word for snacks servied with vodka.

The rest of the trip followed the same pattern. We were to stay on the main river for another day or so and only for the last few miles were we to turn into a tributary which would lead us to our destination. Provided the good weather held we were hoping to get there in record time.

It was on the very last morning, when we were clearing up after the night and preparing for what was to be our final leg, that I noticed that the driver was in a particularly good mood. He was singing, talking to the horses and generally oozing good will. It was not normal for him, so I asked him to share the cause of his good humour with me. He said he was pleased that the trip had gone well and that he was looking forward to a bit of a rest before his next assignment. It sounded fair enough so I accepted his explanation at face value. But when I noticed that his now familiar grin was back again, I knew that something was up. I waited until it was safe and asked him, specifically, what kind of mischief he was contemplating. He said nothing for some time. I was sure he was teasing me and that sooner or later he would tell me of his own accord. So I pretended not to care. It was only just before our departure, at the last moment, when the guard was still out of earshot, that he turned to me and said, "I finished his "samogon" for him last night." I wasn't sure what he meant, so I asked him to repeat it. "The bottle of moonshine we were talking about. There was still a good drop left in it, so I felt, as he had asked us to forget about it, that he should forget about it too. Levels up the score a bit – don't you think? Fair's fair, as they say!!!"

"But you must be mad," I hissed, "he will kill you – he said he would." "Oh, no he won't," he replied, "and if he does, who cares!!!"

\*   \*   \*

When we finally arrived in Vazky Yol, for that was the name of my new camp, it was late afternoon and very dark. The guard signed some documents and vanished, and so did the driver, after shaking my hand and wishing me luck. His parting words to me were, "Be very careful. I have just been told that your predecessor, the previous Lekpom, was hacked to death by his patients here." I was alarmed and wanted to know more but he said he couldn't tell me, as he didn't know, but that he advised extra caution. Very sound advice, but how? I wanted him to find out more and tell me, but he said he couldn't , that he had to dash, and just vanished. Meanwhile I was to produce documents, sign forms, send my things to be de-loused and have a bath in the camp 'bania', a Russian version of the Turkish bath, one of their better inventions, which is the traditional way of keeping clean. The bania helped me to regain my mental balance. After all, I thought, the driver didn't really know anything.

When I was finally shown to my lodgings I was overjoyed. This was heaven. A tiny log cabin with a sloping roof standing in the snow like something out of a children's fairytale. It looked warm and clean and homely. It consisted of just one room, the surgery, but behind a partition stood a perfectly adequate bed. A sizeable iron stove was radiating welcome heat. On a small desk stood a kerosene lamp and above it a glass cabinet with medicine bottles and a few surgical instruments. The feeling of unimaginable comfort overwhelmed me. I wanted to be alone to wallow in all this, to enjoy it, to delight in it.

Many times during the years I have been back in my thoughts to this moment. Incredibly, it ranks as one of the few occasions when I was fully aware of having reached absolute happiness. Why it should be so is difficult to imagine as the 'ingredients' normally associated with this rare condition were simply non-existent. The odd thing is, too, that at the time I was fully aware that I had little cause for happiness, that I was still a prisoner with some five years to serve, that I was 2000 miles from home, that my family didn't know where I was, and dozens more perfectly valid reasons for being thoroughly miserable. I remembered, too, what the driver had told me about the fate of my predecessor and the possibility that it could easily happen to me. I am quite sure that I was fully aware of all these things. I am equally sure that despite all this I was, for that brief moment, completely happy. An American psychologist told me, years later, that he was working on the theory that the way to achieve ultimate happiness was through privation. He may have had a point there.

To my intense annoyance, just as I was settling down to enjoy my solitude, the Camp Commandant came to see me. His name was Patiomkin and he was the senior NKVD officer in charge of the camp. He came ostensibly to welcome me under his command, but in reality he wanted a drink.

His favourite beverage was Valerian, a mild sedative with a fair bit of alcohol in it. It took, however, a long time before I realised the true purpose of his visit. Still, I profited from his presence to get some information on the situation in the camp. I asked him also about the rumours concerning the fate of my predecessor, to which he replied that yes, maybe there had been some problems in the past, but they had been caused through lack of tact on the part of the previous Lekpom. He felt that, had the old Lekpom handled it all with more tact "this" would not have happened. When I pressed him to tell me exactly what had happened he said the matter was under investigation and he would prefer not to say anything for the time being. He did admit, though, that the old Lekpom was dead. What he would not say was why and how. His parting words to me were, "I would be very careful if I were you. Do not get involved with petty crooks. They are the nastiest and most treacherous lot imaginable. Always deal with Grisha, he is OK." When I asked him who Grisha was he did not reply directly, but I guessed that he must be the highest ranking criminal and head of the unofficial camp Mafia. With this friendly warning he shook hands and left.

Predictably, I was very disturbed by Patiomkin's visit. My attempts to forget all about it, and to revert to that state of bliss which I had experienced only half an hour earlier, proved impossible now. The menace was too real. I had to prepare mentally for what lay ahead. I had so little to go on, though. I did not know anything about this camp. "Not to allow oneself to be bullied by anyone..." what did it mean? It was so easy to say such things when they meant so little. I was getting tired and sleepy. I knew I was just going round in circles and getting absolutely nowhere. "I will start worrying about it first thing tomorrow," I said to myself aloud. And as often happens, I immediately felt better.

At about eight o'clock, having completed my unpacking I decided to go to sleep. The prospect of spending the night in a proper bed was too tempting to delay. I warmed some water on my stove and started my evening ablutions when a rude noise at the door gave me an nasty start.

"Open up" a voice shouted "let me in, I need medical attention."

Quickly I put my clothes back on and unlocked the door. A man came in without as much as a nod. I went to my desk and sat down and asked him to take a seat on a wooden chair next to me. He didn't move and just stood near the door. He was fully dressed in his working clothes, including his hat and gloves, and held an axe in his hand.

"What brings you here at this late hour?" I asked as casually as I could. The whole thing seemed odd. He looked at me and said, "You are the new Lekpom?" "Yes," I answered, "I am. And who are you and what do you want?" "You look far too young for a proper Lekpom to me," he said without any sign of friendliness in his voice. "What I want is a certificate from you that I am ill and that I can rest tomorrow." "You know you cannot have such a certificate until I have examined you first," I was getting annoyed. "You sit down here, tell me who you are and what your problem is." I was trying to control my irritation. "You don't seem to understand," he suddenly turned nasty, "we don't want any young boys like you telling us what to do. I will tell you now, if you don't sit down and write me a certificate right away, tomorrow they will find you dead with your brains on the floor, like the chap before you. We don't mess around here, you know. Have a look at this..." and he raised his axe slightly to emphasise the point.

"God," I thought, "do I have to make my stand right now? Could it not have waited a few days? I am so tired, I don't feel like fighting with my bare hands against a man with an axe... Please, God, please..."

My hour had come. I knew I had to face it now. It was no good hesitating. The only thing was how. I was still seated and that was wrong to begin with.

It was imperative to get up without alarming my enemy. I took a good look at him. He did not seem very tall or particularly athletic, but he had an axe and was no doubt quite prepared to use it. He still stood with his back to the door which was slightly ajar, and which opened outwards. If I pushed him hard enough, I thought, he might trip over the threshold and stumble out and then I could try to bolt the door behind him.

I had nothing on my desk in the way of writing materials. That gave me an excuse to get up. I got up slowly. He made a move towards me. I lifted my hand to indicate that he should stay where he was. It worked. He remained standing with his feet well apart, right on the threshold , with the door immediately behind him. I walked slowly behind my partition, trying to keep the flow of conversation going to allay any suspicion. I braced myself for the supreme effort. I knew that that move was going to decide whether I was going to live or die. While still out of sight I took a deep breath, crossed myself and with all the desperation I could muster hurled myself at my enemy. I used the wall as sprinters use starting blocks. I aimed to hit my target in the middle of his chest. It took only three steps, as the room was small, but my acceleration was considerable. The surprise was also considerable. Somehow my right elbow ended right under his chin and connected with a most satisfying "crunch". The result was impressive to say the least. My victim crashed into the door which swung open with a bang. He nearly fell out but grabbed the door frame at the last moment, dropping his axe. I was quite upright by now, so I grabbed the top of the door frame lifted myself sufficiently to deliver the "coup de grace" in the form of a very credible two-legged push-kick just below his ribs which propelled him into the soft snow outside. In the process he lost his hat as well as his axe. They both lay at my feet while, exhausted, I held on to the door frame, panting.

I threw his hat at him , and watched his clumsy efforts to get up. I picked up his axe. "I hope you feel better tomorrow," I said, "if not, you can always come back for more." I was surprised at my own audacity. "Perhaps you will tell Grisha from me that if he wants to talk to me I am always happy to oblige. But ask him not to waste my time, and his, with chaps like you." On this I threw out his axe and bolted the door.

A second later the reaction set in. I started trembling like a leaf. I tried to steady myself while I concentrated on inspecting the door and the window to see if they could withstand an attack from outside. The door was solid timber, three inches thick, with good hinges and sturdy bolts. The window was secured by equally substantial shutters. No danger of either giving way in a hurry, thank God.

I was still shaking slightly. I knew I had succeeded in my initial test, but it was not necessarily the end of my problem. If I had to fight like this again and again, eventually they would get me. There had to be a better way of living with these people in a more normal atmosphere. To steady my nerves further I decided to have a hot drink of boiled water as I had no tea. I put a small kettle on the stove and sat down on the bed to wait for it to boil. That's when I fell asleep.

How long I slept I cannot tell. I was up on my feet long before I was awake, though, as in my deep sleep I heard a banging on my door. It was just a reflex on my part since, although I was standing, I couldn't wake up. My body simply ignored my commands. I forced my eyes to focus. I still didn't know where I was or what I should be doing. I saw the water boiling on the stove. I tried to speak, but I couldn't remember in what language. I heard a deep voice the other side of the door. "Russian", I recognised with difficulty, "It was Russian." This recognition felt like the kick of a mule. Everything came back to me in a flood. I was seized by panic. "They've come back!!! I'll have to fight again..." I thought frantically. My limbs replied a categorical – NO. No more fighting, said my nerves, we give up!! I resolved not to open the door. Let them break it down. I said so in Russian out loud. The deep voice behind the door paused, then laughed and said that nobody was going to break down my door, that his name was Grisha and that he had come to have a chat. Very carefully I unbolted the door and opened it, just enough to make sure that it was not my unfriendly patient. No, it was not. I sighed with relief and confidently now, opened the door.

Grisha came in. My mouth fell open, I thought I was still dreaming I had before me a principal character from some Russian grand opera, a Prince Igor, or Boris Godunov, or Peter the Great. Dressed in expensive furs from head to toe, six foot three or four, he floated in majestically with a slightly sardonic, but not unfriendly, smile. He looked at me from his impressive height and said that he had been told that I had expressed an interest in meeting him.

"Oh, that," I said, " there is no hurry. Any time would do. I only said so as I had a very unpleasant incident with one of your men a short while before, who threatened me with an axe."

"I heard that you dealt with him adequately. He will not bother you again, I think. Is there anything else you would like to discuss with me?" Having said that he sat himself down on my small chair.

"Yes," I said "there is. I hear that my predecessor suffered a fatal accident at the hands of some of your men. Having just experienced a direct attempt on me, within an hour of my arrival, I don't think this is going to help me to carry out my job here. After all you do need medical assistance sometimes."

"Of course we do," he said, "of course we do. I am not going to tell you right now what happened to the other fellow, you will find that out soon enough.

Let me just say this: he allowed himself to be blackmailed by some third-rate pickpockets who, as a result, took more than their fair share of time off, while men who were really ill had to go to work. That's not fair, you will agree. Now, you will have a chance to put it right

"I see" I said out loud, while in my heart I knew that I saw nothing at all. So, as one does in such circumstances, in order to gain time and in the hope of some miraculous inspiration, I started to ask questions. How many men were there in the camp? What were their jobs? What were the norms? What was their general state of health?

While we were talking I observed him closely. I have seldom seen such a magnificent specimen of masculinity. Apart from his size, which was imposing, he had a superb bass voice, very noble features and particularly striking, dark brown eyes, giving one an impression of strength, intelligence and natural authority.

As a result of my questioning I was able to ascertain that the camp numbered some 300 men with, possibly, some 20 more in summer. They were all criminals, therefore not requiring any armed escort and that nearly all were employed in logging work. In addition, during the summer some floating work was generally added. Their state of health was good and on an average day three or four of them would report sick. He also told me that the previous Lekpom had often up to ten men off work, mostly his pickpocket pals wishing to have a rest. All this gave me an idea:

"Assuming that the rough figures you have given me would not alter materially in future, how would you feel if we were to make a gentlemen's agreement so that, in addition to those men who, in my opinion, were really ill and should not go to work, two more were to be given a day off?" I paused and looked him straight in the eye. As I did not detect any objection, I carried on "... and supposing further that these two men were to be selected by you personally, and that you would send me every evening the two names on a piece of paper written in your own hand?"

"Is that your proposal ?" he said drilling me with his brown eyes.

"Yes, it is" I said emphatically.

A huge hand was extended to me in reply.

"It's a deal then" he said "a Fair Deal".

"A Fair Deal" I repeated after him.

Solemnly we shook hands. Shortly afterwards he left.

I never had any more trouble with any of my patients from then on.

Chapter 8

# LIFE AMONG CROOKS

With very few exceptions, everyone who lived in Vazky Yol in 1941 was a professional criminal. At first it seemed odd that there was not a single person about who had not killed, or robbed or cheated and who did not regard his occupation as a normal and legitimate way of earning a living. It was equally strange that all my companions considered their trade in the same way as carpenters, bricklayers, or even doctors or lawyers do. Men introduced themselves as, say, Ivan Ivanovich Petrov, 20 years for robbery, or Andrey Kuznietzov, pickpocket, Moscow Main Station. One could almost imagine that they carried business cards with their professional qualifications showing under their names. The fact that the non-criminal world did not consider their activities as legitimate presented no problem to them. They were crooks and lived among crooks. They accepted that another, non-criminal world existed, but they were glad that they were not a part of it. To them being a crook was not only perfectly normal, but was a source of considerable pride. What we would describe as nice and straight and honest to them was artificial, unnatural almost. The non-criminal world was viewed by them with condescension. They knew such people existed. They had to exist, otherwise the crooks would have no-one to rob or cheat. They would say, for instance, "I was lucky you know. In 1933 I met Vanya who taught me all I know. Without him I would still be an ordinary worker in some factory somewhere..."

The Russian criminals were extremely class-conscious in those days. In fact, class to them was everything. In their hierarchy big-time criminals such as bank or train robbers, were members of the upper class. Grisha Tchorny, the head of the camp Mafia, was one of them. At the opposite end of their social scale were the petty crooks, like pickpockets. The big boys would use them as their valets or messengers and they received very little consideration. All other crimes formed the bulk or the middle class, but even there, there were distinctions.

In many ways this strange society was, in caricature, a replica of the 'normal' world. In it one could find the equivalent of every shade of human virtue or failing. For example, you could readily recognise the ambitious man on his way up, the snob, the social climber, the cheat as well as the honest and generous man. After a while I learnt to recognise the latter. One wouldn't expect to find such men among crooks, yet not only did they exist, but I have known some who were real gentlemen...

It took me some time before I could understand all this. To begin with, I was confused and unsure of myself. My experience in Krug, among the loggers, gave me a certain preparation for this kind of community but there, they seemed more friendly. Here, I had had a nasty shock on that first night with my very first 'patient', which didn't help much and whilst I knew that my subsequent agreement with Grisha was potentially favourable, I was not at all sure if it could be made to work.

In Krug I was Sasha's assistant, a nobody. Here I had an independent position and considerable responsibility. In order to do my job properly I had to be convincing. But how? How was I to establish any semblance of authority over a group of men who, a short time ago, had murdered my predecessor. Not easy for someone aged 20, and a foreigner to boot. It was not long before my determination was to be put to a further test.

In fact, this test came on the very next morning.

I was awakened by the usual clanging sound of a steel rail being hit with an iron rod. Not a pleasant noise. It was five o'clock, time to get up. As I was washing and dressing I saw breakfast queues forming in front of the kitchen windows.

My first impulse was to take my plate and get some food, but I changed my mind. I thought I would rather wait until everybody had gone to work, and have my breakfast alone without the strange crowd – of which, frankly, I was rather shy. Then, almost painfully , I remembered my resolution of the previous night: "I must be strong, I mustn't run away. I must meet the challenge head on..." I recalled that in most previous camps the Lekpoms used to go to the cookhouse to inspect the food. They never stood in a queue. They went straight into the kitchen, something that I thought very natural then. "This is what I am going to do this morning," I decided.

With grim determination I put on my coat and hat and went

straight for the kitchen door. I even forced myself to look at the queuing men without flinching. This was meant to harden me up for the task in hand. I noticed, by the way, that they looked well dressed and well fed, certainly not the poor wretches I had known in the political camps. Some men stopped talking and looked at me, but without much interest. Good, I thought, let's look as casual as possible.

At long last I reached kitchen door. So far no-one had said anything, they just stared . I tried the handle of the kitchen door. It was locked. Nothing unusual in that, I thought, just good common sense. I knocked. No answer. I was facing the door, but felt the eyes of the men fixed on my back now. I knocked again, but harder. I heard footsteps the other side of the door and a voice asking "Who is it?". "The Lekpom" I answered "let me in". I heard someone laugh and walk away. The door remained locked. "I must not give up now, there is no going back from here," I thought. I gathered all my strength and instead of knocking I kicked the door hard.

The resulting noise was quite considerable. It seemed to work. The door opened, but only enough to allow somebody's head to pop out. I was confronted by a smiling Chinese face which asked me in a typically oriental, high-pitched voice: "What do you want?" "Let me in at once," I said as firmly as I could. His smile broadened. He looked at me, then at the queuing men, as if to take them for witnesses of his super-human patience. Then, like a professional comedian, he paused for effect and in a stage whisper, which could be heard by all those present he hissed: "G-o t-o h-e-r-r" ... This, I guessed, was his well rehearsed and very popular party piece, and was rewarded by a howl of laughter. The Chinese smiled and bowed elegantly.

I knew I had lost the first round. It was not the end of the world, but on no account must I lose the bout. That would be disastrous. While I was trying to steady myself the Chinese comedian was driving his advantage home: "See the end of that queue over there. That's where you should be, like a good boy!!!". He pushed me gently in that direction. He got some more laughs from his responsive audience. They all agreed, no privileges for anyone.

I didn't have a clue what to do but, instinctively, turned round and faced the crowd. They were still laughing in a nasty, mocking sort of way. Even the men at the serving hatches remained there with their steaming plates so as not to miss the show. As a result the queue was not moving, but nobody seemed to mind. I looked again at the men nearest to me. There was something which compelled me to take that second look. What could it be? I looked hard, I saw their laughing faces, the steaming soup in their plates and.. then...suddenly – I knew !!!. I dashed to the nearest hatch and asked the man to show me his plate. Laughing, he thrust it right under my nose. I examined the contents thoroughly and waited for the noise to subside. Then I looked up and pushed the plate firmly away.. I raised my voice to full volume, "What diet is this supposed to be?" I asked. "Stakhanovite No.3," he replied. "And how much oil is there supposed to be in Stakhanovite No.3?" I enquired. "Twenty five grams, I think" he said with a shrug. "No, thirty," I corrected him, "and how much would you say is here, in this plate?" "Hardly any," he replied almost apologetically.

I paused to allow everybody to have a good look at their plates. "It seems to me," I declared loudly, "that you are paying excessively for your morning's entertainment". I moved slowly to where the Chinese cook was standing. "Not a bad little business you have here, my friend, not bad at all!!!" The hum of the crowd sounded different now, almost as if it had changed gear. I felt I was gaining, but only just. I could not afford to let go. It was essential to drive the advantage fully home, without mercy. I mounted the single doorstep to gain height and in a theatrical gesture put my hand on the cook's shoulder: "Well Mr. Comedian, what have you to say for yourself?" He looked worried. The crowd was not with him any longer, and he knew it. He started shifting unhappily and making some unintelligible noises when suddenly, I felt that he froze and stared into the middle distance.

I followed his line of vision and recognised the Camp Commandant who was approaching across the compound. "Anything the matter, Lekpom?" asked the Commandant from some distance. The silence was such that one could clearly hear the snow creaking under the Commandant's boots. I looked at the Chinese. He seemed petrified. I looked at him hard. His eyes seemed even narrower, darker. His body language showed submission, regret. I knew it was too early to let him off. Not yet.. The Commandant was now standing next to me.

"Is anything wrong?" he asked again. I looked at the cook,

hard. My pulse was racing. His yellow face was covered in a faint purple blush. I looked at the crowd. They understood, I knew. I took a deep breath and cleared my throat. I could not hold this any longer, I had 'squeezed' all the juice out of that lemon and ... I was now feeling sorry for the cook. "No, Citizen Commandant, not really". I said. "I was just suggesting to the cook that we should open another serving hatch. It would speed up the whole operation, make it more efficient, less queuing." While I was talking I kept looking at the Chinese severely, so as to make sure that the significance of my magnanimity was not lost on him. He looked surprised and... relieved. He even winked at me, in a shy and rather self-conscious way. I was sure now that the message had got through. "Good idea," said the Commandant. "Remind me of this tomorrow." "I will," I said and opened the kitchen door wide, and slowly walked in.

* * *

The next few days following my skirmish on the steps of the cookhouse abounded in similar instances. I had to overcome sometimes real, but more often artificial, obstacles which were placed in my way by petty officials.

I tried to use reason, but often had to resort to varying forms of blackmail. Each battle was progressively easier, though, as my standing improved. The resistance became less fierce and, consequently, the effort required diminished.

I was beginning to build a relationship which, I hoped, would translate hostility into co-operation and mistrust into confidence, friendship maybe. My deal with Grisha Tchorny, which I had concluded on my arrival, was working well. It removed areas of conflict with the petty crooks, who were potentially my most dangerous enemies. The cookhouse staff were very friendly now. In fact Misha, the Chinese cook, turned out to be a very nice fellow, despite his mania for hoarding food. He didn't seem to mind if I ticked him off, even in public. The credit for any improvement in the quality of the food was thus given to me in its entirety. My remonstrations had to be repeated again and again, though, as otherwise, within a few days, Misha would revert to his old wicked ways. But at least I was sure now that there was no malice in the man.

Grisha Tchorny and his court were very kind to me and I felt that since our very first encounter his 'protection' was paying dividends. The word got round that he and I had struck some sort of a deal, and that was quite enough for the resident 'snobs' to consider me as socially acceptable.

This was proved to me beyond doubt when I was asked by Grisha Tchorny to join him in a small reception which he was arranging for a friend of his. This was to be an exclusive affair and only the aristocracy were admitted.

It was to be held in the barrack where Grisha Tchorny lived. This normally accommodated some 150 men. For the occasion, a third of the total area was cleared for the benefit of some 20 members of the 'elite'. The rest had to squeeze into the remaining space. In return they were allowed to watch.

Grisha Tchorny was already there when I joined the party. Nonchalantly reclining on a kind of improvised chaise-longue next to the iron stove, he greeted me by a minute movement of one eyebrow and a suggestion of a smile. Otherwise he remained immobile. He had his fur hat on, but no shoes. He was smoking one of his expensive cigarettes.

It was hot in the barrack and the iron stove was bright red around the top. The rest of the company were already seated on wooden benches, the senior crooks on the bottom tier and the lesser ones on the top deck, their feet dangling. I saluted my host and exchanged friendly smiles with those of his guests I already knew, and started to look around for a place to sit. My host must have noticed this, for he gave a majestic kick to one of his courtiers who took it for an order to make room for me and promptly abandoned his seat. I was embarrassed and protested that I would rather not sit so near the fire, but this was not in conformity with my host's wishes, as I discovered, when one of Grisha's followers gave me a mighty push, so that I arrived at the designated place with greater velocity than I would have wished.

When I regained my balance, I found myself sitting on the couch at Grisha's feet. This was, apparently, where he wanted me to remain, as he said nothing. He lay immobile, his head propped on his hand, smoking. The man next to me offered me a handful of tobacco and a piece of newspaper to roll it into. We exchanged a few platitudes, as befits polite society.

What struck me was that everyone was talking in hushed tones, like in a theatre or cinema before a performance. One could

113

detect a general sense of anticipation except, of course, in the great chief himself, who maintained his imperious immobility and total lack of visible emotion.

Presently the door opened at the far end of the barrack and a man appeared.

All conversation stopped. Everyone looked. Even Tchorny lifted his head by at least one inch. The man, small and thin, with a grey face and red eyes was making his way down the long passageway towards us. The greyness of his complexion indicated his recent arrival from prison. His clothes, the regulation prison outfit, without any of the flamboyant additions so common among criminals in camps, indicated that he had been held at some important prison, perhaps even, a Moscow jail. There was something striking in the way he moved. Each step he took suggested agility and alertness. His arms, bent slightly at the elbows, swung loosely and rhythmically, as if he were about to execute some gymnastic feat of great complexity. He appeared fully aware of being the centre of attention. He did not strike me as a shy man. He seemed to be enjoying the limelight.

Obviously, we were about to witness an event of some importance, as Tchorny was actually sitting up on his daybed, his stockinged feet resting on the wooden floor. Without haste, he handed his cigarette to one of the lesser courtiers and, looking benevolently at his newest guest, lifted himself to his full height. I should have been used to it by then, but his technique of impressing people continued to amaze me. Without any apparent effort Tchorny could project his charismatic personality. Romantic visions of some fabulous eastern potentate invariably sprang to mind. Where does this talent come from? I mused in awe. Grisha Tchorny was sure to have spent most of his adult life in concentration camps. He was unlikely to have had much education and that would have been of the standard Soviet variety. It could certainly never account for his princely bearing. All this comes from within, I concluded. Leaders were born here, they were seldom made.

All eyes were on the two principal figures. No-one stirred. Tchorny spoke first; "Welcome to Vazky Yol Sasha Golob, we have been expecting you for some weeks. This was the voice of a Roman Emperor, I thought, or a Tsar of All Russia. "Come, sit down and meet your new comrades."

Sasha Golob didn't move. He just stood there looking up at the giant in front of him. He, too, looked impressed.. "Friends!" boomed Tchorny's voice as he looked round his audience. Raising his arm in a theatrical gesture, he repeated, "Friends!" This was followed by an extended pause. "He is overdoing it a bit," I thought, mildly disappointed. It seemed to me as if the star was 'drying up', forgetting his lines. I was willing him to get on with it. My hero wasn't performing as well as I would have wished. But the audience was still with him, I could tell. He was performing for them, not for me. For them it was great. Then, suddenly he turned to me as if he had sensed my disapproval, his brown eyes drilling right through me, "...and some Western witch doctors..." he said very slowly. I blushed to the roots of my hair. I was looking straight into those eyes; they burned like hell-fire. Then, the corner of his left eye smiled briefly at me. That was enough. I was back in his fold, unflinchingly loyal, all rebellion gone without trace. Now the audience was all his, one hundred per cent, even the 'Western witch doctor' was his.

"You have all heard of Sasha Golob," he continued, "the greatest cat burglar of all time." Sasha's face smiled thinly, his eyes didn't. I understood now what all the fuss was about. This was indeed an important guest.

Presently Tchorny started introducing the more senior members of the company to Golob. This part of the proceedings followed a fairly formal, almost ritualistic, pattern In each case he would indicate the man, give his Christian name, patronymic, surname, his professional qualifications and his home town or district. Thus he would say Ivan Andreivich Makarov, bank robber, from Kiev.

Sasha Golob listened politely, looked briefly at the man concerned, occasionally inclined his head respectfully if an important crime was mentioned. It was all done very slowly. Once, when a man was introduced who was known to have led a famous bank robbery in Kiev, Golob got up, and went to him to shake hands.

After a dozen men had been so introduced, the rest were dismissed with a general term of "friends and colleagues". Nobody minded. The preliminaries were at an end.

I tried to exploit the confusion and fade quietly into the crowd. I was longing to abandon my seat of honour at the top of Mount Olympus. Tchorny must have read my intentions without so much as a glance in my direction, for I had only managed to lift myself a couple of inches when I felt his huge hand crushing me back into my seat with friendly brutality. It was no use, I was stuck. Nobody, least of all a mere Western witch doctor, was going to abandon his post, unless ordered to. Not when Grisha Tchorny was about. I felt he could see me without looking, he could even read my thoughts. I was helpless. Why he needed my presence at all, I couldn't tell. He must have known I was uncomfortable and this, maybe, amused him. As long as I didn't attempt to slip away, he would leave me alone. My function seemed purely passive, like that of a court jester at a serious state function.

The formal part of the ceremony having been concluded, the conversation fragmented into several little groups. Sitting next to Grisha, I heard him exchanging impressions with Golob, on various people they knew. The others discussed food, or working norms, or arm wrestling matches. After a while, Misha, the Chinese cook, with his two young Chinese kitchen hands, arrived. They each carried a wooden container of steaming kasha, and Misha nursed a large bottle of vegetable oil. It wasn't hard to guess where this came from. I pretended not to notice. After all I was a guest.

The inhabitants of the unfashionable end of the barrack noticed the oil too, I had no doubt, but I knew that they would accept it as a fact of life. When the Elite were having a ball, there was no point in protesting. I looked into the darkness where the 'proletariat' were crowded. Through the cigarette smoke I saw their eyes watching eagerly. They were visibly interested, fascinated even. But were they envious? Was this display of opulence causing envy? I did not see any sign of it in their faces. "Equality, my foot!!!" I reflected, "where can one find it? Certainly not here".

Vazky Yol had its 'Social Register' and you were either in or out. I was just an observer, I was a guest, but I could watch from within. The strange thing was that those not included, the have-nots, did not seem to mind. They enjoyed the spectacle, they knew the members of the Elite, just as cinema goers know their film stars. To them too, this was an unreal, glamorous world outside their reach. They were allowed to watch, and for them it was entertainment. Of course, in this camp, nobody was really hungry. "Maybe," I thought, "hunger is the real equaliser".

Meanwhile the banquet was about to begin. Ten or twelve

wooden bowls were distributed among the guests, half the number of those taking part. "You eat with me." Someone tapped me on the shoulder with his wooden spoon. "Yes, thank you," I replied, feeling for my own spoon in the leg of my boot. I noticed that Tchorny held a metal spoon, not a wooden one.

Misha was dishing out the thick soup. When our turn came, I placed the wooden bowl on the edge of the couch. When it was full of kasha my partner and I started, each dipping his spoon in turn. Camp etiquette demanded that our spoons should not touch. Each one kept well to his side of the bowl to avoid contact. Tchorny and Golob were sharing an ornate china bowl. I could not decide what its original purpose was – not for kasha, that was sure. Its elaborate border caused the hot soup to drip persistently onto Tchorny's socks. When, after a while my partner and I reached the bottom of our bowl, he said to me grandly, "Go on, finish it," and proceeded to lick his spoon clean while I consumed the remainder of the kasha. He then dried his spoon in the palm of his hand, gave it a final rub with his sleeve and held it up for inspection. Pleased with the result , he slipped it into the top of his boot.

Spoons in labour camps were the most personal of possessions. One could share almost anything – except one's spoon. I followed the same procedure except for the finishing rub. For this I used the remnants of a cotton handkerchief. My partner was duly impressed. Despite my unfashionable clothes he clearly recognised in me a young man of quality.

Sasha Golob also finished his soup.

I had lost, meanwhile, the gist of his conversation with Grisha Tchorny. I did not, at first, know what he was talking about, when suddenly I heard him say,

"The trouble is that there are just too many of them. They are weak, they are dirty and they only want to eat. They produce nothing. Why the authorities bother, God only knows. Twenty of our men could produce more than a whole camp the size of Lishky. All camps are full of this vermin. Why they bother, beats me. I would shoot the lot or, better still, let them freeze to death."

When I heard all this I had no doubt what he was talking about: the political prisoners, my countrymen. This issue had become a frequent subject of conversation and unfriendly comment. I always dreaded it, as it placed me in an embarrassing dilemma.

117

Meanwhile the speaker continued: "Have you ever been in a camp where Westerners are?" he looked round, sensing that he was preaching to the converted. Some heads nodded emphatically. "Old Marx was right, after all, when he said that sooner or later the Western world would collapse without any assistance. Do you know that they don't wash? How can such a world exist? And yet, the odd thing is, that many of them seem to be educated people. Those that speak Russian are fun to talk to – that is, provided you don't stand too close. The smell could kill you." He spat eloquently.

The conversation became general now. Many voices joined in. The verdict was unanimous. Those that had been in contact with Western political prisoners agreed with Golob. I knew exactly what they were on about. After all I had been one of this 'vermin' only a few months ago. In Camp 91 I had myself been a "dokhodiaga" or a "goner". If it hadn't been for Maria Alexeyevna I would not have been eating in this exclusive company.

Another man took up the argument. He remembered coming across a Westerner in some transit camp, a scientist, a professor of some kind. One night he spotted him digging in a refuse heap by the kitchen.

"And believe me," he announced to those listening, "I caught him eating, yes, actually eating the half-rotten tail fin of a Treska fish. I gave him hell, you can imagine. I asked him if he knew what he was doing. He just said he was hungry. I promise you, this is all he said!!! A professor, an educated man!!!" He raised his hands in mock desperation. "So I gave him such a wallop in the neck that he started vomiting there and then. Makes me sick to think about it. I even reported him to the guards, but the filthy old man was dead the following morning. Serves him right!!"

Several more speakers joined in: Each one had a story to tell, but these stories varied only in detail and in essence they were all the same. They all asked the same question. How can educated people behave in such an unbelievably stupid way? Of course, I knew it was true. I had myself seen men, intellectuals mostly, do such things. A peasant would rather die of hunger. To him hunger was no excuse for doing something as contrary to nature as eating rotten fish.

So far, I had succeeded in staying out of this discussion. But I knew that it would not be long before the inevitable question was asked of me. " After all I am the only Westerner present," I thought with alarm, "what can I say?" It would be useless to dispute the facts. On the other hand, I could not disown my own kind and join in the general condemnation. How, then, to get out of this predicament with some sort of credibility? "Diversion, change of subject," I thought frantically. "But it must be good, interesting to them. But what?"

For once, an idea occurred to me almost immediately. What bliss. It was still rather sketchy, but at least it was an idea I could start to develop before my turn came...

I looked round and listened. Golob was not talking. He was eyeing me with a mischievous smile. Our eyes met. He knew that I knew what he was thinking. It was still a private thing between us, but not for long. But I had a plan all ready and knew what I was going to say, so I could afford to play it cool.

"Listen fellows," Golob started at last, "listen; we are only asking questions here to which we have no answers. But we have with us someone who can help us, because he knows. He hasn't spoken at all, so why not let him?" he looked straight at me, still smiling. I looked at Tchorny, my ally, but found no help there. He was laughing openly. The joke was on. I had to deliver again... "Diversion, change of subject..." I repeated in my thoughts.

"It may be easier to answer your question if I could be allowed to tell you a story," I started, looking Golob straight in the eyes. "It may seem to you, at first, that I am evading the issue, but things may become clearer if you hear me out to the end." I looked now at Tchorny as if to obtain his blessing. "Why doesn't he answer the question?" a lone voice spoke from the crowd. "Shut up." Tchorny's voice sounded final. "Let him tell his story, if he wants to." Then, turning to me, he said "OK – carry on."

"My story takes us to a city in America called Chicago during the years of the prohibition," I started. Almost at once someone wanted to know what prohibition was, but Tchorny gave him a dirty look and signalled to me to proceed. I tried to imitate the way in which my nanny used to tell me her stories when I was little: in a slow, rolling rhythm with plenty of detail and without any rush. Thanks to Tchorny's iron grip on the assembled company I was able to get into 'gear' relatively quickly.

What I told them was my own version of a film, suitably embellished for maximum dramatic effect, which I had seen in Poland some years earlier. It was a 'Cops and Robbers' story, taking place in Chicago, involving Al Capone. For good measure I threw in Bugsy Malone, maybe even Bonnie and Clyde. I decided to include everything I could remember, plus some extra refinements which I invented on the spur of the moment. I crammed it with stop watches, cine cameras, two-way radio transmitters, aeroplanes , tear gas, super-charged cars and so on.

I tried to include all the latest gadgets for crime detection in existence. I used complicated names and pseudo-scientific terms to provoke questions. This resulted in very useful 'audience participation' which, when I finally ran out of ideas provided me with some handy improvements on the original story. Thus, when I did not know how to get my hero out of a particularly nasty predicament, I would ask: "And what would you have done if you had been in his place?" A number of suggestions would be offered by this highly professional audience, and all that was left to me was to choose which solution best suited my story. "Yes," I would say with approval, "not bad, not bad. But still not quite what eventually happened." I would then add a few modifications to keep them guessing and ensure the element of surprise.

When I had finally squeezed all the excitement out of my tale I turned to Golob and said, "Now, let me answer your question with a question. Could you honestly say that anyone amongst you here could operate successfully among the Chicago crooks?" Golob shrugged his shoulders: "After some time, of course," he replied. "Don't be silly," I heard Tchorny's voice, "you can't even drive a car, let alone fly an aeroplane. No-one here could operate in Chicago."

That disposed of the problem.. My diversion had succeeded beyond my wildest expectations. My companions were very impressed. How was it possible, they asked, that I knew so much if I was not myself a crook? I told them that there were many non-crooks in the West who were interested in studying such cases. I myself knew very little. There were thousands of books devoted to criminology written by famous authors which, I was sure, being experts, they would find very interesting and educational. They had no doubt that they would.

By implication it was clear to all present that a civilisation which could produce such brilliant crooks and, in addition, supply appropriate literature could not be so bad after all. They came to this conclusion without my having to suggest it to them. In a roundabout way it helped them to regard the 'vermin' with a little more sympathy than hitherto. If they, the Russian crooks – the argument ran – would find it impossible to operate in Chicago, then the Western intellectuals would find it equally difficult in Russian labour camps. They arrived at this conclusion with very little help from me.

The evening was a success. My popularity improved. In the weeks and months that followed I was required to repeat my story many times. Whenever there was a bigger gathering in the camp I would be asked to perform: "Karlusha, why don't you tell us some more about those clever foreign crooks." Like children, they would listen intently . They didn't mind hearing the same stories over and over again. Like children, too, they liked me to use the same words every time. They also noticed the slightest change or the smallest omission. In the end I got bored myself, so I tried to invent some new twists to my plots. They objected at first, but later admitted that these additions improved the original story.

I also tried to introduce an element of justice into my tales. It was my private contribution to the improvement of morality in the world. The 'nasties' were always caught and put behind bars. The goodies always won. But my audiences did not mind that at all, since that gave them the justification for being behind bars themselves. If Al Capone, the greatest of the great, had finished behind bars, it made them feel better. In their eyes he was not a failure, quite the contrary. By implication, neither were they. I realised that my moralising efforts were totally lost on them but I felt that at least I had tried.

Within three weeks of my arrival I was a different man. My relations with my fellow prisoners and my confidence in my own abilities were improving daily. I did not have to fend off constant attacks from every quarter. That was a thing of the past.

I was able to introduce little improvements with no resistance from the others. And above all, I was gaining the confidence of my patients. Fortunately, they were a very healthy lot of men, and even my primitive methods seemed to produce very good results.

I was devoted to my job and if anybody fell ill I would do absolutely anything to make them better, even, sometimes, at a considerable discomfort to myself. It compensated, I felt, for my insufficient medical knowledge and the lack of medication. They used to joke, "Karlusha puts so much energy into looking after his patients that they can't help getting better."

My own understanding of the psychology of my companions was also improving. They, too, were getting used to me and my foreign ways. In fact, in time, I discovered that these could be turned to advantage, that by remaining different and maintaining a certain distance, while observing a friendly neutrality towards their more violent solutions, I could remain on the outside and still retain a considerable degree of influence.

I tried to develop my own style. I avoided passing judgement on any of their activities. If pressed, all I would say was that I would do it differently. They learned to accept and, eventually, respect my attitude.

What was even more important I started to feel that I was winning real friends in this strange criminal community. Despite their unfortunate criminal inclinations, despite a completely different philosophy, despite all the terrible things which they had done, or were capable of doing, I began to feel that I was among friends. It sounds ridiculous but, even today, I know it to be true.

# Chapter 9

# RUSSIAN POKER

It was not until late spring 1941 that I first came into contact with the Floaters, or Splavshchiki, as they were called in Russian.

April in the Arctic could be quite lovely and, when the sun was out, it could feel pleasantly warm. I remember standing outside my surgery listening to Misha, the cook. He was in the middle of a sentence when he suddenly stopped and, pointing to the main gate, exclaimed "Look – the Floaters are coming!". I looked. A group of half a dozen men were filing through the big gate. The compound was packed as it was quite late. Everybody stared. To me it seemed a most unexpected sight. The floaters were making for the centre barrack. They looked most impressive in their long boots, carrying their halberd-like booms. Bronzed heroes, returning home for the night. Although hatless, they reminded me of medieval infantry, or Cromwellian troopers, perhaps.

"Are these the chaps who float timber down the rivers?" I enquired.

"Yes, they are the mighty floaters. Crocodile and his team. Duke and his lot will be coming soon, too, I should imagine. I'd better hurry and make sure their food is ready, otherwise, they will give me hell!" He made a move to go.

"Is it true that they have special privileges, that they are actually paid for their work?" I asked eagerly.

"Yes, they even get coupons, just like the NKVD guards. But," he shrugged his shoulders, "I wouldn't want their job! I'd rather clean latrines, you know. It's a very risky job, not worth it..."

During the next three months I was constantly involved with the Floaters. It was difficult not to be, they were such a high-profile group of men. They were the favourite topic of conversation, they also supplied most of the gossip and, unfortunately, also drama. But in addition to my professional involvement, in treating their numerous cuts and bruises, I made friends with a number of them.

We had just two teams of Floaters at Vazky Yol. Each team

numbered only five or six men. One team was led by a man nick-named Duke, a tall, handsome chap, and the other by a tough, stocky character, nicknamed Crocodile, or Crocky to his mates. Crocky was a particularly strong swimmer and, like the reptile after which he was named, showed an impressive set of white teeth which seemed too big for his mouth. There was no love lost between the two leaders. I heard rumours of some recent quarrel, but no-one wanted to talk about it so, for me anyway, the whole thing was a bit of a puzzle.

As in the case of Lumberjacks, the Floaters were very fussy about their appearance and were particularly 'sharp dressers'. Their working clothes were quite unique, spectacular even. In fact, I suspected that this was the principal reason why there was always a waiting list for this difficult and dangerous job. After work they spent a lot of time and effort in looking good. They reminded me of Sasha in that respect, except that they used a great deal more cheap after-shave and smelled of violets and roses which, fortunately, Sasha had not. They were also very keen on tattoos. A nasty little Chinaman, nicknamed Mandarin. was the principal tattoo artist and he was kept busy, throughout the summer, embellishing their bodies with the most elaborate designs.

Being a political prisoner I was not allowed to leave the camp, so I never saw the Floaters at work but, listening to them talking, I became very familiar with details of their working life. It was, indeed, a very difficult and risky job. Both on land and on water they had to handle masses of timber, and all they had in the way of equipment, was the long wooden boom, with a steel hook at one end of it. I remembered, from my lumberjacking days, that logs were stacked in huge piles on steep river banks.

I had been told that in the Spring, when the ice had gone, the Floaters would begin their work. They would remove the retaining fence, thus allowing the timber to roll downhill until it hit the water. This was, possibly, the riskiest part of the operation as some logs did not roll straight. Unaided, they would often cause huge pile-ups. In order to prevent this, the Floaters would watch for the first signs of trouble and, before serious obstruc-tions could form, one of them would dive into the falling avalanche and correct the flow so that the movement was not hampered. It's not difficult to imagine what the smallest misjudgement could bring about. Armed only with their booms they were usually able to guide hundreds of tons of rolling timber on their intended path.

Once in the water, the logs would form a floating carpet which, propelled by the current, would travel downstream until eventually it reached the designated sawmill some considerable distance away. That part of the journey was also hazardous, as similar pile-ups were apt to form in the water at the slightest provocation. The Floaters would ride the carpet like water skis, constantly directing the alignment of the logs to obtain unimpeded movement.

Frequently, they ended up in the water and their Cromwellian boots, while very useful whilst riding the timber, would weigh them down in the water and interfere with their swimming. If a loss of balance were to occur while a pile-up was forming, the result could be fatal. The weight of the logs would see to that!.

The working week in Vazky Yol was not a seven-day cycle. It was called the decade and, as the name suggests, consisted of ten days, nine working and one rest day. The official working day was twelve hours long.

The Floaters worked very hard. They also played hard. Their favourite game was poker. The rules were basically the same as in the West. There were a couple of exceptions. One was that, for more important games, an umpire was employed. His job was to ensure the fairness of the proceedings and, often, he would be asked to deal the cards. I was sometimes required to umpire to which I agreed most reluctantly as I had never been interested in card games, and to me it was a real bore.

As a non-player I was considered to be completely independent and an ideal candidate for supervising the game. I often ended up sitting for hours on end trying to look interested, and presiding over endless games well into the night. I also had to learn the rules.

Some of these rules were very odd, particularly regarding the penalties applicable to players who got carried away and over-played. Such penalties could be ridiculously cruel. The Floaters played, mostly for coupons, unlike ordinary mortals, who used bread, sugar or tobacco as currency.

One summer evening I was working late in my surgery. I had finished with my patients and was catching up on my paperwork. The evening was hot and I had both my door and window wide open. The mosquito season had not yet begun so, one could afford to do this without fear of being eaten alive. I was about to pack up when I heard steps coming towards me round the corner.

It was the Mandarin. He came to ask me if I could lend him some glasses. This, as he well knew, was something I never allowed as my surgery was very short of the most basic equipment, and glasses were difficult to replace.

"Please, Karlusha, don't be mean, at least two, I am desperate. Crocky told me to get them from you, just for this evening, for the game, the big game." He winked confidentially.

"The big game? What do you mean?" I asked. "Oh, didn't you know? I thought everybody knew that it was going to be tonight," he continued, in his irritating way. "Now, look here," I said firmly, "you have a bloody nerve. You come to me when I am busy, wanting me to do you a favour and you haven't got the basic courtesy of telling me what is going on. Go away, and don't bother me!" "You can come and watch, if you like," Mandarin's high pitched voice continued, "I am sure it will be all right but, please, give me the glasses. I am in the most frightful hurry. They want to start soon." He sounded both desperate and insincere.

That was not good enough, I told him. Unless he told me the whole story – no glasses. He swore that all he knew was that Duke was playing Crocodile at poker and that the game was about to start; that Crocodile had sent him to fetch the glasses; and that he was sure that if he did not get them, this minute, he would die the most horrible death. So I gave him the glasses and let him go.

I was most intrigued. I didn't understand, in the first place, why these two men never played each other. So why should they have decided to stage this encounter in the middle of a decade, and not at the end of it, as usual?

I resolved that I should not hurry. I was not really invited as I did not consider that Mandarin was qualified to invite anybody. He was just a stooge, a messenger, a nobody. So I decided to stay away.

Time dragged on. I could see no activity in the courtyard. Everybody was there watching this unique contest, and I was here, alone, because of my stupid pride, missing this great event. I knew that it was only I who had invented such a convoluted etiquette, one which could never apply in the rude world of convicted criminals but, as these were my rules, I felt obliged to obey them, stupid or not.

Two hours must have passed when, suddenly, I heard someone walking in my direction; running would probably be more accurate. It turned out to be Andrusha, one of the Floaters on the Duke team. He looked worried. He came to fetch a new deck of cards which Duke had left with me for safe keeping. He said that things were not good, that Duke was losing, and that in fact he would almost certainly have to go for a 'sudden death' play-off.

"Good God," I cried, "is that why you came for a new deck of cards?"

"Yes," he whispered, "and this time he must go through with it, even if it kills him!"

I knew most of the rules, but had to ask for more information from Andrusha.

Basically, the loser could have one more shot at it. One final gamble. If he won, he would redeem all his losses in one hand. If he lost, his existence was at the complete mercy of the winner. The penalty for losing was harsh. It had to be, according to Andrusha, otherwise it would have been abused indiscriminately. Besides, the victor had to show to everybody that he was not 'soft'. In a big game like this the loss of one finger, usually from the left hand, was the norm.

"You had better come as well," Andrusha added, "Your services may be needed, who can tell..."

"Oh, I hope not, this seems to be a lunatic way to behave. It is just a game after all!" I added, knowing that I was about to witness something so firmly established in this crazy, crazy, world which Andrusha belonged to and understood, and which I would never begin to understand.

Still, I had to go now. It was my duty.

The barrack where the Floaters lived stood in the middle of the compound. We had some difficulty in getting in, but Andrusha's loud announcement that he was the carrier of a fresh deck of cards worked wonders and we were almost propelled to the centre of the drama.

Both contestants were standing, their seats empty, facing away from each other, smoking and talking, each one to his own supporters. I looked at the table. Crocodile had a sizeable heap of coupons on his side, while Duke's side was quite bare with only a glass with some mauve coloured liquid in it, and a piece of paper with some notes.

A bottle of methylated spirits stood in the middle, its sinister label with a skull and crossbones clearly visible. I was well aware that this poisonous beverage, the Gulag equivalent of Napoleon brandy, was extremely difficult to come by. A whole bottle, that was really something! The fact that total or, at best, partial blindness was likely if one drank a quantity of it, seemed beside the point.

Andrusha completed his mission and gave the cards to Duke. Immediately, both contestants sat down and Crocodile took the deck of cards, broke the seal, and started a minute examination. Andrusha explained to me the obvious, the new cards belonged to Duke. Duke had the right to demand a new deck for his final hand, but Crocodile had to make sure that all was above board and that they were unmarked, or otherwise untampered with. Each card was looked at back and front and, finally the pack was counted by the arbiter.

While this was going on I managed to squeeze into the crowd so that I could clearly see the whole stage. Outwardly, both contestants looked calm, but Duke's face was tired and drawn and he was nervously sipping the sinister beverage. He even started to roll a fresh cigarette while his previous one was still only half smoked.

I felt for Duke. He seemed to be doomed. I knew that this was a game of chance and that, at this late stage skill was practically immaterial. In theory, at least, he could still win and redeem all his losses. The odds were even. But my instinct said otherwise. In my mind I was working out what to do in case Duke's finger should be cut off. According to Andrusha, this was the likely result of Duke's defeat.

Meanwhile the drama unfolded right in front of my eyes. Andrusha supplied the explanations. I learned from him for instance that, as no new money was to be involved in this final round, the cards would be dealt five to each player; they would then be allowed to discard anything from nothing to five cards and replace them with fresh ones. They were then expected to show their hand. "It will soon be over," he said, looking at my worried face.

It was soon over. From where I stood I could not see any of the cards, nor for that matter could anyone else as both players made sure of that. The arbiter dealt the cards after they had been well

*Obory Manor, October 1939*

*My mother, ca. 1920*

*My father, ca. 1920*

*An early riding lesson, Pototurow 1926*

*The passing-out ceremony, Iraq summer 1943*

*Marysia, Jerusalem 1944*

*As a cadet officer, Iraq 1943*

*Marysia's mother, Baroness Emma Heydel ca. 1920*

*Lieut. S. Maksymiszyn, Italy 1944*

Ulani Krechowieccy czują się dziś w czołgach
nie gorzej, niż kiedyś na koniach.

*Lieut. K. Irzykowski, Italy 1944*

*In my best uniform, Italy 1945*

*At the meet on Tapster Lad (with Liz on my right and Claire on my left)*

*Dandino*

*A birds eye view of Saddlecombe Stud*

*At a show on Windmill Boy, 1988*

*Saddlecombe Stud*

*My English home*

shuffled and cut, five apiece. Duke asked for three new cards, Crocodile for two. There was a long pause. Both players sat immobile, like statues.

Crocodile spoke first. "So, what have you got, Duke?" His voice was strong and relaxed. Is he bluffing, or has he got a good hand? I agonised in silence.

"I think you can order the cook to bring in the meat cleaver" I heard Duke answer, quite casually. "I don't think mine could be a winning hand". He let his cards drop on the table. A pair of kings – that was all. A gasp of horror filled the room. "Do you want to see what I have here for you, your royal highness?". Crocodile's voice sounded relieved, triumphant. "One, two and three," he counted slowly as he laid his cards on the table. Three jacks!!!

Some weak cheers could be heard from his own crew but, otherwise, voices were kept low in anticipation of what was to follow. Everyone knew that Duke would have to suffer, immediately, some form of physical mutilation for having risked and lost in this barbaric, mediaeval tournament, this senseless, pointless act of cruelty. One of Duke's own crew poured him a gigantic measure of methylated spirit which Duke refused at first, but then drank avidly and asked for more which was supplied, immediately.

Crocodile meanwhile got up, stretched and yawned hugely, then shook his head vigorously, returned to the table and, standing by his chair faced Duke looking directly at him.

"Now, what shall we do with you, your Royal Highness? Ha! Any suggestions?" he looked at Duke for a while and having no response, continued. "I would like you to cast your mind back exactly two years, almost to the day. I told you then that, one day, you would regret what you did to me... Remember? Remember?" He shook Duke violently by the sleeve. "Do you remember?" he shouted. "Answer me!" He straightened his back and looked around. "As his Royal Highness is too drunk already, let me remind you what happened. He accused me of being a coward, that's what he did – me, ME, Crocodile... And do you remember why? Because I was smart enough to stop playing while he was winning. I chose not to lose my last few coupons. I chose not to have to do what he has to do tonight. You got trapped in your own snare, my dear fellow..."

I was beginning to understand. This was the reason for the fierce antipathy that existed between these two. This was why they would not play against each other in a friendly way. But this, of course, made things worse. Crocodile hated Duke. He was determined to get his revenge.

Meanwhile Crocodile was continuing his judgement. We all waited for the verdict. What would the punishment be? Crocodile, obviously, was enjoying his role, he was not in a hurry. He knew that Duke was at his mercy, waiting, dreading, agonising...

"You think that your punishment is going to be the usual loss of one finger. one small finger, out of the ten, that you have?... No my dear friend, this would not fit the bill at all. Not for someone who has accused Crocodile of being a coward ... Oh! No."

"Where is Mandarin? Let him come here at once". He said it in a tone of urgent command. "Here I am, Crocky," Mandarin's thin voice replied from behind a pillar while he pushed his way through the crowd.

"I want you to improve the masculinity of this individual by way of the best tattoo you have ever done. Let us have, on his left cheek, a nice big image pointing straight to his mouth. Do you get the drift? Do you think you are able to do such a simple job, right here, on the spot, while we are all watching?" "Yes, Crocky, sure thing, of course I can," and using the pencil and pad on the table, he quickly produced a sketch of the proposed design. Crocodile made some crude adjustments to the sketch and Mandarin quickly assembled his gear and spread it on the table.

Duke sat motionless and expressionless. Mandarin applied his working sketch to Duke's face and waited for the signal to begin. Crocodile nodded nonchalantly, and continued his commentary. "I realise, of course, that what we are doing here is purely a temporary embarrassment to our friend. He can grow a bread and most of Mandarin's work of art will be covered over. That's OK with me. By nature I am a kind and reasonable man – but, while his beard is growing, he will suffer a little." He smiled with 'innocent' satisfaction.

In half an hour the job was done. It looked awful. Mandarin was delighted. Crocodile looked pleased. Everybody else was horrified. We knew that this was the most terrible thing that could happen to poor Duke. Such humiliation. What would he do?...

Duke asked if he was free to go. Cheerfully, Crocodile agreed. Duke stood up and pushed his way through the crowd to the corner where a small stoves stood which we used for making tea. He opened the lid, stirred up the flames, with a small poker, pushed the poker into the centre the fire and calmly returned to the table. He poured himself another large drink, and sat down.

We were watching, mesmerised. Some voices were heard, asking what he was planning to do. Anxious voices, friendly voices... My own mind was blank. I did not dare to think, I could only watch. I felt sick, immobilised by fear.

After a couple of minutes he asked for a mirror. Mandarin obliged. Duke took the mirror and, without looking into it, went back to the stove and pulled out the poker. It was dark red at the very tip.

He pushed it back into the fire, returned to the table, drank the rest of his spirit then, calmly, inspected his face in the mirror; walked back to the stove and pulled out the poker again. Carefully, he aligned the hot metal to where the tattoo was and, with a triumphant expression, pressed the red hot iron against his skin.

I shut my eyes. I had had enough. I could not stand it. The smell of burning flesh hit me so that I could not breathe. At the very same moment I felt a strong grip on my shoulder. It was Andrusha. "Go to him, he needs you now!". He pushed me gently towards Duke.

Suddenly, I realised that it was my turn to act. Thank God, I could do something and not just watch. I pushed everybody out of my way. I called to Andrusha to fetch me a bowl of cold water. It was produced at once. I grabbed Duke by his hair and pushed the injured side of his face into the water and held it there.

"We will keep it there for as long as possible," I whispered into Duke's other ear. "Keep your nose out of the water and breathe normally," I instructed.

Duke obeyed silently. Meanwhile, I heard Crocodile's voice. "What a terrible smell, I am not enjoying this any more, let us go, boys." Mercifully, he and most of the onlookers left the barrack.

I knew that Duke was beginning to feel the pain. He did not say anything, but he was squeezing my arm harder and harder.

Also , I knew that my job had only just begun.

# Chapter 10

# FREEDOM

During the early 1940s the Soviet media did not bother very much about offering their services to the northern-most reaches of the country. These regions were populated largely by forced labour camps, and the indigenous population, on the whole, could not read Russian. We did see an occasional copy of 'Pravda' or 'Izvestia' newspapers, but these were only in demand as cigarette paper or as an extra layer of thermal insulation, to protect us against the winter cold. Besides, the newspapers reached us with considerable delay and – on arrival – would be at least a month old. Radio transmissions, the pride of Soviet propaganda, though powerful, did not cover the whole of the vast stretches of the Northern Provinces. The KGB guards did get some news from the outside world, including letters from home, but these, too, reached them very late. In short, we were almost completely cut off from everything that was happening outside our little community. But the fact is – we did not care. No-one was interested in anything very much, other than their next meal.

During the summer of 1941, however, strange rumours started circulating. At first, most level-headed people dismissed them out of hand. Soon, however, these rumours grew louder and as they originated from men recently arrived from Kotlas, they could not be dismissed quite so lightly.

By the middle of July everybody was talking about the war. To most, it still seemed incredible that the Soviet Union was, apparently, being invaded by its ally, Germany. Even more unbelievable seemed reports that the Germans were advancing fast and that the Red Army was in full retreat. Since 1939 Germany had been billed as the Soviet Union's "glorious ally", whose triumphs in Poland, Belgium, Holland and France were celebrated as if they had Stalin's personal blessing. We had known that astronomical quantities of Soviet raw materials were being shipped from Russia to help the Reich war effort. To the average Russian this latest news sounded like pure fantasy.

With every new arrival from Kotlas, or even from Pechora, fresh disasters were being reported. We heard of the catastrophic collapse of the Soviet defences, of vast territorial gains by the Germans, and that Leningrad was under siege.

So far, officially, we had heard nothing. The authorities were, obviously, unable to decide what to tell us. Predictably, when their silence was broken, the official version was very vague. It did talk of the heroic efforts of the Red Army, of the crippling losses suffered by the invaders, of thousands of German prisoners captured and of their low morale. Most of this we ignored. The fact that Germany was at war with Russia was, however, officially confirmed. That was the only thing which, to us, was really significant.

By and large the majority of my fellow prisoners wished the Germans well.

The logic behind this was rather odd. They seemed to think that, if the Germans won the war and the Soviet system collapsed, automatically life would return to the pre-revolution mode and land would be given back to all peasants. They also believed that a general amnesty would ensue and that they would be freed at once. A lot of nonsense was being spoken, half in jest, half seriously but, undoubtedly the hate of Soviet tyranny was greater than the fear of the enemy. Even the guards looked less sure of themselves. The searches became less ferocious and the shouting less loud.

Everybody was asking for my views as I was supposed to understand the workings of the "perfidious capitalists". Although their curiosity seemed insatiable, they only wanted to hear confirmation of their own infantile hopes. For them I was far too pessimistic. They did not like it, and insisted that my views were biased, that what had happened in Poland had nothing to do with what was likely to happen in Russia. Russia was bigger, Russia was different, the Germans were bound to understand that – they would argue. When I continued to voice my doubts, they just patted me on the back with the words: "If we'll live – we'll see," an old peasant truism.

By the end of the summer we had a pretty accurate view on the state of the war. By combining our various sources we could piece together a general picture . Western Russia was virtually lost to the enemy: Leningrad was still under siege, but holding out, but now Moscow itself was threatened. There was no more any doubt about that. In addition, however, reports from Kotlas spoke of terrible things happening in the territories now controlled by the Germans. Alarming reports reached Kotlas from men who, having been taken prisoner by the enemy, had managed to escape back to the Soviet side.

These men were immediately arrested, we were told, this time by the Soviets (no doubt as potentially dangerous) and shipped to Kotlas. This sounded more than possible and most people accepted it as fact. From these reports a picture emerged which was very much less optimistic than the one which had been circulating hitherto. If this was to be believed, it seemed that the Germans were treating the local populations in an appallingly brutal way, that food was short and villages were being devastated. No land was being handed back to anyone...

Eventually the Soviet media confirmed what we knew already. My credibility was restored and – as a result – I was frequently consulted, now, with considerably more respect, in view of my earlier warnings. "Tell us," they would say, "you understand these things – you must tell us." My non-existent powers of political analysis were being stretched considerably. At first I managed to fob them off with generalities – but they would not leave me in peace. I had to tell them something more than that.

Very reluctantly I decided to share with them my very sketchy knowledge of the works of Adolf Hitler.

So, I told them what little I knew about "Mein Kampf". I said that Hitler had written a book, a sort of 'bible' for his Nazi followers, and that it contained not only his general philosophy but also a fairly detailed programme for the future. I explained that so far nearly everything contained in that programme had occurred just as he had said it would. The conquests of Poland, Czechoslovakia, Belgium, Holland and France, were all in the book. I could not remember .what he had said about fighting the Soviet Union, but the fact that he considered Communism as his number one enemy was never in doubt.

My listeners were fascinated; they were also puzzled: "How could this be?" they demanded, "If Hitler wrote everything down beforehand, why was he not stopped before he even started?" That – I was forced to admit – was a very good question. Still it was easy to be wise after the event. Why, even Stalin had been taken in by Hitler and no-one could accuse him of being naive in such matters. This was the gist of my reply. My listeners nodded wisely. Understandably they were worried. They wanted to know more and more.

"Tell us, Karlusha, what are the Germans like?" they would ask. I told them that I had not been to Germany , so I could not say. I had spent three days in Austria in 1938, that was all. To my listeners this was not a valid excuse. I knew far more than they did and I had to share my knowledge with them, they argued.

"There is no doubt that Germany is a great nation. They have produced great musicians, great poets and statesmen," I started cautiously.

"Have they got great crooks, like Al Capone?" asked Misha the cook, evidently referring to my stories about the Chicago gangster.

"No," I conceded, "maybe not, but what is more important they've got some pretty good generals. You see, what happened in Poland, Belgium, Holland and France was a completely new kind of warfare, using a new military technique. The German generals call this the "lightning war" (or "Blitzkrieg"). They invented it only recently and it has brought them extraordinary success. The fact that big, strong countries like France could be subdued in a matter of weeks is proof of it. They are using this very same method against the Soviet Union right now."

Within a relatively short time I was considered quite an authority on these and other matters. It started to worry me. It wasn't wise to know too much about anything, and in particular about matters such as these. Even the NKVD Commandant exchanged 'friendly' comments with me on the state of the war – proof that the authorities were aware of my little lectures.

Within a few weeks we started noticing the influence of the war on the economy of our little settlement.. Our food became noticeably worse. Sugar was very scarce; even the bread, the basis of our diet, was soggier and more lumpy than usual. We all prepared ourselves for a long and difficult winter. But the Russian criminal, like the Russian peasant, is a very resourceful individual, and thanks to the enterprising and no doubt illegal manipulations of our 'transport department', our camp did not suffer any real shortages.

In our region the winter started early, for already towards the end of October we had quite a lot of snow. We were, of course, much further North than the German armies. Our camp, about halfway between Pechora and Varkuta, was just South of the Arctic Circle. Nevertheless the Russian climate was not helping the Germans and even much further South they seemed to have lost their momentum. Was the climate, once more, going to save Russia, just as it had in 1812.? The similarities between these two wars were remarkable: the fact that the French Grand Army, just like the German one now, was not equipped for winter; that both Napoleon's and Hitler's Russian offensives had started on exactly the same day, 22nd June; that there was no immediate logical reason for either campaign etc. etc. made this into a very interesting study, a point on which my fellow prisoners demanded constant explanations, thus severely testing my meagre knowledge of history.

After a while I noticed that the overall attitude of my Russian companions was also changing. Gradually a note of national pride started to sneak into their utterances. They seemed much less pro-German, and far more likely to support their home side. One could detect a measure of pride, even, when they spoke of the Russian winter, about the toughness of their own race. German successes were no longer the subject for enthusiastic comment. One could almost say that patriotism was back in fashion. These changes could not be attributed entirely to the official propaganda. The reports of German brutalities, and the fact that the Germans were not giving anybody any land, may have had something to do with this. Perhaps ,but not in a big way. I now feel more inclined to think that the average Russian is naturally a patriotic individual, and that the concept of Mother Russia is such an integral part of his make-up that even Communism was not able to destroy this.

The change in mood was also reflected in music. New songs, some quite beautiful, with very romantic and intensely patriotic lyrics, were being sung in the barracks at night. They were quite different from the old-style Communist songs. They were much more Russian and less Soviet in character. The tunes, based on traditional tonal arrangements, though sad and even tragic, still sound good even today. The lyrics, sentimental, but not cheap, went straight to the listener's heart, or, more accurately to his 'soul'. If this was propaganda, it was very subtle.

The war affected us also in other ways. The soldiers who had guarded us hitherto were all replaced by a completely new team. Presumably the previous lot, all young and healthy, were needed at the front. We were now guarded by a much older, much seedier team. They were all well over 50. Even the camp Commandant was new. An NKVD man like his predecessor, but much older, he seemed somewhat untypical in his job. His name was Krepkin. He was very fat and shapeless, with a red, flat, pock-marked face, a big purple nose, and small, blue, bloodshot eyes. He perspired profusely, even in cold weather. He was in the habit of using some sort of aftershave, which resulted in a revolting combination of smells: violets, vodka and mother nature. When he spoke he revealed a set of stainless steel teeth. The stories which circulated about him spoke of his involvement in a famous show-trial where, if true, he was a prosecution witness. His testimony was said to have helped in the conviction and subsequent execution of General Tukhachevsky, (under whom, apparently, he had served). The memory of these trials, stage-managed by Stalin himself in the 1930s, was still very fresh. Krepkin was soon nicknamed 'Smelly' and we all avoided him like the plague.

Our nearest railway station was Pechora, a distance of ten days with a good pair of horses, in favourable weather. Our supplies came, therefore, from a nearer depot, only a couple of days away, and a shuttle was in operation for basic supplies of food and other essentials; it was operated by Vanya, a pleasant, cheerful fellow and a good friend of mine. I relied heavily on his unique talents in order to secure my supplies of bandages, iodine and a few other items for my medicine chest. I also depended on him for cod liver oil, which was desperately needed for the treatment of chicken blindness, now that winter was upon us (a couple of spoonfuls would restore the sight of patients unable to see after dark).

It was about the beginning of November when Vanya returned from one of his regular visits to the depot. I was very anxious to see him and was trying to locate him in the usual places. When I finally found him he greeted me excitedly: "Karlusha," he exclaimed, "I have been looking for you everywhere, where the hell have you been hiding? I have some interesting news for you. Let's go to your surgery and let's talk. Besides, I have some cod liver oil for you and some other stuff too." "Bless you, Vanya, you are a pal!" I patted him on the back, delightedly.

"Here we are," I said, when we reached my place presently, "sit

137

down and warm yourself by the fire, while I make some tea." I put the kettle on and started to unpack the little parcel which he had brought me. "So what is this exciting bit of news that you are bringing me , Vanya?" I asked at last.

He didn't answer me immediately, so I lifted my eyes from my parcel and glanced at him. He was sitting on the couch quite casually but he was looking at me with a very strange smile. At last he said, "You will never believe this, but I have it on very good authority: you may be a free man soon."

"If by "soon" you mean five years and six months, then I will believe you, otherwise I would say you are having me on – and what's more I don't think it's very funny."

This did not sound like a joke, I thought. Could it be that Vanya was involved in some cockeyed escape plan and wanted to involve me in it? Surely, he had more sense than that. He must have known that not one escape had ever succeeded in our region. The local tribesmen saw to that.

"You are not asking me to join some new escape project. If so you know what you can do?" I said.

"God, no!" he responded "who do you take me for? It was I who told you what happened to the pair that tried it, remember?" Yes, I thought, I remembered, it was indeed Vanya who had told me of an attempted escape from a camp much further South. Those men had been tracked down by the Komi tribesmen, with dogs, a few miles from their camp. They broke every bone in their bodies, took out their eyes and delivered them to the NKVD guards in return for a generous reward. The bodies had been left in full view for the rest of the winter outside the camp gates, as a reminder.

"So – what on earth do you mean?" I asked.

"You are a Polish citizen, if I am not mistaken. So, they told me at the depot that all Poles were being set free – a new law had been introduced. I've got it from the best source, almost directly from Kotlas."

It was difficult to get out of Vanya a coherent account of what it was exactly that he had learnt and from whom, but at the end of my questioning I concluded that he had met somebody who had heard it from someone else from Kotlas, who in turn knew the driver of a big shot in the NKVD. The driver had evidently overheard a conversation between his boss and some other official about this news, which was what Vanya was convinced would make me happy. He now felt let down, since my reaction was not what he expected, in fact he was sulking quite visibly.

As I knew I could not get any more hard facts out of him, I thanked him profusely and, after his second cup of tea, let him go.

I was left with my thoughts. They were very confused. I had no doubt that the whole thing must be pure fantasy. The number of people involved in passing the word on, and the distances it had travelled, were sure to have resulted in a most ridiculous garbled account. And yet – what if it were true? Just assuming, for one moment, the totally impossible, the totally, totally impossible, what then?

To my great astonishment, deep in my heart, I felt uneasy. Although I knew that I was just playing games, teasing my own brain with the most unlikely thoughts, I felt no pleasure, on the contrary I felt faintly sick. Why? I could not say, but the feeling was certainly there. I decided not to think about it and willed myself to 'change gear', as it were. No use worrying, I said to myself out loud. On this I went to bed.

During the following week we had to battle against the most exceptionally severe blizzard. Snow and wind immobilised us completely. It was out of the question to do anything out of doors: visibility was down to zero, we could cross the camp compound only in groups of three, holding hands, groping along the barrack walls. If one wanted to cross from one building to another one had to use ropes for guidance, otherwise one was in danger of vanishing without trace. The most difficult problem was to get enough logs to burn in each barrack, from the pile outside, to keep us from freezing. It took us three days to accomplish what was normally done in a couple of hours.

I tried not to think of my conversation with Vanya. The blizzard helped me in this. Somehow I felt safe in our total isolation from the outside world, from the war, from the unknown... The fight against the elements, our helplessness, our inaccessibility, which normally should have worried me, had the opposite effect: they made me feel safer, more secure. In my heart I was hoping that the storm would last for ever.

The storm did not last for ever. It finished as suddenly as it had begun. We woke up one morning to a normal, frosty, semi-darkness, our small windows covered in snow. Snow drifts up to the top of most buildings. Pure, white, fresh snow everywhere. The first few days were spent in digging ourselves out. It was a major undertaking, requiring all the skills and all the experience available, as well as a lot of very hard work. But soon life returned to normal.

I nearly forgot my conversation with Vanya. Somehow I felt that it was just a strange dream, long, long ago.

About a week after the storm, one morning I got a note from Krepkin to come to see him that afternoon at 5 pm. It was a shock and I was very worried.

It did not sound right at all. Normally, when he had anything to tell me he would simply call me during the morning or evening headcount; but to summon me to his office like this, at an appointed hour, was most unusual. It could not be good, I concluded, it had to be bad... I tried to ask around, whether he had called anybody this way before me, but no-one had any ideas. So there was nothing I could do, I had to wait several long hours, and waiting was never my forte.

I started out from my surgery at five minutes to five, to walk some 300 yards to the administrative barrack where Krepkin worked. Even at a snail's pace I reached my goal far too early, so I turned round and walked back as slowly as I could. I had only managed ten or fifteen paces on my return trip when I heard a window open behind me and Krepkin's voice roared:

"Karlusha! Where are you off to? Come this way at once. You were supposed to come to see me – remember?"

"I am sorry citizen Commandant," I tried to explain, "I am a few minutes early..." "You just come straight in; never mind a minute or two, I am waiting."

Not a good start, I thought. He will be even more annoyed, I was sure.

Miserably I went through the main door, past the outer office, where I recognised the clerk's familiar face, straight into the open door of Krepkin's room. I thought I noticed a funny sort of grin on the face of Antoshka, the Commandant's clerk. I did not look at Krepkin, I concentrated on his carpet instead: a red and blue pattern, printed probably, certainly not woven.

I waited with my eyes firmly glued to the fake Persian design. Silence. It felt like eternity... Krepkin's inimitable smell made the air almost painful to breathe. Still the same revolting mixture of vodka, violets and dead meat.

I was not enjoying it at all. Out of sheer desperation, very reluctantly, I lifted my eyes: Krepkin was standing in front of me only a few feet away.

I looked at the big, red face. I looked again trying to focus, for what I saw did not make any sense to me: He was smiling, yes, unmistakably, smiling! His gearbox-like, all-metal grin was confronting me in all its ugliness. Surprise is not a word which can describe my feelings; shock is probably nearer the mark. The Commandant was undoubtedly enjoying it – I was not.

Could this be some diabolical joke, some sadistic game which was meant to frighten me to death? I looked again: No, this did not look like a vicious smile. It looked almost benevolent. His red, watery eyes were looking at me with affection, almost, I thought – certainly without malice. I continued to wait in silence.

When I heard his first words they did not sound like ordinary speech; it was verse – unmistakably verse. And to crown it all I recognised it as a crude translation of a poem by a well-known Polish poet, Vincety Pol. "For many long years holy Poland was asleep, the White Eagle was asleep..." he was reciting slowly accentuating the rhythm with his index finger, "but..." and here he made a dramatic pause "they woke up and..." – another dramatic pause – "you are now a free citizen!!!" He almost shouted these last words. I was totally at sea. I looked at him without any comprehension. There he was – standing as if on a stage, one hand on his heart, the other pointing vaguely towards me, resembling some grotesque monument. Well," he said at last, "you did not expect such good news. I am sure you are surprised. I am glad I am the one to bring you these happy tidings."

Suddenly I realised that this was what Vanya had been trying to tell me just before the blizzard. So he was not the first, Vanya was. But that was not important just now. First I had to get from Krepkin some hard facts.

"Citizen Commandant," I started, not knowing where to begin.

"No, no!!" he cried, and his huge red hand went right up, in front of my nose. A strong wave of the Krepkin aroma hit my senses with renewed intensity, "Not citizen, but Comrade, – you can call me Comrade now!"

His tone reflected the importance of this concession. Its significance could only be appreciated by those who were serving time and who knew that by calling a free man Comrade one invited a sharp reprimand, since a superior being like a free man could never be a "comrade" to an inferior one such as a prisoner, hence the term "citizen". "You can call me Comrade Commandant, in fact," he added graciously, "you can even call me Ivan Ivanovich, since you are an educated young man."

"How do you like that?" he coughed, unable to control his emotions and – evidently – his breathing. I was having serious problems in controlling mine but for a different reason. The air was getting very heavy. "Thank you, I appreciate it very much, Ivan Ivanovich," I replied in my new capacity as an "educated free young man." At this moment he advanced on me, grabbed my hand in his huge, wet paw and started to pump it vigorously. "Oh God," I prayed, "please don't let him kiss me!!" But kiss me he did – with a vengeance. First on the right cheek, then on the left, and on the right again. Three huge, wet kisses. I longed to wipe my face , but willed myself not to, in case this action should spread the damage over a larger area. I let it dry where it had landed.

To avoid further emotional outpourings I pretended that all this was too much for me and asked whether I could sit down. He consented readily. I was offered a chair at a reasonable distance from my benefactor. I felt appreciably better.

"To celebrate this moment with you I have here something which you will not have tasted for a long time," he pointed towards a small table on which stood a bottle of real vodka and some 'zakuski' in the form of bread and sausage. I was impressed. This, I concluded, could not be a fake, this was for real! Real vodka would not have been wasted on simulations. Remarkably swiftly he uncorked the bottle containing the precious liquid and poured out two large measures. "A toast," he lifted his glass high, still holding the bottle in the other hand, "Karl Efstafievich!" – no-one had ever addressed me in such a courtly manner – "let us drink to FREEDOM," and he emptied his glass straight into his mouth without it even touching his lips. "To Freedom," I echoed weakly. The initial fiery sensation gradually changed into a beneficent glow, which spread, radiating pleasantly to the very tips of my extremities. I was aware that something unbelievable was taking place, I couldn't be bothered to find out what and why. "Not now," I repeated in my mind, "not now, later. I must have time to work it all out."

In fact it did not take all that long. Within a few days I was able to piece together some sort of a picture of what was happening. It seemed that the German attack on the Soviet Union had enabled Britain to form an alliance with Russia against Germany. Poland, by virtue of having been Britain's ally all the time, automatically became Russia's ally. It appeared that a Polish Army was being formed in the South of the Soviet Union, for the purpose of fighting alongside the Russians against Germany. I learnt that a Polish general, named Anders, was in charge and that all Polish citizens were expected to join him somewhere in the South. They told me that I would be travelling soon to Pechora and thence by train to Kotlas, where the Poles from the northern concentration camps were being assembled and where Polish officers would tell us what we had to do.

It was easier to obtain the information than to adjust to it. The transition from regarding the Soviets as enemies to embracing them as allies was not easy.

The thought that one was expected to fight alongside the Russians, presumably under their overall command, was most disturbing. The whole thing seemed very odd. Freedom was wonderful in theory, but would it be so wonderful in practice? Now I started to understand why I had felt so uneasy when Vanya first mentioned the rumour, why I was so reluctant even to think about it. My instinct was right even then. I knew I had to come to terms with the new reality now, to try to form a positive attitude to what my instinct was warning me against. Not easy, not easy at all. Secretly, in the innermost privacy of my heart, I was longing to revert to the safety of the status quo. In other words I wanted to remain here, as a political prisoner. I felt terribly ashamed of this feeling, but I knew it was there.

First of all I had to share the news with my fellow prisoners. I was worried that they might take it badly; that they could be envious, even angry. After all, I had spent but a short time in the camps, while they were to remain, here, to serve out their sentences to the bitter end, regardless.

I need not have worried. They were wonderful. They did not begrudge me my freedom. "You are not guilty of any crime, you have done nothing, you don't belong here," I knew they spoke from the heart and meant every word of it. "You go and join your army and help us beat those German bastards!!"

143

I spent a couple of weeks more at the camp before transport could be arranged.

Appropriately, it was Vanya who drove me to the station. From there I travelled, by train, to Kotlas. I was dreadfully sad to leave my friends, my patients. They were just ordinary criminals, of course, most of them violent, some of them murderers. But I had learned to be happy with them and they with me. They never tried to change or corrupt me. When I refused to take part in their crooked schemes, they would just laugh and let me be.

They did not survive the war: most of them, anyway. Some diabolical mind in the NKVD devised a scheme aimed at using this great mass of men to help the Soviet war effort. Special units were formed consisting entirely of criminal prisoners. Their job was to de-fuse German minefields. The method was simplicity itself: The prisoners were sent in waves straight over the minefields – while the NKVD stayed behind, with machine guns trained on their backs. They would be required to go forward and explode the mines – with their bodies. When one unit had been fully 'utilised' the next one was sent in. Anybody hesitating or turning back was shot. Their choice was to go forward and be torn to shreds by mines or to go back and be shot!

I have often agonised about which way I would choose to die if I had to make that choice.....

Evidently, my own destiny did not involve dying in the war, either as a prisoner, or later as a soldier. I suspect that, at the time, my 'script' was still being written. In the winter of 1941 the unknown lay in front of me in all its mysterious darkness. I had to brace myself, yet again, and try to meet it as it came.

The war changed my life completely, in a way I could never have expected, but on the whole my luck held, throughout, although at times it was tested quite vigorously.

That, however, is another story.

Chapter 11

# THE ARMY OF SKELETONS

My train journey out of Pechora was a very prolonged affair. It lasted more than six weeks. We sped across the snowy expanses of Soviet Russia, first in a southerly direction and later to the South-East, around Moscow and then headed due East, towards the Ural mountains. The train was mostly occupied by Polish ex-prisoners, on their way to Buzuluk, where our armed forces were being assembled. Also, on the train, there were some ordinary Soviet civilians, who came and went in pursuit of their individual business.

During this long trip I had a dream, a nightmare, to be more accurate. I dreamed I was in the Army. I knew it was the Polish Army as all the soldiers had Polish badges on their headgear. We were not in uniform but were still wearing our prison clothes, including particularly nasty prison rubber boots. I dreamed that I had arrived in a great hurry from some distant place, early in the morning. I had come to a vast open space where, in deep snow, I could see a large number of tents. I was sure they were tents as they were flapping in the wind, a cold, cutting wind.

Just as I came in I heard the bugle sound the reveille. From absolutely nowhere, apparently from the frozen ground, thousands of shadowy figures started rising. They were all thin and strange looking. They swayed in the wind. They moved in stiff robot-like movements as if sleepwalking. I watched in awe, as a little while later they started forming into lines, endless lines, still swaying in the wind. I felt that I ought to join them, but couldn't. An invisible force was holding me back and I could only watch.

As I watched, the sun came out. This 'Dali-like', surrealistic scene was now drenched in sunlight. In utter horror I looked at their faces: they had all horribly white faces. I soon realised I was looking at bones. They were grinning in the sun the horrible grin of death. Their hands were all bones too, dry bones, so were their legs and feet. In fact all the mass of men in front of me was a mass of skeletons. I watched, petrified, as an officer appeared in front of the lines. He too was a skeleton, but he was in uniform. He marched, as if on stilts. His movements, too, were the laboured movements of a robot, as he ploughed through the snow. Presently he halted and stood to attention, as if ready to give a command. From where I stood I could not hear the words of command, but saw the lines re-form into marching order and the whole unit started marching towards me. I tried to move out of the way, but couldn't.

I woke up with a scream, much to the alarm of my fellow passengers.

There was a young woman in the compartment, an ordinary civilian, who gave me a knowing look. Without a word she took my hand and held it in both her hands for a brief moment. It worked like magic. This silent gesture of compassion, of comfort sent the horrible picture back to the world whence it had come. I felt much better.

I made friends with her, later. She did not want to hear any explanation from me. She just said that she understood these sudden fears and knew she had the power to make them harmless. She was a very nice Russian girl from the suburbs of Moscow. She said little, but seemed to understand everything.

When eventually I arrived in Buzuluk, the provisional Polish army HQ, I was immediately redirected to Totskoye, where the 6th Infantry Division was being formed under General Tokarzewski.

The scene I found in Totskoye was uncomfortably reminiscent of my dream.

The tents, the snow, the wind, were the same. The men were not skeletons, though. They did not grin the grin of death. They all had skins, very pale skins, perhaps, and they were all swaying in the wind, as they were very thin and weak, but they were not dead and to my surprise were remarkably cheerful. This gave me the confidence, the certainty almost, that there was hope, that we were an Army, and that all would be well in the end.

The tents were surprisingly effective in this snowy plain. They had double skinned canvas roofs. They were all dug into the frozen ground to the depth of some 6 feet, with only the double-skinned canvas roof exposed to the elements. Most tents were equipped with a small stove, newly built from clay, complete with a short length of galvanised iron pipe, protruding from the gable end of the canvas and which served as a flue.

146

The stove was fed with wood, which we collected daily and which was stored in the tent. This provided a remarkably effective source of heat. One of us, in turn, would sit all night, and feed the stove with this fuel. I do not remember suffering from cold in the tent at night, even though, on these plains, half-way between the Volga and the Ural mountains, the outside temperature at night was seldom much above minus 40 Celsius.

What we found difficult, though, was the fact, that despite our poor physical condition we were expected to operate as if we were a proper army. Our daily routine included exercises and 'square bashing' which lasted for hours and which seemed a little overdone. The food was as bad as in the labour camps, in fact it was frequently quite a lot worse, since the rations we received from our Soviet hosts were not only insufficient, but had to be shared with thousands of Polish civilians, who were there 'unofficially', without the knowledge and permission of the Soviet Authorities. The remarkable phenomenon of cheerful acceptance and almost enthusiastic compliance with the energy-consuming military drilling on an empty stomach, still amazes me to this day.

Personally I was in much better shape than most of my colleagues, having had some exceptionally good months behind me, in my job of medical assistant in Vazkey Yol. My superiors spotted that immediately, and soon I was selected to join a special unit, a battalion of candidates for the officer cadet course.

It was a great honour and distinction, but it was physically even more demanding, in view of the intensive schooling which we were expected to undergo. The wounds on my legs, which were still open, the residue of my near-fatal bout of Tsinga, were playing up now quite embarrassingly. I was determined that this should not impede my military advancement and tried to conceal them from my superiors. I knew that nothing could help me, nothing other than proper food – which, I also knew, was simply not available.

From the early morning to the late afternoon we were practising our military skills, carrying sticks instead of rifles. We were, continuously rehearsing the antiquated technique of infantry attack, which involved a lot of running and rolling in the snow.

By some devious means I managed to acquire a pair of perfectly good Soviet army boots which enabled me to move with greater ease in the snow. I was also more agile and better

147

balanced than most of my comrades. The NCOs who were supervising our training started to use me as a guinea pig to demonstrate, in front of my unit, how certain exercises should be performed. I was often excused from the exercise itself which was invariably repeated ad nauseam. Thus I was able to save valuable energy.

I found yet another formula for saving energy. It was a discovery I made quite by chance which helped me to avoid a lot of tediously repetitive exercises and hours and hours of square-bashing. I found that if I volunteered for latrine cleaning I would be left alone all day and nobody would interfere with me at all.

Maybe because of the unglamorous nature of the job I had the field entirely to myself, without any jealous competitors breathing down my neck. My job was to remove the contents of a ditch, load it into a small sleigh, take it to a nearby wood and spread it, judiciously, under the trees, with great benefit, no doubt, to the ecology of the planet. What everybody overlooked and I established, to my own benefit, was that because of the very low temperatures the substance that I was dealing with was frozen solid and was not obnoxious at all.

I was thus left to myself with a job, which could be completed, easily, in a couple of hours, but for which my superiors allocated a whole day. As a result I could indulge in my favourite pastime, that of daydreaming. While my body was engaged in this menial activity my soul was wallowing in most fabulous dreams. Usually they included some imaginary battle scenes in which I was participating, or sequences of blissful country life or, sometimes, visions of riding a magnificent Irish hunter across my own fields of ripening wheat.

In contrast with these non-intellectual activities I had, every evening, a unique opportunity of improving my mind. I became friendly with a young chap whose name was Edward. He lived in the same tent and was the first true intellectual I had ever met who was approximately my own age. In his way he was a genius. He had a considerable influence on me. He was the son of very brilliant parents. His father had something to do with the theatre, producing or directing plays, and his mother was a writer of learned books on subjects ranging from literature to the history of art.

Edward's looks were also rather striking, of a type somewhere

148

between a youthful Lord Byron and Julius Slowacki, the famous Polish poet. His dark brown, slightly wavy hair was longer than the army normally permitted. He told me that even the battalion barber could not bring himself to cut it short. His large, brown, intelligent eyes, had a slightly bored, languid expression and gazed from under dark, silky, arched eyebrows. His fine, aquiline nose added a further touch of distinction. The weakest of his facial features was his mouth. It was thin, small and rather mean looking, but changed radically when he smiled. He had the most radiant, engaging and charming smile imaginable, unfortunately rarely seen, as he preferred to remain pensively sombre and sad-looking. While his face was impressive, his figure was not. He was thin, short and slightly stooping in posture. He was best seen sitting down, preferably in a semi-reclining position. Physically he was a weakling.

The most extraordinary thing for me was that he treated me as if I were his intellectual equal, which could not be further from the truth. It flattered me immensely, though. It worried me, as well, as I felt I would lose him as a friend if he were ever to discover what my true intellectual level was. I was trying to postpone the inevitable by various means, principally by saying nothing. I could not imagine what made him talk to me the way he did, since at first I mostly did not know what he was talking about. Still, I was compelled to listen, to think and in the end to learn.

There was another young man in our tent, named Janek, who was a very different type, earnest and friendly and not at all complicated. He always told the truth and, if he did not know something he was not shy about asking. Of average intelligence, he was not at all highbrow. He helped me a lot in my little game of deception: If he was around when Edward started on one of his complicated monologues about some obscure piece of literature, it was Janek who asked the questions. Thus I could maintain my knowledgeable silence and later, if all went well, could even risk an unoriginal comment.

Edward was a great admirer of Ibsen. His mother, he said, had translated some of Ibsen's poems and plays and he knew most of them by heart. His personal philosophy was quite similar to that of his literary hero. Like Ibsen he believed in the freedom of the individual and rebelled against the predominance of the majority. In many ways he was not democratic. He was more of an elitist.

149

His main problem was that he was physically weak. Much too weak for the demands which the army was imposing on him. He had spent a relatively short time in Soviet captivity, most of it in prison, from where he had been sent directly to Buzuluk. So he did not go through the ordeal of labour camps, which I was sure he would never have survived. The current regime was definitely too harsh for him and he knew it, but his pride did not allow him to quit. Janek and I did our best to cover up for him by taking on certain energy-consuming jobs, like the night vigils by the stove.

Although this would gain him a full night's sleep it did not seem to help. He began to sink deeper and deeper.

Even for those of us who were relatively strong, life was fairly miserable and above all very boring. Although we were supposed to be training as candidates for an officer cadet school, there were very few lectures and it was nearly all just pointless exertion. The monotonous routine of senseless drilling, plus my solo sessions at latrine cleaning, seemed to be going on for ever, week after week. The intellectual stimulus of my conversations with Edward did help a lot, but these were centred on a sphere which was too remote for me. I enjoyed the challenge but did not relish the subject.

There was to be one exception, though, one event which introduced an element of magic into our dreary lives. This experience seemed so wonderful at the time that it is difficult today to appreciate its full significance. It made such an impression on me that, even now, I remember every single detail, literally, as if it had happened yesterday. On the evening in question, after returning from exercises, we were told that the Army Theatrical Unit was giving a show near the divisional HQ, situated about 3 kilometres away from where we were, and if we wanted to attend we had to report to the duty officer by a certain time. I was very keen, so was Janek, but poor Edward was too tired. He just wanted to sleep. We persuaded him that the effort was worth it, that it would cheer him up. Although he thought the whole thing was slightly beneath his dignity, he finally agreed to join us. So at about 6 pm we formed into a marching column, under the command of a sergeant and went.

What confronted us, on arrival, was an impressive-looking stage formed in a very ingenious way. Three flat-backed army trucks were positioned to stand side by side, thus providing a raised area.

The stage was illuminated by the headlights of two more lorries standing to each side of the audience. As there were not enough seats, the spectators at the back of the auditorium were obliged to stand. I was worried about Edward who, after a full day's work and the additional march of 3 kilometres in the snow, could be feeling faint. But he seemed all right. In fact he looked almost excited. The sight of a stage seemed to animate him.

After some time, when the audience had settled and all lights had been switched full on a little orchestra appeared on the stage. Apart from the upright piano, which had already been there, there was a violin, a viola, a cello and a saxophone. As an opening number they played a snappy little tune, which met with an ovation from the audience. I kept an eye on Edward. He seemed all right for the time being. The introduction was followed by a couple of comedians, who cracked jokes and then sang a song . They too proved a great success.

But all this was nothing compared with what was to come. After some more preliminaries the main attraction of the show was announced. Her name was Renata Bogdanska. When she walked on the stage I was sure she was the most beautiful woman that had ever existed. She was, to me, simply divine. Although I remember to this day every word of every song that she sang she was so stunning that I cannot recall what she was wearing. It could have been anything from a glamorous evening gown to a simple khaki uniform. But this is probably the point: her beauty was such that it did not matter what she was wearing, all the props, such as dresses or jewellery were superfluous. This blonde goddess was the personification of perfection. And when she started to sing, the impact was almost unbearable.

She sang in a lovely melodious voice directly to me and for me. There were several hundred men around, but I was convinced that it was all done for me. It does, no doubt, sound ridiculous and exaggerated, but this is how it felt at the time. The impression of this experience remains with me to this day. It made all the difference to my will to go on, my will to survive, my will to try to regain the life which, I had thought, could never come within my reach. In the final analysis it made the difference between life and death.

There is really no need to go into more detail regarding this event. It was, no doubt, following the well-established formula of 'entertaining the troops'. If somebody had given me this defini-tion at the time I would have probably knocked him down. The sight and sound of this glorious creature was to me a mystical mystery, a religious rite, an act of faith, whatever one might call it, but certainly not 'entertainment of the troops'.

This single apparition did more for my soul than a thousand heroic speeches of a thousand orators. It shook me out of my neg-ative mode into a positive attitude towards the mountainous dif-ficulties which lay ahead, it changed me from a moral vegetable into a motivated individual ready for anything.

As we were marching back to our unit after the show I looked at Edward. I could see that he too was moved, he had tears in his eyes. The effect on him, on this intellectual genius, had been sim-ilar. After a while he turned to me and said – "It is the simplicity of it all that really gets you, isn't is? The Greeks knew it well. The power of the word and the power of music is best set against an empty stage. It magnifies the effect."

I knew what he was talking about , but I did not agree. One could not explain it in terms of technique. It was more than that. It was more fundamental, deeper. I could not put in into words and, for once, I did not try. I just kept humming Renata's song: "Maybe a day, or a year, who can tell..."

\* \* \*

Edward did not survive that winter. We found him one morn-ing, barely breathing, on the floor of the tent. He died shortly afterwards.

For some time, prior to this, we had been nagging him to go to the medical orderly and get some vitamins or cod liver oil to help him with his chronic weakness.

He kept refusing, and insisted that he did not wish to advertise the fact that he was physically inadequate. A strange sort of logic for someone as intelligent as he was, but finally we persuaded him and he went. As I expected, he was given cod liver oil and some vitamin C in tablet form. This seemed to help him quite a lot. He started sleeping better and, presumably, absorbing his food, mis-erable though it was. He was moving with greater energy and, for him, became quite cheerful. He was so much better, that one night he insisted on taking his turn at the stove. Janek and I tried to talk him out of it, but he was adamant.

At about four in the morning, I woke up. Inside the tent it was freezing cold.

My first thought was that Edward had dozed off and allowed the stove to go out. With great difficulty I managed to light the kerosene lamp. My fingers were completely numb. The flickering light revealed the dreadful truth. Edward was lying on the tent floor and breathing very irregularly, in a terrible rasping, gargling way. It did not look good. I knew it was serious. I woke Janek up and he the rest of our sleeping companions. Someone started the difficult process of re-lighting the stove. I asked Janek to get the medical orderly and, if possible the doctor. To me it looked very much like a stroke.

We decided not to move Edward from the floor, but tried to make him more comfortable where he was.

The medical orderly proved quite useless. He didn't even have a stethoscope. Edward's pulse was very weak, at times non-existent, and above all, most erratic. The orderly and Janek went to fetch the doctor, who lived by the divisional HQ. I calculated rapidly: 3 kilometres could be covered, in the snow, if one hurried, say in 30 minutes. If the doctor was there and had at his disposal some form of transport, he could be with us in 45 minutes. I prepared myself for the worst, and for having to assist another human being through the final barrier of life.

By the time the doctor arrived Edward was dead. He died peacefully and imperceptibly. I did not feel anything just then, I just felt very cold.

The death of Edward filled me with despair. Janek was also badly shaken. Suddenly I saw the grotesque pointlessness of our situation. We were indeed an army of skeletons, after all. The fact that we were alive was not important. We were useless, useless and doomed. The hunger, the cold, the exhaustion would kill us all, before we had a chance to fire a single shot.

The fact that we had skins did not mean that we were not skeletons, like in my dream, all dead to the last man. Not in battle, oh no, that would be far too good for us; but dead of starvation, of exhaustion, of exposure. How many were we? Fifty thousand or maybe even one hundred thousand, but who cared? We were all doomed.

As an army we were worse than useless, we did not have a single rifle between us and, even if we had, we were too weak to pull the trigger. What was the good of practising these silly infantry manoeuvres, if we could not attack anybody, or even climb a hill, as half of us would die from the effort?

I went on with my duties, as best as I could, but I had no more enthusiasm left in me. I was drained. I knew from experience that such a state of mind was, in itself, a formula for death. I had 'dropped my wings,' as my Russian prison mates would have said. But I did not care – the sooner the better, I felt.

Then one day, at about midday, when I was at my latrine duties, I heard someone whistling. I recognised the lovely melody that Renata had sung that magical evening, a million years ago. It filled me with rage. Who dared to be cheerful, while I was in mental agony? I looked up: It was Janek.

"What the bloody hell possessed you," I glared at him. But before I had a chance to say any more he raised his hand and said, "I know, I know, but listen to this. I have some good news, some wonderful news. It has just been announced, at lunch time, that we are all going South. Uzbekistan or Turkmenistan, they say. Glorious sunshine and fruit and spicy food. It would do wonders for your wounds..."

It all sounded terrific, but I wanted to be careful, not to accept as fact something which was probably just rumour. But Janek assured me this was official. He had seen it in black and white in the Army bulletin that morning.

Janek had to run back to his work. I was left alone. I was able to indulge in a lovely session of day-dreaming, the first for a long time. And the little tune came back to me and all of a sudden I started to hum Renata's favourite melody: "Maybe a day, or a year, who can tell..."

Yes, who could tell?... Who indeed?

# Chapter 12

# UZBEKISTAN

While I was struggling to survive the long winter on the Russian steppes to the East of the Volga, I was in no position to discern the momentous changes that had occurred to the West of it. Just as well, since it would have depressed me even further. One short glance at the map would have sent shivers of alarm down my spine, for without a doubt the 1941 map of Europe was not a reassuring sight. One did not have to be an expert in strategy to conclude that, in effect, Hitler had won the war. To all intents and purposes the European continent belonged to Germany. The few nations that were still shown as independent were not independent at all.

Italy and Spain were totally committed to supporting the Reich. Sweden and Switzerland, technically neutral, remained unoccupied only as long as it suited Berlin. The rest of the European continent was either incorporated into the Reich or under its direct occupation.

The magnitude of these changes was in itself unprecedented, but when taken in conjunction with the speed with which it had been achieved, the overall result was almost beyond belief. Germany, after all, had begun re-arming in earnest in 1935 and had gone onto the offensive in September 1939. By June 1941, within six years from producing her first tank, and barely twenty months after firing the first shot, she had Europe at her feet.

Great Britain still stood alone. The invasion and eventual occupation of this fortress could only be a question of time. She had just the Royal Navy and the Royal Air Force to bar the way and these were stretched to the limit. Coastal defences were negligible. With America and the Soviet Union maintaining their military non-involvement, Britain's days seemed to be numbered. Hitler appeared invincible. He had won what he had in spite of his generals' objections, acting on a hunch, with insufficient forces, just following his own convoluted instinct.

Historians tell us today that in the end Germany lost the war as a result of two fundamental errors which Hitler committed in June 1941: that of attacking the Soviet Union and simultaneously declaring war on the USA.

I have no quarrel with the latter assertion. There truly was no need for the Reich to have confronted America. Hitler should have known that. He should have remembered that it was America's participation and industrial might that had finally decided Germany's defeat in the Great War.

But what I do dispute is the supposed inevitability of the failure of his assault on Russia, code-named Operation Barbarossa. It is my view, even today, that if Hitler had adopted a less hostile attitude towards the Soviet civilian population he could have won the Russian campaign very quickly – quickly enough to free his Eastern armies in time to defend himself from any invading force from the West, or from anywhere else for that matter.

He would have gained access to Russia's oil supplies and even, conceivably, to Russian or Ukrainian volunteers or mercenaries willing to do the fighting for him.

There is no doubt in my mind that the USSR would have collapsed very quickly if the Germans had not been so brutal. I was there myself and I knew it at first hand. Most Russians, or Bielorussians and certainly most Ukrainians were waiting for them with open arms. We have all by now seen contemporary photographs of Ukrainians welcoming the Panzers into their villages with bread and salt. Instead of tanks or machine guns, a few loudspeakers would have done the trick, calling on the Soviet civilians to cooperate and promising them land and prosperity. Stalin's murderous repressions against his own people were fresh in everyone's minds. They could easily have proved to be the most powerful of weapons. The whole of the Soviet empire would have collapsed.

Instead, Hitler ordered massacres, the burning of villages, the extermination of Jews and, above all, incredible cruelty to the prisoners of war. Operation Barbarossa was lost in the hearts and minds of the Soviet people and not at Kursk or Stalingrad. In the end, they decided that the devil they knew was preferable to the one that was coming from the West.

Stalin realised this and took full advantage of it.

* * *

We did leave Totskoye for the South eventually, as we had hoped we would, but not directly. We spent a short time on a collective farm first, helping the local women to bring in the much belated harvest. We were in the depths of winter and all their menfolk had gone to war months before, so our task was doomed from the very start. Our feeble efforts did not redress the combined effects of the war, the winter and of the collective farming system. When we were eventually ordered to leave, the sum total of our endeavour was not impressive and a long way short of the target. Still, to me it was a welcome change from the futile and boring routine of the previous months. The food, too, was a little more plentiful than before. Otherwise I have not retained many memories from that short interlude, except one. I still remember, most vividly, driving a pair of oxen alone, in a blizzard, at night and knowing that I was hopelessly lost, not something I would recommend to the faint-hearted. I confess that walking knee deep in snow for hours, probably in circles, plus the effort of driving the reluctant animals before me exhausted me so much that I was seriously considering giving up, lying down in the snow and quietly freezing to death. Oxen in my personal experience, unlike horses, are not endowed with the instinct for finding their way home under adverse conditions. The fact that I am now able to tell the story had nothing to do with any skills either mental or physical on my part or on the part of the animals in my care, but to the purest chance. We literally collided with another sleigh driven by a local woman who knew precisely where she was and where she was going.

Our journey to the promised land took place a few weeks afterwards. Like all train journeys at that time, ours was a slow and very roundabout trip, but eventually we began to notice a marked improvement in temperature. When at long last we reached Uzbekistan it was really hot. We were delighted. Our elation did not last long though, as on arrival at our destination we realised that the warm climate was not going to solve any of our problems. In fact, if anything, it made them worse. All the bacteria and viruses which had lain dormant in the cold climate of the Northern regions, suddenly hit our population with unbelievable ferocity. Typhoid, hitherto rare in our midst, began to decimate our army and the civilians alike. Our medical staff had no drugs and were helpless. Dysentery raged unchecked and uncheckable. The little fresh fruit and green vegetables that were available, and which we needed so badly, were almost useless for fear of contracting other diseases. Wagons laden with corpses could be seen each morning unceremoniously speeding towards makeshift cemeteries. I was told later that during those months we lost more people, civilians and soldiers alike than in the whole of the Italian campaign.

Our camp was near Shakhrisyabz, a fairly big town in Eastern Uzbekistan. It was a particularly nasty place, where typhoid was commonplace and sanitary conditions were well below the average, even by Soviet standards.

It was in that camp that I was first assigned to an infantry officer cadet school. Then one day an officer came looking for volunteers to join the Armoured section of the school. I was one of the first to enrol. In my view anything was better than the infantry, for which I had never had any enthusiasm. I thus found myself in the nucleus of a company, about 90 strong, all volunteers, all looking for something a bit special. Soon we were separated from the infantry battalion and little by little our unit began to find its own identity.

In the early Spring of 1942 the officer cadet school was sent for a time to Kazakhstan, to a little village called Vozniesieniovka, not very far from Alma Ata. In was inhabited almost entirely by Ukrainians (no doubt forcibly resettled by Stalin during the '30s). As usual at that time, there were only a few old men about, and the rest were all women. I remember this time with particular pleasure. We had practically nothing to do, we just rested. The early Spring in that region is simply enchanting. We lived in a neat little village situated on a vast fertile plain with the snow-capped peaks of the Pamir mountains majestically looming on the horizon. We were far from the disease and pestilence of Shakhrisyabz, and we had enough to eat. In fact some of our more enterprising colleagues discovered a source of additional sustenance. For a very few cigarettes, or even less chocolate (which we received on rare occasions, compliments of the US Army), we could obtain from the local women generous quantities of eggs and sufficient granulated sugar to produce, together, quantities of 'Gogel-mogel'. This delicacy was obtained by beating raw eggs with lavish quantities of sugar, thus producing a substance which seemed not only delicious but highly nutritious as well, and it undoubtedly contributed to rebuilding our severely weakened immune systems. I ate so much of it then that I have never been able to face touching the stuff since then.

It was in Vozniesieniovka that we first heard the unbelievable news that some Polish units were being allowed to leave the Soviet Union to join the Allied Forces in the Middle East. We were all by then well trained in not expecting miracles or favours. So we did not even talk much about it among ourselves.

But we did dream. No-one could prevent that, least of all ourselves. To be able to leave this God-forsaken country, to be given at last some proper equipment with which to train' We could then become a real army! And to have food' That, too, was included in our dreams, Gogel-mogel or no Gogel-mogel!

But it was not to be, not for us this time round, anyway. The dreaded NKVD refused to include us on their lists for shipment back to Uzbekistan, and by the time that we finally arrived there, we were too late. The first wave had gone and no-one could tell if there would be another one.

So there was nothing for it; we had to wait and hope. The waiting and the hoping, and some training too, was to be done in a place called Vrevskoye, a little town in Uzbekistan between Samarkand and Bukhara.

It was in Vrevskoye that our little band of volunteers became a proper unit.

And what a good unit it eventually turned out to be! For the first time since joining the Armed Forces in Totskoye, I realised what a wonderful thing it was to have the feeling, more, the conviction that one was part of an elite force, well disciplined, well turned out, where the old cliché of 'one for all, and all for one' was not just an empty phrase, but a matter of actual fact.

We had just two officers who were responsible for shaping us in that way: the school commandant, Captain Jerzy Rędziejowski and Lieut. Wladyslaw Sypel who had come with us from Kazakhstan. Rędziejowski was a charismatic figure, particularly gifted at inspiring young men to discover self-esteem and self-confidence. "A tank commander fears no-one but God," was one of his catch phrases. I still use it, frequently, to myself when faced with a difficult situation or an unpleasant encounter. He also encouraged us to develop our initiative. A professional officer who had served in one of the few Polish armoured units in the September '39 campaign, he had both authority and experience, which we all admired and respected.

Lieut. Sypel was only a couple of years my senior. He was a good organiser and fought hard to keep our school going, which was sometimes an uphill task. He was always very kind to me and later, when we both served in the same line regiment, we became good friends.

Our camp was located in a pleasant shady orchard, and the surrounding countryside was criss-crossed with deep, fast-flowing, irrigation channels, which the locals called *Arik* and which proved to be a good source of clean water. There, we were far enough from the infected areas and could keep relatively cool and meticulously clean.

Our training was severely limited by a total lack of equipment. We had no weapons of any description, and for driving lessons we used one three-ton army truck which could only be spared for a few hours at a time. It worked out to just a few minutes a week for each of us behind the wheel. Those of us who could drive, even a little, were regarded with great respect and double de-clutching was given the status of a major skill, worthy of universal acclaim.

The instructors were mostly our own colleagues, usually those who being a year or so older had one, or even two years at university behind them. Thus, for instance, basic metallurgy courses were the responsibility of Eugeniusz Czauderna, while mechanics and rudimentary engineering were taught by Tadek Bobak.

There was also one interesting character who had a considerable impact on our little group. His name was Sgt. Wincenty Kokowski. Sgt. Koko, as we called him, had hitherto been a professional NCO, serving in one of the armoured battalions. He was much older, in his late thirties, and could never have become an officer before for lack of academic qualifications. Since these had been lowered for the duration of hostilities he decided to attend a cadet school. Because of his experience and abilities he enjoyed a special status and was, in fact, our senior instructor. He spoke Polish with a strong German accent (having been born either in Silesia or the Poznan region) and although a patriotic Pole, he retained many Teutonic mannerisms which amused us immensely. It was he who taught us a rather special parade step, for which we became renowned in the garrison and which we demonstrated frequently to the delight of the young ladies of the Polish ATS battalion. He also conducted exercises designed to acquaint us with tank drill and formation manoeuvres. As we had no tanks, what it meant was that we were running around in teams of three, pretending to be tank crews, while he was shouting orders, in his special clipped Germanic voice. Should one 'crew' step out of line, or take a wrong course, Sgt. Koko would stop us at once and describe in a most realistic way, the grisly fate that would befall the erring tank. This usually included horrific details of human flesh burning freely, while the rest could do nothing to save them. Surprisingly, we found these exercises great fun and loved him dearly, despite his exaggerated severity.

The other activity which kept us busy was the production and staging of variety shows. One of our colleagues, Jurek Maty-kiewicz had a particular talent for putting new, topical words to the music of old operettas. We used a village hall, which proved ideal for the purpose, found some excellent musicians complete with instruments and our shows proved to be a great success. We must have staged half a dozen performances within a few weeks. I sang in a rather romantic duet with a very pretty blonde to the Franz Lehar aria from the 'Merry Widow,' "Vilia, oh Vilia".

Although I was, at the time, deeply disappointed that we had missed our opportunity to leave Russia with the first wave, in March-April, in retrospect the period in Vrevskoye was a very important one for the formation of my character. I experienced there things which were to stand me in good stead for the rest of my military life. The bond which forms between young men of the same age who share the same purposes and ideals is something which is valuable in any organisation, but in the Army it is vital. The fact that we were denied arms and equipment may have been a blessing in disguise, because then other qualities could develop more freely and naturally. Rędziejowski had a great influence on me. He developed in me a boldness which for a future officer was a vital factor. I had hitherto tended to wait until things happened before reacting. He taught me that it is often better to anticipate events firmly and decisively.

We still had our problems. Although we were not hungry, as we had been in Totskoye, we were not well fed and food was still very much on our mind. And, above all, we were still in the Soviet Union. That in itself was something nobody could get used to. Anything could still happen, anything at all...

\* \* \*

Finally, on 13th August 1942, together with the rest of my officer cadet school, I boarded a ship at Krasnovodsk, a Soviet port on the Caspian Sea. Our destination was Pahlavi in Persia (today called Iran). We were about to leave the USSR, having spent nearly two and half years there. A mere 230 miles separated us from another world, which had seemed an unattainable paradise.

As I was settling down on the deck of the rather scruffy steamer, I made every effort not to feel elated. It was far too soon for that. A lot could still happen. We had lived through so many false dawns already. The last six months had been spent in futile anticipation. Even dates had been given, only to be postponed and eventually cancelled. Could this finally be the fulfilment of our dreams, or would they, at the last moment, order us to disembark?

My feet were very sore, covered in huge blisters, and the tsinga wounds, the relics of my Taiga days, felt hot and itchy. It was, in a way, a good thing as it took my mind off the forbidden subject and dampened the feeling of elation which I was at such pains to control. The reason for my physical discomfort was that we had spent the previous night and the best part of the day marching furiously. We had covered 40 kilometres with only a couple of stops. The blisters on my feet and the smelly wounds on my legs reminded me of that. For several days prior to this we had been waiting for a signal to join the long queues at Krasnovodsk. The holding area, where we had been kept on full alert, was near enough to the port, a couple of hours' drive by army truck. But no trucks had arrived. Then, the previous night, Capt. Rędziejowski, the school commandant, had announced that there would be no transport and that if we were to make it, it would have to be on foot. The 40 kilometres had to be covered in under 10 hours.

Even at the end of our marathon march, when we got there well within the time allotted, things did not look good. Our ship was still loading but it appeared full already. There was considerable doubt whether we could be squeezed in, as there were many civilian families who had a higher priority than us. The ship's captain told us that, at best, we had a 50/50 chance. But, he said, if we could make ourselves really useful he might still have us. Would we help to load the civilians? Yes of course, we said without hesitation. So in addition to our forced march and no sleep we worked like demons, on the theory that if we were really helpful they would not have the heart to leave us behind. It worked. But as a result the ship was terribly overloaded The waterline was above the permitted level. One of my colleagues came to me and said, "I hope you are a strong swimmer. I can't swim, so I have no problem. Unless this weather holds, the Caspian fish will have a feast. I wonder how the authorities could have allowed such over-loading?"

"Put yourself in their shoes," I replied. "If they had left us behind we would have died in Russia. If we sink we will die at sea, but at least we will have had a chance. The other way we would have had none." "And what if we go down at sea, but are rescued by a Russian ship?" he asked, "we will have had a good soaking in the water first and then die in Russia after all. I think I would rather sink in the first place." We both laughed.

When I finally saw the crew making preparations for the ship to cast off I felt relieved. Perhaps we would be allowed to remain on board after all. A little earlier I had been told that ours would be the last ship for the foreseeable future. And we were leaving, I could see, so many people on the quay, old people, little children, with hopeless, pale, tearful faces. Their last chance had gone, maybe for ever.

The ship gathered speed. We were pointing South-West, towards the setting sun. Sea gulls escorted us noisily, drowning the receding cries of children on the shore. It seemed that we were in luck.

I concentrated now on dressing my wounds. They looked a mess. The ordinary blisters did not bother me quite so much; it was my scurvy wounds which looked very inflamed, hot and weepy. The forced march was obviously the cause of it. But it had been worth it. Anything was worth it. The port of Krasnovodsk was disappearing into the distance. I was leaving the USSR behind, that strange, malevolent land of lies, death, and cold; of barbed wire and living skeletons; the richest land on earth, yet one incapable of feeding its own people, let alone those whom they had enslaved.

I carried two canteens filled with boiled water: one to drink and the other to dress my wounds with. One of the few things which was fairly plentiful in the USSR was boiled water. One could get it, on tap, at every railway station or public building. It was called kipiatok and was the outward manifestation of a phenomenon called Kultura, which, although literally translated means 'culture', has little to do with what we would understand the term to mean.

The Soviet version of 'culture', apart from boiled water, would include such things as 'de-lousing' facilities, or the provision of spittoons in public places, or the use of handkerchiefs for blowing one's nose in preference to the less 'cultured' alternative, the bare-finger method.

When I finished my surgical chores the moon had already risen. A big silver disk hung over the horizon, roughly where Krasnovodsk had been. The sea was like a mirror. Not one ripple disturbed the calm of the water before us. In the wake of our ship two deep furrows glittered in the moonlight. The picture was enchanting, unreal. I was still refusing to give in. We had a long way to go, I kept repeating to myself, anything could still happen. But my determination was wearing thin. The smell of the sea, the warmth of the August night, made it even more difficult.

And then from down below I heard the sound of human voices singing. Shy and faint at first, but steadily rising. A familiar tune, a prayer sung below deck by the civilian passengers, filled the air. It was a hymn to the Holy Mother of God. A mournful tune which I normally disliked, but which that night carried the extraordinary power of true prayer. The sound and the manner in which it came faithfully mirrored my own feelings of gratitude and suppressed joy.

My sleeping companions started to stir and a few of them sat up and listened. We looked at each other. And then softy, softly at first, one by one, we started to join in. Strong, young masculine voices added force and depth to this already miraculous sound. Before long the whole ship was one big song, one tuneful prayer. 'Ave Maria'... The Mother of God, the Queen of Poland, Her own children praised Her and thanked Her for delivering them from barbaric bondage, from hell on earth, from the frozen steppes where only hunger and disease reigned.

The feelings I had so desperately been trying to suppress burst out in me like a flood. I could not control them any longer. As I sang my heart out, my soul was so full of joy that it hurt, I was aching with happiness. Even if a storm came, I thought, and we

164

were to drown this very moment, the joy I was feeling now would make it worth while. The thirty long months which lay behind me faded in my memory into a hazy cloud, less painful, less horrible. Everything seemed pure and holy and good.

As I watched the small ship, bathed in moonlight, suspended in semi-darkness, vibrating with the sounds of the truest prayer on earth, I felt huge warm tears rolling down my cheeks.

# Chapter 13

# A CASE OF INSUBORDINATION

Among the many coloured photographs of my horses which cover the walls of my dressing room at Saddlecombe, there is a frame containing a modest arrangement of three black and white photos with not a single horse in it.

These are the only pictorial records of my army days in my possession which I felt were worth framing..

Pride of place among them is given to a rather blurred photograph, taken in some distant desert location in the Middle East in summer of 1943, featuring three generals, three other officers and one cadet officer. The generals, in order of importance, are: Gen. Wladyslaw Sikorski, Supreme Commander Polish Forces in exile, Gen. Wladyslaw Anders, Commanding the 2nd Polish Army Corps and Gen. Gustaw Paszkiewicz commanding the 2nd Polish Armoured Brigade. The other officers include Lieut. Stanislaw Masztak, commandant of the 2nd Armoured Officer Cadet School, Lieut. Ponikiewski, Gen. Sikorski's Naval ADC, and I think that the man standing behind Gen. Anders is Lieut. Romanowski, Gen. Anders's ADC. Finally, the young cadet in the picture is myself.

The occasion was the passing out parade and the picture records the moment of the handing out of the diplomas.

This photograph, in addition to bringing back personal memories, has a certain historical value. It must be one of the last records of Gen. Sikorski's visit to the Middle East and one of the last official pictures taken of him before he died, with all his entourage, in an air crash off Gibraltar on his way back to England. The accident is still the subject of much speculation and sinister implication. On a totally different scale, perhaps, it has to my mind certain similarities with the death of President Kennedy a quarter of a century later, not only in that there are still many unexplained aspects which tend to contradict the findings of the official enquiries, but also that the more answers one gets the more suspicious are the questions that seem to come up. The

166

matter has, as far as I know, continued to remain largely unexplained.

On a personal level this picture brings back to me a whole array of memories, some pleasant and some unpleasant.

But I think I had better start from the beginning. After landing in Pahlevi in August 1942, for the subsequent 10 months we were truly roaming the whole of the Middle East – from Persia to Iraq, and then to Egypt. We lived in camps, some big, some small, nearly always in the middle of more or less inhospitable deserts. Having been acclimatised to the cold Russian weather, our bodies had to learn to adjust to dry desert heat, often reaching 50 degrees Centigrade. Even in winter, whilst the mercury could drop at night to near zero, the days could be as hot as European summers. We were living under canvas, of course, and had to learn to cope with frequent sand-storms, something that is difficult to describe and even more difficult to survive.

The so called hamsin is a climatic phenomenon which has a depressing influence of the average human being. The hot wind, carrying with it sand and grit, can last for a week at a time and is capable of uprooting even the most carefully secured tent. The sand gets everywhere, in one's eyes, mouth, nose, ears and, of course, one's food. According to Islamic law a man will not be punished for killing his wife if he does it while that wind is blowing. I was unable to establish whether the law is equally forgiving if the opposite happens and the wife sticks a knife into her husband's back under similar circumstances, as I never had an opportunity of consulting a learned Islamic lawyer on this point.

On the positive side our training was progressing well. Slowly at first, we started receiving arms and finally even armour, beginning with ordinary infantry carriers for preliminary training, and eventually progressing to proper tanks. Half-way through we were issued with Sherman tanks, which we knew we were going to take with us into action.

It was a busy time but a happy one too. In the early summer of 1943, the end was in sight and we knew that our time together was drawing to a close. We would be made full cadets soon and sent to various line regiments. (In the Polish Army one was not automatically commissioned at the end of the course). Shortly after our arrival in the Middle East, both Capt. Rędziejowski and Lieut. Sypel were transferred elsewhere, and we were given new officers. This was a pity as we never again enjoyed the same level of guidance and inspiration from anyone after them. Towards the end of the course a man called Lieut. Stanislaw Masztak was in change, a good officer, but lacking Rędziejowski's charisma and finesse.

I felt comfortable in what I was doing and found my task easy. I had little difficulty in fulfilling the demands imposed on me, and throughout the course, was consistently placed among the top few in overall classification. At the end of the course I found myself in third place, beaten only by two of my colleague-instructors, Tadek Bobak who finished first, and Genek Czauderna who was second. They were both a few years older and having spent some years at university before the war, whilst technically remaining cadets like us, were given the task of instructing us, each one in his own speciality.

It so happened that the end of our course coincided with the visit to the Middle East of our Commander-in-Chief, Gen. Wladyslaw Sikorski.

I cannot remember how and when, but somebody had the idea that it would be really good if we could get the General to take the salute at our passing out parade. The idea caught on and we went with it to our C.O., who also expressed enthusiasm and promised to start the necessary enquiries.

In a few days the answer arrived. It was a categorical 'No'. Lieut. Masztak told us to forget it, the General was far too busy and could not spare the time. We were very disappointed and, judging by the expression on our C.O.'s face, so was he.

Disappointment is not a state of mind which sits well with young men, and very soon ideas were being discussed how to try to remedy the unsatisfactory state of affairs. We decided that the real reason why the General was not coming was not that he was too busy. It was simply because there was no-one bold enough to present the idea to him and to do it really well. It could only be done if we got to see him face to face. He was bound to agree.

Every commander-in-chief likes to be seen by his troops, we theorised, and young cadets, after all, were the 'future of the army'. It was a dead certainty. And besides, we were sure that in his heart of hearts, even Lieut. Masztak would be delighted if we were to make a private attempt and succeeded in getting the General to come here.

So rapidly a plan has evolved: we would mount a small 'delegation' made up of three cadets, to go and find the General and simply ask him. Our confidence was unshakeable. But there was a question first: who would have the privilege of taking on this job? The answer almost suggested itself: the top three cadets, that is Bobak, Czauderna and myself! Czauderna, could not or would not do it, so we co-opted Tadek Antosewicz, or Antos to his friends, and although not placed terribly high on our league table he was a good, smart sort, perfectly game and he had contacts among General Anders's entourage which might prove useful. The plan was that we would each ask individually for 4 days' leave, then go and find the General, and the rest was sure to be a simple matter.

The execution of the plan went without a hitch; we were granted leave and left separately, planning to meet at some convenient spot and then travel together, by thumbing a lift all the way. We still had a problem: we didn't know where the General currently was, but this was immediately resolved. Antos happened to meet a driver on General Anders's staff and we were assured that the C-in-C was in Jerusalem, which of course was a long way from Iraq. Still we decided to have a go.

We were lucky. Army traffic between Iraq and Palestine was intensive, and travelling day and night, crossing various deserts on the way, we reached our goal with a rapidity which even today seems remarkable. Rather sleepy and only a little tired we arrived in Jerusalem and went straight to the Polish H.Q., ready for immediate attack.

From now on things started to slow down. It fact we got stuck at the very first control post. The officer in charge of reception insisted that we should produce some document to convince him of the bona fides of our mission. We had none. The fact that three smart young cadets assured him that they were an official delegation, did not seem to cut any ice with him and he told us quite plainly to clear out.

Dejected and somewhat deflated we were preparing to leave, when suddenly the front door opened and a strange looking figure entered the office.

He looked distinguished, middle-aged and although wearing a khaki outfit, did not look like a military person. I noticed his face. It was vaguely familiar.

While I was straining my brain to try to remember who he could possibly be, the unhelpful officer got up rather smartly, which proved to me that the mysterious newcomer was considerably senior to him.

I decided to play my hunch. There was nothing to lose and, perhaps, something to gain. I approached the newcomer, saluted smartly and said:

"Excuse me Sir. I am cadet officer Karol Czosnowski. I believe that you will remember me." The distinguished figure looked at me closely. "Are you by any chance Klima Czosnowska's son?" he asked. "Yes Sir, I am!" I almost shouted in reply. "Oh! My dear fellow, I am so pleased to see you. Last time I saw you, you were much younger. How is your lovely mother, have you had any news from her?"

I still didn't know who he was, but at least I had found somebody important to talk to. A moment later I introduced my two colleagues and eventually a conversation developed during which the purpose of our mission could be made known to my important acquaintance.

But my would-be rescuer was still firmly in the past: he was describing at great length his recollections of a ball at the Viceroy's residence in Lwow, before the First War, when he had had the pleasure of dancing a waltz with my mother. Moving though his account was, it wasn't getting us any nearer to our main purpose and time was slipping by, so again I had to force the pace a bit.

"Sir," I said in a confidential tone, "You seem to know your way about this H.Q. Could you possibly help us to see General Sikorski? It would be a tremendous help to us." "Why don't you call me Uncle Olo, as you used to?" he asked me instead. "Yes Sir... I mean, yes Uncle, thank you I will, but please, can you help us?" I wouldn't let go.

'Uncle Olo' – who could he be? Olo in Polish is a diminutive for Alexander. I could not remember, for the life of me, any uncle of mine called Alexander who could remotely fit his description. Still having an uncle was obviously a plus, so I persisted and repeated the question, now addressing him as uncle.

"The only thing I can do for you is to take you with me to see the General's Naval ADC, on the next floor up. From then on, you will be on your own.

"Oh! Thank you Sir!" I exclaimed, correcting swiftly to "Thank you Uncle!"

Uncle Olo then asked the miserable duty officer to telephone upstairs and tell the General's ADC that he was in the waiting room. I listened keenly for possible clues as to my newly found uncle's identity. I got it! I heard the officer's voice: "Consul Alexander Zaleski, is here to see you, Sir." He then listened to the ADC's reply and announced with a smile, "Yes Sir, he will see you now."

So I knew who he was at last. I remembered. He was in fact not a true uncle at all; he was a first cousin of the husband of my mother's sister, hardly a relation, but I was not complaining, I was perfectly prepared to embrace him as a true blood relation under the circumstances.

I looked at my companions in triumph and said: "OK then chaps, let us follow Uncle Olo..."

At the top of the stairs uncle Olo was slightly out of puff, so we paused before knocking. We followed at a respectable distance and when we finally entered the office we were faced with a small desk, behind which sat a slim figure of a Naval officer, smartly dressed in a white uniform. He got up slowly and smiled at the Uncle. It was a thin, diplomatic smile. The face itself was cold and hard. A tough nut to crack, I had no doubt. The two men talked for a while about something entirely different, a diplomatic reception of some sort, and when they had finished Uncle Olo signalled to us to approach.

"And these three young men came specially to speak to you about a matter of great importance to them. I would be most grateful if you could hear them out. One of them, in fact, is my nephew," he added with a smile. On this he shook hands, first with the ADC and then with us, and still smiling benevolently left the office.

We were now alone with the hostile individual. He gave us another icy look and said unencouragingly, "Yes, what do you want?"

Bobak, who was our leader, delivered his little speech. Briefly, clearly and with dignity, quite unperturbed by the unfriendly atmosphere, he explained the reasons for our request. Half-way through, I knew what the answer was going to be. The ADC was not given to hiding his contempt for those who dared to waste his valuable time.

Before he had time to say a word, though, the door opened and the figure of a middle-aged man in uniform appeared. He held a paper in his hand and was walking slowly towards the ADC, reading as he walked.

My heart stopped dead, for quite some seconds. "Bless my soul!" I thought, "the General in person!". This was a real stroke of luck. While the ADC rose to his feet slowly behind his desk, the three of us, as if pulled by one magic string, sprang to attention with such vigour that the whole building seemed to tremble. The General looked in our direction briefly, then at the ADC and then, slowly, started to walk towards us. 'Now,' I said to myself, freezing inwardly with tension, 'this is the moment we have been praying for. Please God, don't let us lose it...'

"Hello," said the General, looking at us calmly, "and whom have we got here? Three smart cadets..."

Bobak drew himself up a further couple of inches and in his best baritone voice replied, "Sir! The delegation from the 2nd Armoured Officer Cadet School, to ask you to attend our passing-out parade". I looked at the General. He seemed smaller than I had imagined from photographs, but his face was remarkable, unforgettable, something the photographs did not convey. His eyes, in particular, were full of wisdom, profound wisdom.

"Delegation, eh?... I see. And when is your great day?" he asked.

"Next Saturday, Sir," Bobak replied.

The General turned to his ADC, who immediately started telling him of all the other engagements he had to attend that very same day. He also added that nothing, absolutely nothing had ever been mentioned to him before now, about this or any other passing-out parade.

"And what are your names?" asked the General turning back to us.

Each one of us rattled out our rank and name in the best military manner.

"Czosnowski?" the General turned to me, "would a lady called Rena Czosnowska be any relation of yours – she used to host some excellent balls at the American embassy in Warsaw before the war?"

"Yes Sir," I replied, "she is an aunt of mine, my father's second cousin."

"It's a small world," commented the General to himself and then turned to his ADC again and uttered the incredible words, "I want to attend that parade, next Saturday. Please cancel my other engagements accordingly."

The ADC cringed. "But Sir," he protested, "I have already accepted..."

The General looked at him in his inimitable way and said quietly: "Do it, just do it!" smiled briefly at us and said, "See you next Saturday, then "and disappeared behind the door.

If eyes could kill, we would have been dead there and then, the three of us. The ADC was livid. In an icy tone he demanded the briefest of details from us and then with visible disgust dismissed us from his office.

As we marched smartly through the door, I looked over my shoulder. With a deep sigh, he was reaching for the telephone to start the unenviable task of demolishing the arrangements that he had spent so much effort in preparing for this trip. I felt almost sorry for him.

When we left the building and turned a couple of corners for good measure away from the H.Q. we stopped, looked at each other and then... exploded into the wildest fit of frenzied yelling, back-slapping and similarly undignified manifestations of unbridled jubilation. We even involved some rather reluctant, large, middle-aged Jewish ladies, who happened to be passing by, by dancing with them a few rounds of a Viennese waltz, in honour of uncle Olo's memorable ball at the Viceroy's residence.

We stopped as abruptly as we had started, straightened our uniforms, adjusted our hats and boarded the first bus bound for Tel-Aviv, where we were sure of catching a long-distance lift in the direction of Baghdad.

"Mission accomplished," we repeated to ourselves with lazy satisfaction, as a rather rickety Arab bus took us South.

* * *

Our arrival to the camp was the biggest anti-climax that anyone could have possibly imagined. Instead of the wild enthusiasm which we felt we were fully justified to expect, we met with hostility. Our colleagues, even our best friends, didn't want to see us. The news that we had accomplished the miracle, the ultimate, the impossible was of no interest whatsoever to them. It was as if we were on a different planet. We just could not imagine what could have taken place.

It wasn't until we bumped into Lucek Mroz, an honest, uncomplicated, frank individual that the full horror of the situation started to become apparent to us.

It emerged that our sudden appearance at the H.Q. in Jerusalem had been immediately made known to some high official on General Anders's staff. Presumably he was the man who had issued the instructions not to involve General Sikorski in our ceremony. Brigade command was then alerted and rapidly Lieut. Masztak summoned, accused of disobeying direct orders and of failing to maintain appropriate discipline in his unit.

The results for the school were immediate and painful. The Army has its own methods of making its authority felt and impressing on the unfortunate culprits who is the real boss. The school was subjected to several days of incessant and gruelling marching, drilling and inspections, including night 'red alerts' which were sounded every hour on the hour, just to make certain that nobody could possibly get any sleep. No wonder our popularity was at rock bottom.

"What in God's name made you do it?" was the best we could ever get, even from our best friends. "Wait until Masztak is told that you are back... I don't envy you your lot..."

Lieut. Masztak was indeed in a bad mood. He was pale, drawn and signs of sleeplessness were clearly marked on his face. He gave us a real rocket.

"Men have been shot for lesser crimes... Yours is a case of blatant insubordination... You have endangered the good name of the school..." etc., etc.

I was very sad and was really sorry that that our success, our triumph, what we had intended as a real coup for the 'glory of the school', was being turned into a common crime, a 'case of insubordination'. On the other hand, in a way, I was not surprised. It had been bound to happen. I had disobeyed orders, irrespective of my motives. I had to pay the price, but I was sorry for my friends. Although I knew that, at the time of our departure, they had been fully behind us, wishing us luck, urging us on, all that was now forgotten, as if it had never existed. Such is human nature. The last few days had, from their point of view, been punishment for something they had not done, which in many ways was true.

Strangely, I cannot remember any of the physical discomfort which I must have suffered during the days following our return. I know that we had to be subjected to the harshest form of disciplinary action, short of a firing squad, which could be dished out in the remaining days preceding the parade, to expiate our sins and to level out the score with the rest of the school. Justice, even military justice, required some relation between crime and punishment.

Every army is pretty good at that. In our case it involved, no doubt, sleepless nights, standing in full gear for hours in the heat of the desert sun in the middle of the day and considerable physical effort, of the most useless, soul-destroying kind, all specially designed to demolish the last remnants of pride and joy that, only a few days before, our personal achievement might have produced.

But still, remarkably, it did not touch me at all. All this has been wiped from my recollection. What I do know is that incredibly, the sense, more, the conviction of having achieved something worthwhile was left intact in me. The certainty that my luck, my star, my destiny would still be smiling, would be with me and would supply all the help I would need if the necessity arose, remained within me unaltered.

The parade itself was a subdued affair. We went through the motions and succeeded in projecting what every commander would want to see: plenty of vigour, good turn-out and devotion to duty. I personally knew that the School's heart was not in it. The whole incident, whilst correct and impressive, was lacking in the youthful enthusiasm which was so tangibly abundant before this had happened.

Still, the photograph remains. Every day when dressing I glance at it, there on the wall, among my other pictures. And, from time to time, I take it off the wall to have a better look, to try to recapture the faces, the movements and the flavour of the occasion.

I ponder about the strange twists of fate which were to befall the figures in the photograph. The main one, General Sikorski was to die within a month. His Naval ADC would die with him. Most others are gone now too, though not in a violent way.

175

And the young man in the black beret, receiving his diploma. I know it was me. Would I do it again today, would I undertake a wild mission, as a member of an 'unofficial delegation' for the glory of my unit so as to secure the presence of some important person at a ceremony?

I think not. But then, of course, I am no longer 22.

# Chapter 14

# A SOCIAL CALL

The day after the passing out ceremony I collected my new posting. My request had been granted and I was to join a cavalry regiment. I was delighted, as the regiment in question even before the war would have been my first choice. So I was now a cavalry-man and could wear on my black beret the miniature of the amaranth and white lance-pennon of the First Krechowiecki Lancers.

Unlike British regiments, Polish military units could not claim a very long and uninterrupted regimental history. They had all been formed during, or shortly after, the First World War since prior to that, for over 100 years, Poland had been under foreign occupa-tion, partitioned between Russia, Prussia and Austria. The tradi-tion of my new Regiment therefore went back only as far as 1915. But even then, during those twenty odd years the Regiment had fought in three wars: the First World War, the Bolshevik War of 1920, and the September Campaign of 1939 and could claim credit for some gallant operations, including a number of mounted charges, rare at that time. As early as 1917 in fact, the young Regiment had scored a really major victory against con-siderable odds. While operating near the town of Stanislawow, in Southern Poland, it had first dealt with demoralised Russian bands of marauders looting the town. Later in the day, this was followed by a mounted charge led by the Colonel himself, against the combined German and Austrian forces, which had proved decisive. That was the battle of Krechowce from which the Regiment takes its name. There is a unique dimension to this action, in that, in the course of one day, a Polish cavalry unit had inflicted painful defeats to the forces of all three occupying powers.

I had another reason to feel pleased, for I had been invited to join the 3rd Squadron of the Regiment, under the command of Capt. Marian Karpinski, whom I had known before the War. He had in fact served in the unit of cavalry which had been stationed on our estate, in what used to be the old stud buildings near the town of Dederkaly, and he remembered me well from those days. It felt really like home from home. Although, Karpinski was visibly pleased to see me and had obviously used some influence to get me into his squadron he was ostensibly very strict with me, in case anyone should think that I was getting a 'special deal'.

We were now preparing for war in earnest. Intensive manoeuvres were being held in the desert of Egypt under full battle conditions. We were brushing up our skills and getting to know our crews. I was given command of one tank, a Sherman, like the ones we had been training on in the Cadet School, in a troop headed by a Senior Sergeant by the name of Franciszek Dobrowolski. Like Karpinski and myself, he too was from Volhenia, a small-holder, whose farm had been located not very far from Obory, so he had known my father by sight.

Predictably, he too, made every effort not to give me any 'fancy ideas' or any hope of an easy ride. In actual fact, at the very beginning of our association, I had one or two rather rough incidents with him. I soon realised that when he had a few drinks inside him, he could get rather aggressive. This taught me to stay clear of him at such times. Fortunately, this policy worked and I had little trouble from him from then on. For those who are not familiar with the procedure in the Polish Army it may be helpful to explain that upon graduating from the Cadet School one was not commissioned automatically. This usually came later, after the candidate had proved himself in his unit. Senior Sergeants, meanwhile, would outrank a qualified cadet in every way.

In the early Spring of 1944 we were stationed in Gaza, in Palestine, on what was later to be called the Gaza Strip. Our tents were right on the beach so we could have a most refreshing early dip in the sea before breakfast. I decided that as I had not been to Jerusalem, not properly, (other than that rather lightning visit to the Polish H.Q, to try to induce General Sikorski to come to our passing out parade), this was the last moment to do it, otherwise it might be too late. I so wanted to see the holy places. I applied for the remainder of what was still due to me by way of leave, which in fact was just a couple of days, and set off as soon as I could.

The only person I knew in Jerusalem was my cousin George Baworowski, who held the job of either consul or vice-consul at that time. Uncle Olo Zaleski had told me about him during my previous lightning visit to the City. Israel or Palestine, as it then was, is not a big country so it did not take me long to get from one end of it to the other and I arrived in the City without difficulty. I went straight to the consulate.

George, or Izio, received me at once, and appeared to be genuinely pleased to see me, which was kind of him. He was ten years my senior and had, before the war, been in the diplomatic service, so although we knew of each other's existence that was about all. The first thing which he suggested was that I should go and see the Heydels, old friends of the family, who, he told me, were also living in Jerusalem. The Middle East, in those days was full of Polish refugees, so although I was pleased to hear that they had made it to safety, I was not surprised. "They will be so happy to see you," he said, "I know this may seem a bit boring for you, making social calls on some old acquaintances from Lwow, but it is only a small effort and it will be really appreciated. They do not see many people here nowadays." With some additional prompting, I promised to go. In fact, I went there at once, to get it out of the way so to speak.

The Heydels lived in the Arab part of the city, at an address which sounded grand: Abushakra House, Katamon. It was not grand at all. In fact it was small and considerably run down. I rang a bell and the door was answered by a fairly scruffy, big Arab woman, who looked at me with the utmost suspicion. When I enquired if the Heydels were home, she shouted at the top of her voice, in very odd sounding French, "Un soldat pour vous voir, Madame la Baronne."

The words in themselves may have been correct, but the manner in which they had been delivered sounded funny. So, trying to keep a straight face, I told this would-be parlour maid that the Baroness knew me well and that there was no real need to make any fuss. Reluctantly, she let me pass.

My hostess was sitting on a small terrace overlooking a tiny garden. She had the radio on, listening to music and, apparently, had not heard the maid's warning yells. My sudden appearance surprised her. Still, Izio had been right, she was absolutely delighted. I remembered her from Lwow. She hadn't changed much, still looking very beautiful. My sister Krystyna and I used to call her Aunt Musia. Her younger daughter Teresa sat beside her. They had not been well, either of them, the older lady showing the first signs of paralysis, while Teresa had been ill for as long as I could remember. Since very early childhood she had been suffering from a terrible disease, TB of the bones, incurable in those days and, when not bedridden, could only walk with the aid of an iron brace over one of her legs. Remarkably, they both remained vivacious, active, and full of optimism and fun.

"Teresa," said her mother, "go upstairs and tell Marysia that Karol is here."

While Teresa went in search of her older sister, my hostess gave me a brief account of the last few years. She did it well and with humour, skipping lightly over the difficult bits and highlighting the amusing ones. I listened smiling, being at first more conscious of the manner in which it was delivered than of the actual contents of the account, until I realised what an epic story I was being told. I had been expecting a tale, which I had imagined would be typical of those who had had the good luck to have escaped, in contrast with the unlucky ones, like myself, who had failed. What I heard instead, adroitly disguised as a drawing room story, was an account of considerable adversity.

The Heydels had escaped into Romania in the first days after the Soviets entered Poland. It was a snap decision and they went more or less as they stood, taking practically nothing with them. There was no time to lose, as news had reached them that Romania was about to close her border, due to the colossal influx of refugees trying to leave Poland.

The crossing itself went uneventfully, apart from the terrible congestion before the border. It was in Roumania, during the journey, that Teresa had started to run a temperature. It was her leg: the TB bacillus was active again. There were no hospital facilities en route so despite the congestion they pressed on and managed to get to Bucharest. On arrival there, without any money to speak of and knowing no-one personally in Roumania, Aunt Musia nevertheless somehow succeeded in making contact with a Romanian lady, a Princess Bibesco, a relation of an acquaintance of hers from Lwow, who in turn recommended her to another lady, Princess Elisabeth Ghika.

It was Princess Ghika who took the whole matter into her hands immediately, found a good surgeon who operated on Teresa at once in a hospital in Bucharest, and then sent her to a convalescent home on the Black Sea coast, in Carmen Silva, where, incidentally, she had to have several more operations. All this was paid for by the generous Romanian ladies. Under the patronage and protection of the Ghikas, the Heydels received support from other well-connected families in Roumania, and it was only when the Germans decided to occupy the country that they were forced to leave again, in the middle of the night, having literally five minutes to pack, this time to Turkey and from there eventually to Palestine.

What an extraordinary, brave and resourceful person, I thought. A penniless refugee, not in the best of health herself, her younger daughter critically ill; in a totally unknown country and under conditions of peak overcrowding and yet through her charm, her resourcefulness, her diplomacy and a remarkable talent for making and keeping friends, she had succeeded in winning the support and genuine affection of her benefactors, which without doubt had saved her daughter's life. She remained in touch with her Romanian friends and corresponded with them for the rest of her life, even when later all the Romanian aristocracy had themselves to flee the country before the communists took control. Remarkable.

Now they were very lucky, she continued, they had this nice little house, the International Committee for Refugees were paying the wages of Matilda the maid, and Marysia had found a job as a secretary in the RAF headquarters in Jerusalem. Her wages, plus a very small allowance from the Red Cross were, I gathered, the only income at their disposal.

In the fullness of time Marysia came in.

Her entrance, this simple act, produced in me a very strange sensation, a feeling of light. It was remarkable. So much so, that I felt a subconscious urge to look round to see what had changed. Nothing had. The sun was shining, as before, the sky was pale blue, there were no clouds to be seen anywhere, there were no other lights about either. Where could this extra light be coming from? I was astonished. I got up to greet her.

Marysia had changed quite a lot since I had last seen her, back in 1938. A girl, something of a tomboy perhaps, had turned into a strikingly good-looking young woman. She was standing in the doorway gazing at me with a steady, mildly curious blue-green look in her eyes, half friendly, half shy. She smiled very slightly, a slow, almost lazy smile, but full of warmth, like a child's. The eyes held me, unblinkingly, again like a child's.

I said the usual things. I asked her if she had remembered that we had danced together at teen-age tea dances, if she recalled the skiing excursion we had made together with her brother and other friends.

She was slow to reply. This did not make me feel uncomfortable, not in the slightest, quite the reverse, I felt in excellent form. I even pulled her leg gently – observing that it had taken her so long to come down to greet an old friend and dancing partner. To which she said simply that she had a good book, and that besides, she remembered me quite differently, 'a good little boy' she said, from which I understood that she no longer thought of me in those derogatory terms.

Under their mother's prompting Marysia and Teresa went to help the clumsy Matilda to make tea, after which Aunt Musia suggested that the girls should show me some of the city sights.

We walked down the hill very slowly to enable Teresa to keep up with us.

As in many similar cases, I noticed, her sister's handicap did not seem to impede Marysia's urge to walk normally. She was so used to Teresa's disability that she took it for granted. It was I who felt awkward, and purposely slowed the pace down. Marysia was now visibly relaxed. Her mother's presence had obviously had an influence on her behaviour. I looked for the light. It had nearly gone, but a little glow still remained.

We finally reached a vantage point, from which the panorama of the whole city could be seen. The girls pointed out to me the principal buildings and other main sights. Marysia then turned to me and said, "Now that you have seen all this, could you please give me a cigarette?"

I was surprised, shocked one might say. I asked innocently, "Does your mother know that you smoke?" "Don't be so silly," she giggled mischievously, "of course not. I smoke only in the office, where the RAF boys keep me supplied – never at home... What a thought..."

She was a good sort. Now that she was more herself I had a good look at her. It was her complexion which most likely emitted this extra-terrestrial glow, that had struck me so strongly at first sight. That and the expression in her eyes. I had never seen anything like it. It seemed as if they radiated this light from behind their surface, which illuminated her face and the rest of her in this extraordinary way. The impression was further increased by the fact that she didn't blink when looking at me. She just held me in a steady, warm, confident gaze, which seemed to soothe and attract me at the same time.

I did not get to see any of the sights of Jerusalem, after all. I thought it would tire Teresa too much. So I took them to the cinema instead, a rare treat for them. We saw a film with Alan Ladd; a cops-and-robbers story.

When we got back it was nearly eight o'clock. I said that I had to go at once otherwise I would never make it. I had to report back at Gaza by 8 o'clock the following morning.

Much against my better judgement I was persuaded to stay to dinner and worse still, to stay the night. I slept on a very small couch in the sitting room.

Marysia walked with me to the bus stop the following morning. I knew I was late, but she insisted that there was plenty of time. Arab buses were invariable unpunctual, she assured me. She looked fresh and beautiful. I felt proud to walk next to her. A young woman looks so much better in a coloured summer frock than in khaki, like most of the girls I was used to seeing in the forces.

As we were rounding the street corner I saw, to my horror, that the bus I was supposed to catch was just pulling away. The next one would be a full hour later. "Goodbye... thank you... must run..." was all I was able to yell, as I accelerated towards my receding target. "You will never make it," called Marysia calmly, as I was vanishing into the dust, fully committed to beating the world speed record for the 60-metre dash.

I made it, but only just. With one foot on the bottom step of the bus and one hand firmly gripping its door handle, I risked a final look back. She was standing in the distance, waving, gently glowing her radiant aura...

I managed to get back to my squadron in record time. I was just one hour late. No-one would notice such a small delay, I was sure. How wrong I was! "Where the hell have you been?" Capt. Karpinski demanded with a most ferocious glow in his eyes, "don't you know we have a war to fight?..." Oh, yes, the War indeed. I had almost forgotten about that, for the last day and half at least.

Yes, I had allowed myself to lower my guard, to think forbidden thoughts, to plan perhaps, to dream... All that was out of place, of course, now I remembered.

In fact the War took over my life again with the utmost intensity. The order to embark was received in the course of the same day and we were instructed to pack up and proceed to Port Said. We were leaving the Middle East for good.

Next stop was Italy and the War.

The iron grip of destiny was on me again. I felt it holding me hard.

"What will be will be," I repeated to myself, as I boarded the ship for what was likely to be the greatest test of my life.

Half-way between Port Said and Taranto I received my commission.

I was a Second Lieutenant now, a real cavalry officer.

# Chapter 15

# FLAVOURS OF WAR

We landed in Taranto, in Southern Italy, around the middle of April 1944.

The brand new 'pips' on my epaulettes were causing me to feel a little self-conscious. I still tended to look over my shoulder when soldiers referred to me as 'Sir', in case there was a 'real Sir' standing behind me. Almost immediately, I was put in charge of my troop, with three Shermans under my command, and with Sgt. Dobrowolski, who hitherto had been my boss, as my deputy. I was, of course, very careful with him remembering his fiery temper and the hard time he used to give me when I had been under his command. But I need not have worried. For the rest of the war I had nothing but support and loyalty from this mature and brave man. I remember him with affection.

In various stages, we were shifted about the Southern part of the Italian peninsula, until one day in May we found ourselves just South of Monte Cassino. No-one at that stage of the war could possibly have remained unaware of the significance of this fortress. For some six months prior to our arrival the now superior Allied war machine had been stuck, trying to subdue this last obstacle on its way to Rome. Everybody had had a go and had failed. The best units from the still mighty British Empire had been used, to no avail. Even the fabulous Ghurkas had been sent in and had had to retire empty-handed.

When we arrived in the area the magnitude of the problem became immediately apparent to me. An enormous mountain overlooked a perfectly flat plain. The size of this pile of rock and the steepness of the approaches to the summit made my head swim. On the very top of it, somewhere in the clouds, loomed the walls of the monastery, which the Germans were determined to hold and the Allies determined to conquer. At the foot of the mountain ran a principal road, linking Naples with Rome, one of the old Roman roads, Via Appia if I am not mistaken. It was this road that all the fuss was about and this, we were told, was the reason for having to take the monastery.

I never understood then, and still don't understand now, why the generals seemed to insist on conquering the unconquerable, instead of just pressing ahead and leaving the encircled enemy behind. It seemed to me then, and still seems to me now, that much smaller forces would have been needed to 'isolate' the spot than to have to storm it. But, as the poet said: "Ours not to reason why..."

By the way our forces were grouped, one could immediately tell that the Poles were to be the next ones in line to have a crack at Monte Cassino. I had always had a bad head for heights and I must confess that I was dreading the thought of having to climb those precipitous slopes in a tank, particularly as I knew that the Third Reich was determined to use all its available fire power to make it as unpleasant for me as was humanly possible. It would have been far better, it seemed to me, to die on the flat expanses of the lovely vineyards that stretched away from the mountain. They looked much more like my type of country.

In the event, however, we did not take part. We remained in reserve. While my Regiment watched from a safe distance, the drama unfolded as if it were on a stage, right in front of our eyes. It was an awesome sight. The attack was preceded by a tremendous artillery bombardment, reinforced by the combined air forces which were brought over in waves. It seemed that after that kind of pounding every insect, every living cell was certain to have died, and yet... as soon as the bombardment eased and the actual attack began, the still visible ruins of the monastery came to life and fire, deadly accurate fire, was laid on the little spots of men and tanks, crawling up the impossible slopes. The mountain itself, which had presumably been covered with trees before the war was now almost bare, just a few mutilated trunks, like distorted limbs, sticking out in agony from the mass of exposed stone. Because of the bareness of the terrain we could, from our vantage point, see quite a lot of the action. I was glued to my field glasses, suffering the torments of a passive observer.

At one stage I was sent to the foot of the mountain with some message or errand. The harvest of this macabre game could be seen quite clearly from there. Men with Red Cross bands on their sleeves were carrying stretchers with bodies, some dead, others dying. I watched for a while and then decided that watching could not do me any good. It was probably worse than doing it myself. At least one had other things to think about.

The action on Monte Cassino was, by the very nature of the terrain a mainly infantry operation with the Sappers, as usual, in the very forefront having to clear the masses of mines which the Germans had planted on the main approaches. The defenders had been there for a long time, so they had every inch of the slope covered by the most accurate fire including, of course, all the mined areas. The carnage was immense.

In support of the infantry, tanks were being used. We could see some of them which had toppled over and rolled down the precipitous slopes and remained upside down at most nauseating angles. Several of my school chums were in the 4th Armoured Regiment which was given this uninviting task. I was worried about them. I did not like to look at the faces in the stretchers in case I should recognise one of my old friends.

The battle raged for days. Then news came, triumphant news: Monte Cassino was ours! If we polished our field glasses and strained our eyes, we could just make out the white and red colours of the Polish Flag flying over the monastery walls. The Poles had done what everyone before them had failed to do: they had conquered the unconquerable and proved to the world that Poland was alive, very much alive!

When we were ordered to leave our positions, and passed right under the awesome mountain, it was still smoking. The degree of devastation was phenomenal.

And yet, despite it all, the devastated, precipitous slopes were covered with blood-red wild poppies. It was uncanny.

It wasn't long afterwards that somebody composed a very moving song about the poppies on Monte Cassino. Each chorus of it ended with the words that, in years to come, the flowers will get redder since they had grown out of Polish blood.

The action that followed the fall of Cassino was mainly a tank operation. It took place on the plain at the foot of the mountain and was, appropriately, named Piedimonte. The 6th Armoured Regiment was to take the lead there. We were placed on red alert, in the knowledge that should the going get difficult our Regiment was to be used for the decisive push. But, here again, we were not needed. Fierce and bloody though this battle was, it was over before our presence was required.

After that the German resistance collapsed. The enemy retreated at great speed. Soon, the Americans entered Rome and I started wondering if perhaps the war would be over without my having fired a single shot, which would have been a pity.

While we were pursuing the, as yet, invisible enemy, I had the opportunity of catching up with some of my old chums who were serving in the other regiments, and who had taken part in the fighting. I wanted to find out if they were all right. Remarkably, the ones I was most anxious about had survived unharmed. When I finally saw Tadek Bobak and Fred Virski, with whom I had shared a tent at the cadet school, and who were both in the thick of it at Monte Cassino, I asked them to tell me what had it been like on that mountain, in a real tank action? The reply they gave me was not what I had expected: "Mad chaos, infernal noise and a sharp smell of cordite..." was all they said.

*  *  *

My Regiment's turn came in the battle for Ancona. Ancona is a port town on the Adriatic coast, on the point of the 'calf of the leg' of the Italian peninsula.

It was apparent that the Germans had decided to make a stand there. The country of the province of Marche, of which Ancona is the capital, is fertile, undulating and thickly covered with vine-yards and olive groves. It was also intersected by several small rivers and many canals and did not offer ideal conditions for tank warfare, as both visibility and manoeuvre were severely impeded.

The first obstacle which we had to tackle was a small river called the Chienti. This job was given to the 2nd Squadron. My squadron took positions immediately behind them, waiting for further orders.

I had one particular friend who was to take part in this action . He had been an officer attached to our cadet school in Iraq where he had had a minor job as an instructor, but had never been exceptionally effective or successful at it. Still I liked him a lot. He was a gentle, charming man, the type who wouldn't hurt a fly. He was really totally unsuited for the army, and possessed of a sensi-tive, even artistic temperament. He took a great liking to me and despite being an officer while I was just an apprentice cadet he

188

treated me as an equal, or even perhaps looked up to me. This flattered me immensely. His name was Bronek Rogalski. Bronek was inclined to be rather pedantic and fussy, particularly as regarded his possessions, and his little tent (being an officer, he had a tent to himself) was a model of orderly perfection. His dress reflected his personality and even during the most severe sandstorms he never seemed to have a hair out of place. Unlike other Polish officers, he always carried a swagger-stick with him. It gave him, he believed, a distinguished 'English' look. It was so much part of him that he carried it everywhere, even when going to the shower.

Bronek was serving in the reconnaissance squadron and, for the purpose of this operation, was attached to the 2nd Squadron. He was getting ready for battle and his armoured cars were a short distance ahead of my troop, just over the hill. I was standing next to a scout car, waiting for possible orders, when suddenly I recognised the familiar figure of Bronek running in my direction, in a very agitated state. He really looked quite upset.

"Karol," he cried, when he saw me, "Karol... I seem to have lost my stick... Can't find it anywhere... You haven't seen it by any chance?" I assured him I had not.

"Well then," he said calmly, "this is it. I now know that I shall not survive this battle. My time has come. Goodbye, dear boy. Everyone has to go sooner or later..." and perfectly composed now, he went back to his tank, leaving me completely speechless.

Well before dark, before the day was out, we heard that Lieut. Rogalski had been killed while looking for a suitable ford across the Chienti river.

* * *

My own initiation as a warrior came during the battle of Osimo-Castelfidardo, which followed shortly after the crossing of the River Chienti.

What was it like? Was I nervous, afraid? Yes, of course I was, but not entirely in the way one would expect. I was afraid of being afraid; of not being able to control my fear and of disgracing myself in the process. It wasn't so much the fear for my life, but the fear of my own nerves, my reflexes, all the subconscious systems that each of us possesses, for a very good reason no doubt, but which, during the war, one has to learn to 'switch off',

189

or override, if one is to be of any use. Once this 'override' was in place, and I felt I knew what I was doing, I was all right.

Having acclimatised my nerves, the next problem was confusion. Tank warfare, the real thing is, at first, very confusing. There is so much to do and so much to think about all at the same time. Training and manoeuvres are a help, of course. Without them one could not cope at all. But there is so much more that one has to learn in battle. It takes some experience to be able to tell who is shooting at whom and, even more specifically, who is shooting at you and from where. You must be able to tell where the other friendly tanks are and how they are moving. You must meanwhile listen to the radio messages from your superiors and from the tanks under your command, and tell your own tanks where to go and what to do. And, of course, you must give your own crew concrete orders where to go and what to fire at. This is just basic, of course, but to be able to evaluate all the elements correctly in battle does take some experience. Many do not reach that stage, like poor Bronek Rogalski, and fall at the first encounter.

Eventually everyone develops his own system. I found it, for instance, much less uncomfortable if I had my headphones resting loosely on my neck, instead having them over my head. I was able to evaluate the noises around me, while still following the cacophony of voices coming out through the radio. I found that listening to the battle noises around me was just as important as seeing what was happening.

Capt. Karpinski led our squadron in his own inimitable way. He was an instinctive commander, the type who 'feels' the situation, rather than working it out on the map. He did it with flair and considerable panache, but not in the most orthodox manner. Instead of directing the 16 tanks under his command by radio, as the book prescribes, he preferred to do it on foot, trotting in leisurely manner from tank to tank and either signalling or simply telling us what he wanted us to do. If the pace increased or the enemy fire grew too intense, he would hop back onto his tank and we would hear again his familiar voice on our earphones. This style involved a lot of risk and I often saw him under intense fire. At times we felt sure that he was dead or at least seriously wounded but in the end, apart from one or two minor injuries, he got away with his unusual technique. He was amazing.

\* \* \*

It may sound terrible today but, reduced to its very essence, war is about killing: killing one's enemy in the greatest possible numbers, without getting killed oneself. One had to do it according to established rules, of course, most of which were set out by the Geneva Convention, but just the same, he who kills the most of the enemy is, by definition, the better soldier. It doesn't sound very nice, put that way, but there is no doubt that, in honest truth, this is what war is all about.

I do not know how many men I have killed but I have no doubt it was quite a few. To me at first, though, this did not feel like killing. All I was doing was using my formidable guns on some distant target and either nothing happened or, if I was lucky, I could just discern in the distance, that my efforts had been rewarded and bits of enemy equipment would be flying in the air and presumably, somebody would have been either killed or maimed. Fair enough, one would say. They were trying to do the same to me, I got there first, so they died and I lived. In due course one would go to the spot to see the result. There would frequently be a few bodies lying about. This would prove that I had done my job and that they had failed to do theirs. Obviously, the fact that they were dead had been the result of my shooting, but still I did not feel that I had killed them.

Until one day, I killed a man 'properly'. By properly I mean that we were at point-blank range. Only then did I realise what it feels like to kill. It was not an experience that I could shake off easily, irrespective of the obvious logic that justified it. The fact that my victim would have killed me, if he could, did not make it any easier to bear.

It was in the later stages of the battle for Ancona. The terrain there, as I have already mentioned, was undulating, with many streams and canals which made our progress at times painfully slow. My troop of three tanks was, in theory, supporting a company of infantry, but as often happened, the infantry were nowhere to be seen. There was not much shooting going on so we were advancing slowly, hoping that the foot soldiers would catch up with us sooner or later. At one stage we arrived at another of the now familiar streams. It fact it was not a proper stream, this one was dry, but the banks were steep and the crossing looked rather treacherous.

If there was no-one on the ground to help us find a suitable passage, one of us would normally jump out of the tank and under cover from the others would look for the best way to get across. A risky operation, but less so than getting stuck at the bottom of a steep bank at the mercy of the dreaded Panzerfaust snipers (hand-operated anti-tank weapons). So I grabbed a Thompson gun, hopped out of the tank and crept quietly from behind my vehicle, while my crew kept a sharp look out. Very cautiously, I advanced to the edge of the dry stream bed. I saw that a little way to the right there was in fact a likely passage, where the banks offered a better grip for the tracks. I signalled to my sergeant indicating my intentions and carefully advanced near the promising spot. No-one was actually shooting at us and our guns were silent too, so I decided to have a better look.

Using the bank as protection and keeping as low as I possibly could in case I was being watched, I reached the actual spot. It looked all right. I was about to signal to the Sergeant the direction for the crossing, when suddenly something caught my eye, something which I felt sure I had not seen before: a little log cabin neatly hidden in the bushes. It looked perfectly innocent, a shepherd's refuge, or a tool shed. There would be thousands like this anywhere. What I did not like about it was that it was located so near to the spot which was so obviously suitable for the passage of heavy armour.

It had to be either investigated or destroyed, it could not be ignored. One option was to return to my tank and train my gun on it and blow it out of the ground, the other to go and have a look. I chose the latter, as I did not know where our infantry was, nor did I have any idea what was happening elsewhere along that line.

I signally to my Sergeant what I was about to do and still using the high bank as a screen I crept towards the back of the cabin. When I was only a few feet from where it stood I could see that it had a wooden door and that it was slightly ajar. I listened. No sound came from that direction. In fact, apart from the occasional bird, all was remarkably still.

I decided to play it by the book. I found a good solid step from which to spring over the bank. I planned to make one stride on the level ground, kick the door open, and shoot at anything that moved inside the cabin.

I took a deep breath, held my Tommy gun in the correct position, 'at the ready' and like a bat out of hell... I went. The jumping movement was good, I remained in balance while kicking in the door. The hearty kick that I delivered proved much too hard, however, and the thick door instead of remaining open bounced back on me and hit me hard on the right elbow, smack on my funny bone, sending a mighty current straight up my arm and making the whole limb feel numb.

It was at this moment, probably because of the cramp which I felt in my right hand that I squeezed the trigger. A long burst of automatic fire echoed around me. The next thing I heard was a heavy thump of something falling. I blinked. The inside of the cabin was dark, compared with the bright sunlight outside. I could only make out silhouettes. Meanwhile the door swung open again aided by the wind. The shaft of light revealed a human body hanging over the logs, its arms outstretched before it, lying face down, with the posterior sticking up in a most indecorous way. The arms were still moving pendulum fashion. The rest was ominously still.

I could not regain the feeling in my right arm, which was still completely numb. Obstinately, it kept refusing to obey my orders, so I transferred the gun to my left hand just in case, and tried to think. I remained like this for a good few seconds, when I heard steps on the outside and the voice of Sergeant Dobrowolski, calling softy from behind the river bank: "Sir, are you all right?" When I called back that I was, he and another man came in with their guns at the ready.

Dobrowolski inspected the scene with professional indifference. He couldn't have done better himself, he declared. A very professional job. One shot got him at the base of his throat and went straight through the back of the brain and the rest 'nicely located in the heart area'. He pulled the body up and sat it upright. He took out the man's identity card and gave it to me to read. Still half dazed I read: "Otto Eisenschimmel, born Essen 1918". It gave his rank as Sergeant and the name of the SS unit to which he belonged. "I suppose you will want to keep this as a trophy, a souvenir of your first successful hand-to-hand encounter," Dobrowolski said smiling. Otto Eisenschimmel's dead blue eyes were now looking straight at me with a mild expression of surprise.

"Put it back where you found it," I said rather harshly, "and let us get out of here." Dobrowolski gave me a knowing look and reluctantly obeyed. Before leaving, though, he pointed to the anti-tank Panzerfaust which Otto Eisenschimmel had had waiting for us, and to the excellent view he would have had of the very point over which we were proposing to cross.

"You may well feel very proud of yourself, Sir, to have spotted this trap. We would all be burning nicely if this bastard had been allowed to have his way," he concluded.

I never told him how it had really happened. I never told him how I felt. This memory, though, will remain with me for the rest of my life. That July afternoon in 1944, I understood what it felt like to have killed someone at point-blank range. And it is not a good feeling. It is really awful.

*   *   *

Like all human activity, the deadly business of war has its lighter moments. Danger, the proximity of death, fear itself perhaps, make incidents which in themselves may not be all that funny, absolutely hilarious. The ability to laugh is, perhaps, one way of retaining some sanity in the otherwise crazy world of slaughter and devastation.

Let me recall just one such incident which provided us, at the time, with 'comic relief' and in which, involuntarily, I was the chief comedian. It took place one morning just before a battle, when all officers were in the process of rejoining their units, having finished the daily briefing session given by the Colonel. As I was emerging from the improvised briefing room, I saw in the distance that my squadron was beginning to move off. Capt. Karpinski and the more senior officers jumped into a jeep and drove off. There was no room for me, so I had to run.

I was fairly loaded with papers, maps and even a small box of ammunition which I had just collected for our hand guns, plus my field glasses, dangling from my neck and my Smith & Wesson revolver hanging from my belt, so running was not easy. As I trotted awkwardly down the hill, not gaining much ground on my receding chariots, I suddenly felt the elastic which supported the trunks I wore under my overalls break, and I experienced the embarrassing sensation of my under-clothing slipping lower and lower down my legs with each and every stride. My efforts to limit its rate of descent proved useless. I had my hands full and could not risk losing any of the things I was carrying so I could do nothing to counter the forces of gravity which were bent on embarrassing me. My steps, as a result, became shorter and shorter and my progress slower.

Fortunately, after a while the tank column stopped and by using some intricate footwork, mercifully, I reached my tank. What now remained was to hop on top of the vehicle. A simple task, it would appear, for an athletic young subaltern in a hurry. Not any more, as I found. The first attempt failed. I found that I could only lift my leg a few inches off the ground. Useless. I tried again. Also no good. Just as I was preparing to deposit the things I was carrying on top of the tank and lift myself onto it using only my arms the front tanks started to move again. Everybody was looking at me wondering what was the matter. Obviously no-one had guessed, as yet, what my problem was. Desperate situations require desperate measures, I decided. There was nothing for it, I had to resort to a policy of reckless destruction.

In full view of everybody, I unbuttoned the front of my overalls and while clumsily holding under my left arm the objects I was carrying, I pulled desperately hard with my right one at my blue boxer trunks underneath. To my considerable relief they were not top quality Sea Island Cotton, they were an inferior wartime product of Italian manufacture and obligingly split as I intended. I then threw them boldly into a ditch. Freed at last of my shackles, I was able to hop effortlessly onto my tank and dive into the turret.

There were several versions of this story which circulated for a while, to the great amusement my colleagues. Most of them maliciously attributed the necessity for the sudden removal of my underwear, to digestive disorders, caused by my excessive nervousness in anticipation of the battle. Barrack-room humour delights in such simplistic entertainment.

* * *

It seems strange to me that war, a process which is meant to destroy and is fundamentally evil, is also capable of creating incredibly good and noble things. While predominantly bent on destroying life and matter, it can give birth to spiritual phenomena which peace can seldom, if ever, equal. It has been known to inspire the human spirit to soar to heights which are altogether unattainable under more normal 'pedestrian' circumstances. Love is the first thing that comes to mind. Paradoxically, it seems to thrive in the face of death and can sometimes explode like Spring in the Arctic North, eager, thirsty, unquenchable. Self-sacrifice is another. It is widespread under wartime conditions, almost an everyday routine occurrence which one tends to take for granted in respect of oneself and of others.

Friendship, too, flourishes to a degree which, in comparison, renders its peacetime equivalent feeble and half-hearted. The true unquestioning dedication between men in war can sometimes reach heights which are not only unreachable in peacetime but which cannot survive peace itself. Such feelings are born of danger and can only live as long as danger lives.

I had two friends in my squadron with whom I was linked by such ties. They are both dead. One was killed in action, the other died after the war at an early age. I think of them often.

When I first joined my regiment in August 1943, as a qualified cadet officer, Stach Maksymiszyn and Kazik Irzykowski were also cadet officers but of considerably greater seniority, both having qualified before the war. They treated me with friendly indifference.

It may seem strange, but I know very little of Stach's background. Judging by his surname and his looks, he must have had some Hungarian blood in him. He was handsome, of the dark lean variety, rather taciturn, with a sharp, cutting sense of humour. He was the archetype of a romantic war hero, dashing, fearless, dedicated, dependable and at his best under pressure . I knew that he originated from Stanislawow, a most unromantic provincial town in Southern Poland but I am sure I didn't know it from him. He spoke rarely about his past and for that matter about himself. He was a joy to work with in the field. I always knew what to expect of him. He was at once bold and shrewd. He always knew exactly what to do. When we fought side by side, his troop and mine, we would seldom talk on the radio, one little gesture would suffice. If he went forward I would support him with my fire and vice versa. It worked beautifully.

I knew a little more about Kazik. He was more conventional and easier to read. He came from Zakopane, the well known ski resort. His good looks, light brown hair, blue eyes, lean aquiline features and engaging smile gave his face an open, intelligent look. So much so that the wartime propagandists chose him as a model and his portrait appeared on army posters. His looks must have possessed the characteristics which in the eyes of the hard-nosed professionals were symbolic of the virtues which they were trying to promote. I co-operated with Kazik even more than with Stach, particularly in the later stages of the war, by which time Stach had already fallen. He was less instinctive than Stach, more reasoned and liked to consult with me a great deal more than his friend. Stach just knew what was right. But I felt very comfortable with Kazik, too, and trusted his leadership completely. He was very professional in everything he did and never allowed himself the slightest opportunity for exuberance or bravado, which one couldn't always say of Stach.

Tanks in Italy operated principally in the daytime. At night we normally withdrew some two or three miles to the rear where we refuelled, re-stocked our ammunition, repaired any damage to our equipment and got fed and watered. Such operations lasted well into the night. We would sleep three or four hours at best. Sometimes, when our infantry was unable to reach us and we had to remain in the front line for the night, all these activities had to be carried out right there, often under fire. Our command, of course, tried to keep such incidents to a minimum, as they exposed us to the danger of sudden attack. I can remember at least half a dozen occasions when we had to hold the line through the night. In such cases we adopted a 'hedgehog' formation, in a circle, or semi-circle, with guns pointing to the outside. I remember one night in particular, when we had to remain on a road, in line, as we could not spread into the surrounding fields. Had the Germans attacked us there we would have found it pretty uncomfortable. Fortunately they didn't.

It was during these long nights when we were resting and re-fuelling that we could sit down and talk, the three of us. Our crews would be doing the physical work and we would review the day's activities, have a cigarette and even a glass of wine. I remember those long nights with pleasure. The immediate danger was temporarily gone and although we could not sleep, we could relax a little. The nights were warm and the world seemed at peace for a change. Surprisingly, we relaxed by talking shop. We were passionately interested in improving and refining the use of armour in battle. For us the greatest problem was our speed of reaction, which was never fast enough. A tank, and even more so, three tanks acting together could not react instantaneously to any given situation. If only we could succeed in reducing this delay, this slack so to speak, by a few seconds our problems would lessen in proportion. So during these long nights we would analyse the day's experiences and try to adjust our technique.

Every few weeks we would be allowed a longer break. Our squadron would be taken right back some ten miles behind the front lines. The first 24 hours we would spend sleeping and eating and sleeping again. And when we could sleep and eat no more we would get back to talking. The subject again would be 'shop' but this time it would be much more 'futuristic' almost bordering on science fiction. We would allow our imaginations run free and amused ourselves by re-thinking the very concept of the tank. It seemed to us that if we could devise a one-man tank, a terrestrial equivalent of a fighter aircraft, then most of the slack which we were so concerned about would be gone. Our 'design' of the perfect tank combined the best features of the German Panther, which we admired very much, and some of the characteristics of the Russian T34, but all this with one important difference: that ours would be a solo vehicle. We knew that the technology for this existed, so all this was perfectly viable but nobody had, as yet, started making it.

We found these sessions extraordinarily stimulating. It seems to me strange today, but such was our dedication to the 'cause' that three perfectly normal, healthy young men spent most of their free time in this otherwise futile, theoretical, pipe-dreaming.

This happened most of the time, but not all the time. Sometimes we would go out 'spaghetti hunting'. This involved a meal at a local trattoria, a simple sort of restaurant which served delicious local food and afterwards, if it happened to be a Sunday, we would go to a village hall where there would be dancing. These Sunday village dances could be very amusing. Invariably they involved the election of a beauty queen, which the Italians called Reginetta. When the result of the selection was announced and the local beauty had been duly crowned with her paper crown, the custom was that whoever wanted to dance with her would line up in front of her, so that she could select her dancing partner for a dance of honour.

The stage was thus set for Stach to demonstrate his incredible magnetic power over women. He would stroll nonchalantly and join the line. When the 'queen' reviewed her guard of honour Stach would smile at her, his inimitable charismatic smile, and the result was immediate. She would not even finish the inspection and just fall into his arms with total disregard for protocol.

Kazik and I didn't even try to compete and contented ourselves with less pretty partners and although we pretended that Stach's successes bored us to tears we were really green with envy. How did he do it? we asked ourselves in a mixture of annoyance and admiration. We never asked him, for fear of giving the game away. And how was it that he remained so cool and emotionally uninvolved, even with the prettiest girl? It seemed that he was a superman, made to some higher specification, and that we ordinary mortals could never compete with him.

Until one day he came back from a three-day leave, which he had spent alone in Southern Italy and he declared that he was in love, yes, truly in love. Her name was Veronica, a music teacher from Naples and she was sheer perfection. Unusually for him, he was very talkative and told us all about her, how they had met, how they danced, how he met her family and how much they loved each other. Kazik and I could not believe our ears. This cool Casanova who had, hitherto, treated women as toys, playthings, had suddenly turned all sloppy and sentimental... It had to happen sooner or later, it was inevitable. Even a cool customer like Stach, we decided with some satisfaction, had eventually to meet his match.

The squadron was now preparing to get back into action which was centred in the general area of the port town of Fano, some 50 kilometres North of Ancona. We knew it was going to be an important operation and that our squadron was to take the lead.

During the next couple of days Stach grew progressively more silent and withdrawn. His euphoria had vanished completely. He sat for hours studying a map, a most unusual thing for him to do. When we asked him what was bothering him, he said that he wanted to prepare himself for the task ahead. He did not react even when we pulled his leg about Veronica. He said that it had nothing whatsoever to do with her and went back to his map. Kazik and I just looked at one another and nodded wisely: it could be nothing else but love, we concluded.

I know now that it was not that at all. I know that what he had been experiencing was a phenomenon which has been familiar to fighting men over the ages: a sudden and acute awareness of his mortality, perhaps a shiver of premonition, or some cold, eerie message from somewhere unknown, warning him that he was soon to die.

Fortunately for me, I did not witness the fulfilment of his foreboding. When it actually happened I was not there, as I had myself been taken off the battle-field, and was already on my way to hospital. Full details of this battle, however, were given to me later by Kazik as well as by Capt. Karpinski, so I can almost see the events as they unfolded. It was the battle of Monte Chiantello on 19th August 1944.

The final move started late in the afternoon at about 5 pm. The squadron was acting alone without infantry support. Aerial reconnaissance reported a considerable concentration of artillery, conventional as well as anti-tank, both static and mobile. All their anti-tank guns were of high calibre and had considerably better penetration than ours.

Speed was necessary so as to outsmart the German superior armament. In fact after only 1 kilometre from move-off the squadron met three Hornets (self-propelled anti-tank guns) and succeeded in destroying them quickly. Soon afterwards Stach with his troop surprised a static enemy artillery position which he silenced and then, in a typical gesture of defiance, crushed the German guns themselves into the ground, using the weight of his own tank for the purpose.

A little while later, two German tanks were seen retreating but were soon destroyed by another troop, one a Mk.VI and the other a Panther. The brisk momentum was maintained to the end, but just the same, it took the squadron about three hours of solid fighting to reach the top of the hill.

At this point the infantry was brought up in personnel carriers so as to consolidate the conquered territory. It was nearly dark, by then, and time for the tanks to withdraw. Monte Chiantello had been taken, the objective had been achieved, and our losses were light.

At that stage Stach may have felt that his premonitions had been groundless. The action had been a success and he personally had acquitted himself well. But his fate had already been sealed.

As the column threaded its way down the hill over the narrow

200

country track, thickly covered with pulverised clay, a huge cloud of yellow dust rose to the sky betraying to the enemy the presence of heavy armour. The frustrated German artillery, furious at having suffered yet another defeat, really let rip. They literally plastered the area with all they had. And one of these projectiles had Stach's name written on it. It crashed right through the open cover of his tank turret, setting it ablaze.

Miraculously, two members of the crew, the driver and the front gunner, managed to jump out. Severely burned and shocked, they were seen by their colleagues rolling frantically in the dust, trying to stifle the flames. No trace of Stach, his radio operator or his gunner, though. The tank was by now a blazing inferno, all ammunition exploding inside and sending huge cascades of fire into the air. Nobody could even think of coming near this volcano to try to rescue them. The German artillery, too, kept up its barrage well into the night. Those that had jumped out, as frequently happens, did not remember a single thing about the explosion. They didn't even know how they had got out...

It was only early the following morning that the fire burned itself out so that Kazik and Capt. Karpinski could climb on top of it. The tank was still quite hot, and the inside was totally wrecked, shredded out of all recognition by the fire and the violent explosions. Of Stach and the others there was no trace. They were still hoping that they had jumped out and were perhaps either lying unconscious somewhere or wandering dazed, not knowing where they were. Until someone noticed a lock of jet black hair with a piece of skull-bone attached to it which had partly melted on the outside of the engine area, just behind the turret. It could only have been Stach's. All hope of finding him and the other two alive had now gone. They were dead and had probably died instantly.

Kazik came to see me in hospital, a few weeks later, and told me all this in greater detail. He was shattered, just as I was. We had both lost a friend, a companion, a role model; and with his death something had died in us too.

When in the Spring I resumed command of my troop again, we worked together a lot, Kazik and I. As previously, he would take command over our six tanks and we would make a whole series of neat little sorties to great effect. One such sortie nearly finished in disaster. It was at the battle of Bologna in Spring 1945. Our manoeuvre proved so successful that we found ourselves deep in enemy territory, with the rest of the squadron miles behind, unable to join us. We stayed cut off for three days and three nights, without any support, with very little ammunition and hardly any fuel left. I watched Kazik. He was magnificent. Cool, professional and very shrewd as well. We were being pounded by all the heavy artillery which the Germans had on this sector, and fended off several pretty determined night attacks by a crack German SS unit. It was really touch and go. When we were finally rescued we had just four artillery shells left and half a magazine of machine gun ammunition.

Shortly after the end of hostilities, to my utter surprise, Kazik announced that he was getting married. Not to his very nice lady friend whom I knew and liked, but to someone he had known in Zakopane before the war. When I met the lady in question I was sure it would be a mistake. They were not suited, that was totally clear to me. It was, I suspected, a mariage de raison, which with Kazik's nature was doomed from the start. I gathered that on the social scale of pro-war Zakopane her family had held a higher position than his, hardly a reason for two future émigrés to marry.

She struck me as an ambitious but earthbound young woman, totally dedicated to her medical career, who would not be inspired by his romantic idealism which was so much a part of his make-up. I told him openly what I thought and, as often happens, he took it badly. Relations between us became strained. When we both came to England and got demobilised we seldom saw one another and if we did it was mainly at official reunions. The old intimacy seemed dead.

Until some time in summer 1973, when someone telephoned me: Kazik was terminally ill. He was dying and he had expressed a wish to see me, if this was at all possible. I went at once, of course. He had been teaching, I was told, at a girls' convent school in Pittsford in Northamptonshire. I had already been aware that he and his wife had parted company a long time before, so he was living alone, in a little apartment in the school complex where he worked.

They took me to Kazik's rooms. I could barely recognise him. An aged figure was sitting in an armchair, pale and drawn. It was only when he smiled that I could see some similarities with that propaganda photograph of his, when he was at the height of his

202

glory. At first the conversation followed the cautious, tentative path of two old friends who had lost touch with each other. It was only when he excused himself, saying he was feeling sick and asked me to leave the room that I protested. I reminded him that I was a qualified Lekpom and he did not have to be pompous with me.

I helped him with his immediate problem and when he could talk again he looked at me and said, "Stach chose a better way. At least he died gloriously. Now look at me..." he smiled bitterly. I took his hand and looked straight into his eyes. "You don't have to pretend with me," I said. "This is the reason that I am here, to help you face what you have to face. God only knows we did it so often before, together, remember?" "Of course I remember," he said in a much more relaxed tone. "I was hoping that we could talk like this, you and I. That we could be completely open, not have to pretend. You said just now that we had faced danger together before. Yes but it seemed easier then. It seems easier to die when one is young. At fifty-two it is hard. Besides, in my case, we are not dealing with danger. In danger there is hope. What I am facing now is certainty. The only thing they can't tell me is exactly when..." I looked at him again. "Are you afraid?" I asked him, almost in a whisper. "Yes, of course I am. Not so much of dying, but of the uncertainty," he replied.

At that moment I felt as if the clock had been turned back 28 years. We were back in 1945, we were real friends again, comrades in arms. Death had reared its ugly head once again, and our friendship returned, strong as ever, as if nothing had ever happened. I could talk to him without fear of committing an indiscretion, with certainty that he would tell me the truth. "Have you seen a priest?" I asked carefully. "Oh yes, the nuns organised all that. I am as ready as I shall ever be. A nice old-fashioned type, too. I feel quite at peace inside...".

He started to feel sick again, but this time he asked me to call one of the sisters, to give him a pain-killing injection. It was she who told me that it would be kinder if I were to leave.

He was suffering badly, she said. I asked him point-blank and he agreed. Yes, he said, she was right, he was in a bad way and the pain was now getting to him. Perhaps, if he rested it might ease a little. "Goodbye, my dear fellow. And thank you for coming. It must have been a terrible bore for you to come all this way to comfort an old pal. But this has helped me more that you can ever know..."

We embraced. He smelled of disinfectant and surgical spirit. His back felt like a heap of bones, with no muscle left under the skin. "Pray for me..." were his last words. I just bowed my head, in silent agreement.

He died that very same night. The funeral took place a week later. All those from the Regiment who still lived in England came to pay their last respects. The only absentee was his wife.

\* \* \*

But let me go back to my main story a long, long time before all this took place. From the beginning of June 1944 the Italian front ceased to be the centre of attention. We were upstaged by the invasion of France. All that was best was now switched to Normandy and we felt distinctly neglected. This manifested itself in many ways. The air cover which, hitherto, had been freely available was visibly reduced, the replacement of equipment damaged by the war became considerably delayed, and the press seemed to have lost all interest in our achievements. We felt like second-class citizens. This was true not only of the Polish Corps, but affected equally the British and the American forces. Predictably, our progress suffered. We were no longer the blue-eyed boys who had to be assisted in every way available. We had to await our turn.

Nevertheless, we were making some progress. Ancona had been taken and the drive North began. We were fighting along the Eastern coast. At the beginning of August we were given a few days' rest, during which Stach made his eventful trip to Naples, which I have mentioned before. We knew that the action was now taking place to the South of Fano, a small port town on the Adriatic coast. We also knew that our turn was coming soon.

On 19th August in the afternoon we were ordered to move into position. Our objective was Monte Chiantello, a steady slope some two and half kilometres long, which was, we were informed, fairly well defended. We went in without any infantry support. As I was driving past the other squadrons of the Regiment, I noticed my old friend and instructor from the Cadet School, Wladek Sypel.

He signalled to me, indicating heavy artillery bombardment

ahead. He even suggested that we should close our covers. I waved back in acknowledgement, knowing that I would do nothing of the sort. I always felt claustrophobic with closed covers. It was impossible to hear anything that was going on outside. So we pressed on. Still some distance from the hill itself we received fairly accurate mortar fire. Mortars in themselves did not present much danger, unless they happened to score a direct hit. I ordered my driver and front gunner to shut their covers. The other tanks in my troop followed suit, but I left my cover open.

At that precise moment my own turn came. On a perfectly ordinary afternoon, while following a perfectly well rehearsed routine of moving into battle positions for another copy-book attack... a black soft velvet curtain descended on me and I was swallowed by darkness, as if I had ceased to exist.

\* \* \*

The next thing I saw was an angel. I knew at once it was an angel because of the beauty and radiance of the image in front of me. No terrestrial being could possibly look like that. If it was an angel I must be in heaven, I concluded calmly, although for the life of me I could not recall ever dying. But as I had not died before and had no experience in this matter, so to speak, it was difficult for me to tell for certain, so I had to give it the benefit of the doubt. I decided that I had died, even if I had not remembered doing so, and was now in heaven and was looking at a proper angel.

After a while the angel moved. A beautiful white hand came into contact with my forehead and gently brushed aside the hair which had fallen over my eyes. The lovely lips also moved and formed a heavenly smile, full of warmth and love. Those lips kept moving as if in speech, but I didn't make any effort to listen, as I was sure angels had their own language, Latin most likely. But no! The words I heard were perfectly comprehensible to me. This was a Polish angel, I concluded with amazement and delight. How very considerate of St. Peter to have sent me such a beautiful Polish angel to welcome me.

It took me a little while to accept that I was not in heaven and that this was not an angel. It was a Polish nurse, in fact, and although her face was possessed of heavenly beauty she had other features which convinced me of that. I knew that angels were neither male not female, but this one was definitely a girl. I could see that even in my enfeebled condition.

I did not feel well, I knew. I had great difficulty in moving, and parts of my body would not move at all. In addition I felt a severe pain at the back of my neck.

Presently, a doctor came. He told me that I was partially paralysed and that they were sending me by plane to a big hospital in Bari, in Southern Italy, where he hoped they would be able to put me right. No-one at that stage could tell me exactly what had happened to me and why I was so badly disabled. The doctor told me, however, that he was going to give me an injection which would help me to relax completely for the duration of the trip.

While the heavenly nurse held my hand, he pushed a needle into one of my arteries and I immediately started to feel the return of the now familiar black velvet curtain descending gently over me.

The last things which faded from my vision were the warm, angelic eyes of the beautiful nurse.

# Chapter 16

# YALTA

Of all the catastrophes that have occurred during my lifetime, the most painful for me was the Yalta Declaration. This largely forgotten historic event caused me more anguish than even the outbreak of the Second World War. It may sound ridiculous but I can explain: I find it easier to come to terms with a wrong which is inflicted on me by my enemies than that which it is caused by my friends or, in this case, my allies. The war was the brain-child of Adolf Hitler, who was no friend of mine. The Yalta Agreement, by contrast, was negotiated by my Allies, on whose side I had been fighting, risking my life, whose uniform I was wearing and who, in theory at least, had entered the war to defend my country. The fact that America may have been the chief culprit on this occasion does not absolve Great Britain, since its leader signed the Yalta Agreement without any apparent objections. At a stroke of the pen, therefore, without any prior consultation with my leaders, my Allies sacrificed my country to my other enemy for the sake of expediency, so as not to upset 'dear old Uncle Joe' Stalin. This is why I feel sore. Wouldn't anybody?

But first let me recall the facts: on 11th February 1945, at an obscure sea-side resort in the Soviet Crimea called Yalta, an agreement was signed which was hailed as the blueprint for post-war Europe. The Big Three, Franklin Roosevelt for the USA, Winston Churchill for Great Britain and Joseph Stalin for the Soviet Union, laid down the principles which were to govern the world after the end of hostilities. 'The game is nearly won, so let us decide who takes what' would be a crude way of describing the purpose of the gathering. But first, the broad principles were announced: the unconditional surrender and the division of Germany into three occupation zones, the foundation of the United Nations and, somewhat surprisingly, the elevation of France to the role of a victorious power. And then the diabolical part was outlined, under the heading of "The new order in Europe". And this is precisely how the fate of many countries, including my own, was unilaterally and irrevocably altered, ruined, one might say, by three individuals whose only mandate was that they happened to be in power in their own countries at that moment in time. And not for long, either: Roosevelt was to die within two months and Churchill would lose his election two months after that. Stalin survived victorious for a few more years, to preside over his empire, now substantially enlarged, courtesy of Messrs. Roosevelt and Churchill.

But let us go back to the "New order in Europe". Poland, as usual, was singled out. The whole country, in defence of whose frontiers the war had ostensibly started, found itself shifted Westwards, as if in some macabre arabesque. She was deprived of all her Eastern provinces, which were incorporated into the Soviet Union, and was 'compensated' with a considerably smaller acreage of German territory. This in itself was a blow. But that was not all. The lofty language of the Declaration could not disguise the fact that Poland, from then on, was to become a Soviet satellite. Expressions like "free democratic elections" or "more representative government" could, for those who were familiar with the Soviet jargon, mean only one thing: the inevitable advent of communist rule.

A similar fate awaited all the other countries of Central and Eastern Europe. In effect, everything to the East of Berlin was now to come under the dominance of the Union of Soviet Socialist Republics. In a fit of generosity towards Joseph Stalin, the Western Allies agreed to most of his demands and at a stroke allowed the Soviet Empire to enlarge its already colossal territory by extending its hegemony over Poland, East Germany, part of Austria, Czechoslovakia, Hungary, Romania, Bulgaria, Yugoslavia, Albania, Lithuania, Latvia and Estonia. The fate of nearly 150 million people had thus been altered beyond all recognition.

It has been suggested that the blame lay principally with Roosevelt who, having fallen under the spell of Stalin, insisted on conducting the vital part of the negotiations with him alone, and deliberately excluded Churchill. This may well be true. I have no doubt that the American president grew to like his Soviet counterpart, that he was immensely impressed by the courage and determination of the Red Army. All that may have had a great deal to do with it. But just the same, Winston Churchill cannot escape criticism, since he was there and signed the agreement and by this very fact alone must take his share of the blame.

I was about to rejoin my Regiment, having spent some time in Rome, convalescing after my long stay in hospital, when news of this extraordinary event started to trickle in. It was at first very difficult to separate the hard facts from the usual wartime propaganda but, as the true picture started to emerge, we were all speechless with disbelief. How on earth could this have happened?, I questioned myself and everybody around me. How could the Western Allies be so naive as to let this monster have his way and allow him to gain so much? Didn't they remember that he had been the first ally of Hitler in 1939? Didn't they know that he was as bad as Hitler? What of the millions of innocent people who had perished and were still dying in Soviet labour camps? What about Katyn and all the Polish officers murdered by the NKVD, whose graves had just been discovered?

Nobody could offer me any real explanation. The few British officers I knew weren't interested. "It will all turn out for the best, old boy, you will see," they would say, in an infuriating, patronising way. Or, "Stalin is not such a bad fellow, you know. After all he has helped us to beat Jerry and his chaps were pretty good at Stalingrad." Or even worse, "You Poles seem a bit paranoid about this business. Stalin has promised, surely, you should give him a chance..."

As we all know now, it didn't turn out for the best. Yalta marked the beginning of the cold war and it didn't take all that long for the Western leaders themselves to realise what they had done. I read in one of the many biographies of FDR that in April of that year, just before he died, he realised what was happening. Even he could see that Stalin was taking hold of his 'sphere of influence' and treating it as his own. Churchill too, had second thoughts. Having lost the election in July 1945, he reflected for one year and in 1946, at Fulton, Missouri, delivered his famous 'Iron Curtain' speech, warning the world against the wall of secrecy behind which Stalin was indulging in his repressions. He was shutting the stable door well after the horse had bolted. Could he have forgotten that it was his signature at Yalta that had given Stalin the licence to do the very things of which he was now complaining?

From February 1945, it became painfully clear that if we were to fight this war to the very end, we would be fighting for somebody else's cause, not our own. If we were asked to die for the sake of freedom, as ultimately every soldier is, we would be dying for somebody else's freedom. Our freedom had been signed away, sold down the river, if you like, irrevocably, stupidly, unnecessarily, without as much as asking for the views of those who would be most directly affected. I am sure that had Gen. Sikorski been still alive then, there would have been an international scandal. He would not have allowed this vile act to go ahead without vigorous opposition. After his death, our remaining leaders were of insufficient calibre to command the right kind of attention. Gen. Anders protested, of course, but he was a soldier, not a politician, and his first reflex was the reflex of a soldier, which is to obey.

For me personally, Yalta was a catastrophe. I knew that, if I survived this war, I would never go home. I had no home to go back to. My home, my land, my inheritance, the nest where my family had lived and prospered for 300 years, was now in the Soviet Union. From now on I was no longer a Pole, born in Poland. At best I was a Pole who had been born in the Ukraine, a potential citizen of the USSR. And this was totally unacceptable to me.

So these were the immediate consequences of Yalta for me on at a personal level. There were, of course, wider implications too over which, fortunately, I could have no influence. These concerned the future of the Polish Forces in exile. The main question was what our attitude should be regarding our continued service in the Allied forces.

In other words: should we go on fighting this war as before, or should we pull out? As I have said, the Allied cause was no longer identical with our own. If we went on fighting we would, in reality, be like a mercenary army, fighting in somebody else's war. I did not envy our leaders. They had a difficult decision to make.

Characteristically, they decided we should carry on fighting, and predictably we, the line soldiers, obeyed their decision without as much as a grumble. We all felt that if we carried on, despite Yalta, the Allies would be honour-bound to help us.

We were wrong. They did not help us. Our Eastern provinces were lost and, it would seem, will remain lost forever. Poland, together with the other unfortunate countries who were the subject of the 'The new order in Europe', remained under Soviet rule for the duration of the Cold War. Like them, we had to wait until the collapse of Communism itself, before regaining any semblance of freedom.

It was to take a while – fifty years to be precise.

# Chapter 17

# THE MONKEY AND THE RAZER BLADE

The memory of Rome, as I saw it in 1944, still lives for me in the old films of Roberto Rossellini. When, increasingly rarely now , I see reruns of his great classics, "Rome – Open City" or "Bicycle Thieves", the effect is guaranteed: floodgates of nostalgia burst wide open.

The military catastrophe which had befallen Italy in the preceding months, culminating in their separate unconditional surrender to the Allies, stripped the Italians not only of their material well-being but, most painfully, of the already pathetically depleted residue of their national pride. They displayed the symptoms of a defeated nation to a degree out of all proportion to the extent of their defeat. The phrase: "Noi poveri Italiani" – we poor Italians – frequently heard at the time, was to us Poles a source of uncharitable amusement. After all we had all experienced the privations of the Soviet labour camps and sampled the true miseries of war. By our standards the Italians didn't know what they were talking about. In our eyes we were the champions in suffering and resented the unjustified whinging of a nation which seemed , to us, still relatively well off.

Stripped of her glamour, looking distinctly uncared for and unloved, Rome was still a magnificent city. Her 'bone structure' was good. So good, in fact, that despite the uncombed, unwashed, unmade-up look, she remained beautiful. True, her fountains might have run dry, her palaces might have assumed that blind look, with boarded up windows and doors, the streets might be deserted, with no traffic, other than an occasional army truck, and her most elegant shops might have turned decidedly shabby but, despite it all, it was still magic. It seemed that the shabby present was powerless to take anything away from the golden past, the glorious past when Rome was the capital of Christendom. Perhaps, even the fact of not having to pretend that she was modern, slick or sophisticated, gave her the majesty of a true aristocrat. The dry fountains, the blackened columns, the missing

212

roof tiles emphasised that the City was at peace with its past, was comfortable with it and did not need to be 'tarted-up' to look marvellous.

My love of Rome dated back, in fact, to the Spring of 1938, when with my school, I had visited it for the first time. The occasion was the canonisation of a Polish saint, St. Andrew Bobola. We travelled there by train and stayed only 5 days, but for me it was more than enough to enthral me. It was an interesting period, for we arrived at the height of Mussolini's revival of Italian nationalism, and Rome was at her most glittering.

Il Duce, aware of his nation's notorious lack of pride in its past, tried to persuade the Italians that they were the heirs, the most legitimate, the most direct descendants of the glorious Romans, who had ruled the world for seven hundred years. He cleaned up the city, uncovered the Roman Forum, opened up grand avenues, restored old monuments and built new ones. He made the triumphal arches look as though they were meant to be triumphant, unashamed of the purpose for which they had been built, made the Colosseum look colossal and turned Piazza Venezia into a stage for the delivery of his own heroic speeches.

Did the Italians like it, did they approve of his efforts? Who can tell? It sounds like a cliché today, although it did not at the time: but the only good thing most Italians attributed to Il Duce was ... that he made the trains run on time.

When, with my regiment , I landed in Italy in the Spring of 1944, things were at their bleakest. The Italians were suffering from an acute attack of inferiority. There was no defiance in their defeat, nor any trace of magnificence. No wonder the Germans despised them. They were most un-Wagnerian in their darkest hour.

The Allied armies, too, viewed them as a fairly harmless ex-enemy, not to be taken seriously. The fact that everything was for sale, that a packet of cigarettes could open any door, while a carton would buy you a Renaissance painting, that you could gain the affections of an Italian Rita Hayworth look-alike for a pair of nylons, or that Hedy Lamarr's twin sister would willingly spend a passionate weekend with a total stranger, in exchange for a NAAFI blouse – did not impress anybody as particularly edifying. To get involved seriously with an Italian girl was considered unworthy of an officer and a gentleman. This was, no doubt, the normal reaction of any invading army, which, like it or not, is what we were.

When I re-visited Rome in the winter of 1944. I was convalescing after several months spent in a military hospital, in Bari, in Southern Italy. My injury was the result of an artillery shell that had exploded on top of my tank. during the previous summer's campaign. The blast ripped off the turret cover and caught the top of my head, damaging two vertebrae in my neck, and causing partial paralysis. After several operations, the surgeons succeeded in restoring me to near normality, after which I was granted an extended leave. This I elected to spend in Rome, for I wanted to have a good look at the city I remembered from another era.

I was to stay at the Hotel Imperial, in the Via Veneto, in the very heart of Rome. For the rest of the war this hotel served as a hostelry for officers of the Polish forces. It was run by a very pleasant Polish cavalry captain, who, as I was the only other cavalryman present, took a keen interest in my welfare. He gave me an excellent room, which I had to share with just one other chap, an artillery lieutenant. When I told my host that I wanted to spend my time getting to know the city, he very kindly offered me a Jeep and driver to take me round the places I wanted to see. I thanked him, but declined. I said I preferred to do it in my own way, on foot, and at my own speed. He understood.

And that was precisely what I did. I walked for miles. I got myself a good map and a small guidebook and walked and walked, for days on end. My fellow officers considered me a nut case. In their eyes, I was insane, completely cuckoo. Fancy going round old churches and looking at some dilapidated ruins, they would say, when there was so much 'real' beauty around. Their definition of beauty differed somewhat from mine in so far as theirs was to be found in the dance halls and cafes. In the evenings, I would join the old captain, at his table. I liked him very much. Although, to me he was old (he must have been well into his forties!), he was tall and slim and very distinguished-looking. His regiment was the Carpathian Lancers and in the evenings he would wear their rather spectacular uniform (which was the envy of the rest of the army). He looked really smart. He was also very good company, with a charming sense of humour and a vast range of interests. He also knew everybody worth knowing in Rome.

At the end of the first week the captain asked me to join him at a small reception which he was giving, that evening, for some selected Italian friends. I accepted. It proved to be a very distinguished gathering indeed, including a cardinal and several Roman grandees with their wives. The great advantage to me was that most of them spoke reasonably good French, so despite my rather poor Italian I found no problems in communicating with them. I noticed that there was one young woman among the guests. After a while, the captain came to me and said, "I have a job for you. Go and talk to that young lady, who is here with her mother." I understood that this was the real reason that I had been invited. "Nothing is for nothing," I thought to myself while allowing myself to be introduced.

The two ladies were sitting on a sofa in the corner. The mother was a beauty, the daughter was not. She was still very young, nineteen I learned later, and whilst her features were very good, she lacked her mother's presence and poise. She had a studious look about her. Her very intelligent, calm, rather beautiful eyes were those of an intellectual, not of a debutante. She spoke excellent French and was surprisingly easy to talk to.

All my worst fears of having to talk all evening to some stupid teenager vanished. When she discovered that I was interested in Roman architecture she got very excited. I found her excellent company and a source of valuable information. We parted good friends. I felt that I had acquitted myself rather well with the task allotted to me by my host. He complimented me on this too, which I thought very good of him.

The following morning the captain's batman brought me a note: "Please see me before you leave this morning." After breakfast I called at his suite. He told me that he had received a message from the girl's mother asking us both to lunch that day, followed by a private tour of the Vatican. It appeared that she was related to the Pope and that she had the freedom to visit the Vatican whenever she wanted. I jumped at this unique opportunity. This was really an unexpected bonus. I spent the morning polishing my shoes and giving my buttons an extra rub, so as not to look like a poor relation beside the elegant Carpathian Lancer.

At the appointed hour we drove in the captain's Jeep a few blocks to where our hosts lived. On the way I was given a brief outline of who was who. The girl's father, the descendant of an old Roman family, was commonly referred to as the ambassador,

215

although nobody quite knew where this distinction had originated. The mother, who was referred to as the "contessa", came from an even better family. They were very rich, although a part of their fortune was in the North of Italy which at that time was still cut off by the front line.

I gathered that the captain admired the contessa very much and was a frequent visitor to their apartment.

I had never been to a fashionable Roman household before. In fact I had not as yet visited any Italian household, and even while in the Middle East I had only seen the places where Polish refugees lived and an occasional hotel or restaurant. So I can safely say that I was fairly unspoiled. What I saw here took my breath away and I had to keep pinching myself to make sure that I had not died and gone to heaven. The marbles, the carpets, the paintings, the furniture – were so magnificent, that it hurt. I was desperately trying to look natural, but I knew I was completely spellbound.. We were shown into a smallish room, which I later learned was the morning room, and the good captain, no doubt noticing my confusion, described to me in minute detail the interesting paintings and objets d'art it contained, no doubt to make me feel more at ease.

In a little while, the contessa came in. She looked ravishing. The captain was at his most suave and courtly. I felt very shy. She turned to me and said, "Marita will join us shortly. She is still dressing. Wants to look her prettiest for the lieutenant here," and she gave me such a wickedly seductive smile that for a moment I forgot that she was a respectable matron and not my date for the day.

"Anyway," she continued, "I was telling my husband about you and he thought that he knew your family well. Are you not related to the old Conte Isidoro, who lived in Rome for years with his family in Via Gregoriana?"

"Yes," I replied, "he was my great-uncle, the younger brother of my grandfather." "So, I feel you are almost family," she exclaimed. "The old Contessa's cousin married Prince B., who was a fairly close relation on my mother's side. But anyway, I must not bore you with genealogy, I know the young hate this sort of thing. I did when I was your age."

Very amusingly, she then told us of the arrangements for the afternoon. After a while Marita came in, looking much younger than the previous evening and quite natural and very friendly. She called me Charles, pronounced the French way and explained that Marita was short for Maria Teresa. The natural way she fitted into this grand setting impressed me enormously. It was her home, after all, I had to remind myself.

The afternoon was a great success. We were taken to the Pope's private apartments by a very worldly monsignor, who showed us the main treasures there and gave us very good tea afterwards. He also conducted a very witty and, I thought, rather unecclesiastical conversation with the contessa, who sparkled like quicksilver. Marita must have noticed that I found it odd and said to me when we were out of earshot, "Mother was a terrible flirt when she was young and she is always telling me that, at my age, I should be more flirtatious too. She thinks men like it." As far as I could see mother was still in pretty good form, but I thought it was probably just a game. Marita was certainly not overdoing it.. But, on the other hand, she was not the type. She was more in earnest about everything. Imitating her mother would not have been natural to her.

My attitude towards Marita was perfectly relaxed now. She was very nice, a good pal. She told me that her greatest ambition was to be treated by men as if she were a man and that she found the romantic notions farcical and ridiculous and she wanted just to be good friends with them. She hoped I would feel that way too, which would make her very happy, as she thought we had a lot of interests in common. This suited me fine and I told her so.

I saw a lot of her in the next few days. She said there was a pause just then in her educational pursuits and that she would like to show me the kind of Rome that tourists never saw. That was, if I didn't mind. I didn't – not in the least. What was more, she too liked walking. We saw churches, lots of them, big and small. She had a particular liking for the little out-of-the-way places, and knew of extraordinary hidden treasures, which I was sure few people ever saw. Her knowledge was quite remarkable for a person of her age and – to me – quite surprising for a young girl.

We also spoke of philosophy, which was her other passion. She was reading this at the university she attended and in this, too, she had very definite views. Philosophy to me was an unknown subject but she was able to guide me through the, at first confusing, terminology, with such skill that relatively quickly we were able to converse quite convincingly on this subject too.

I really liked her a lot and found her quite remarkable.

All the time I was in Rome, I kept in fairly close touch with my regiment. It was winter now and there was little activity at the front, so several of my colleagues were able to visit Rome and I had the opportunity of keeping well up to date with the situation. My leave was due to end in about a week and I was really looking forward to rejoining my regiment. It was stationed now near Ancona in a little town called Osimo. I told Marita all about it and she said she was sorry that she was going to lose the only true friend with whom she felt really at ease.

The following evening the contessa asked me to join her and her family at the opera. They had, I learned, a private box at the Teatro Reale, which, despite the war, was giving several perform-ances a week. Madam Butterfly was on the programme and the cast was to be exceptionally good.

I was very interested, never having been to the opera before, but having heard a lot about it from my father, who was a great opera enthusiast, as well as from Boris Ivanovich in the San Gorodock field hospital, back in Russia.

The evening proved a great success. I met the ambassador as well as Marita's brother Riccardo. They asked me to supper after-wards. I loved the music of Puccini and knew many arias well, having 'sung' them myself, during my private 'operatic sessions' with Boris Ivanovich in the depths of the Taiga.

My Italian hosts, particularly the ambassador, felt that the per-formance lacked the required sparkle, that the production was drab and the conductor inadequate. To my unspoiled mind the whole thing was wonderful.

As usual the contessa was most entertaining. She told me that she liked to devise her own private happy endings to all operas and that in this one, for instance, Madam Butterfly mismanages her suicide and Pinkerton, moved by remorse, comes back and finding her still breathing promptly hires the best surgeons who soon have the lady on her feet and on the way to the USA, where they live happily ever after.

She said that she had all the Italian composers sorted out in this way, but was, regretfully, unable to do anything about the

Germans, Wagner in particular, whom she said , in the strictest confidence, she found a bit of a bore.

After supper, the contessa asked me if I could come and have tea with them the following afternoon, as she understood from Marita that I was due to re-join my regiment very soon. Of course, I readily agreed.

* * *

"So – it's back to your regiment next Friday," said the contessa, pouring the tea for me. I watched her hands. They fascinated me, not only by their beauty, but by the incredible grace of their movement. They seemed to have a life of their own, unrelated to the rest of her person. They reminded me of tongues of fire, slow and silent but at times incredibly quick.

"Yes. This month has passed terribly quickly, thanks to your great kindness to me. I cannot remember enjoying anything as much since leaving Poland four years ago. "She gave me a lovely, worried look. "Oh, yes. I always think how brave you were, so far away from your home, for such a long time. I am glad you were not too bored in Rome. I find it a terribly sad place, with all the shortages, and dirt and privations ... I hope that you will remember something good about it and that, maybe, you will remember us.... and miss us - just a little."

"Of course," I replied, – "I shall miss you all and all this. Who wouldn't? You are really so kind to me, I cannot find words to express all my gratitude..."

"Look," said the contessa, glancing at her watch, "Marita is still at the hairdresser's and I do want to have a little chat with you before she returns."

She replaced her cup and looked at me again, with the same worried look.

"Look, Charles," she repeated, "I am sure it will not come as a total surprise to you, but I feel I ought to mention it, just in case. You are no doubt aware that Marita is very fond of you." She was watching me now quite closely. "I think I am safe in saying... that she is madly in love with you." She paused and took up her cup. I must have looked pretty shocked, as she continued, "I don't blame her, a dashing, brave cavalry officer, like you. I would have no problem in falling for you myself, if I were her age," and here she gave me her usual wicked smile. I couldn't believe my ears. It was crazy. Marita was a friend, a pal, I told myself, we had a secret understanding about it. That was no doubt why her mother was all confused, and was worrying unnecessarily.

I told her about our understanding, about Marita's unromantic approach to friendship between men and women, about the intellectual interests we shared.

She listened patiently, but looked rather bored. At last she said, "This is Marita all over. She has these silly notions. She is young. I was telling her that a girl must be a girl and act like one. But she was afraid she would frighten you off, hence this charade of hers." I still couldn't believe her.

"Let me talk to Marita," I said, "I am sure I can sort it out without any difficulty. Leave it to me."

"I am her mother. She is my baby. I know her better than you do. It is, of course, your decision, your choice, but I beg you: be gentle about it. Be kind. You are her first love... and if I know Marita, most probably her last."

By now my head was spinning. I did not know what was happening to me. Events were taking place which I felt unable to understand, let alone control.

My knowledge of the world was very superficial. My understanding of women was close to zero. All the girls I knew were either serving in the Forces, like me, or were in the nursing service. They were subject to the same discipline, the same rules as I was. All my little romances, so far, had been of the usual transitory kind and all my partners had known what was what.. But this was incredible.

Then an idea came to me. I could not be a serious contender, I thought, after all I had nothing, I was a castaway. What mother could ever think of her daughter getting emotionally involved with a man who was a penniless soldier, a junior officer without any prospects at all? So I played that card.

"Oh – how typical of your race," she replied. "You are a proud Pole. You want to be independent. How charming. But don't worry. Marita has money of her own, quite sufficient until your affairs sort themselves out, with the war and all that. And if the worst came to the worst and – God forbid – you could not regain your Polish possessions, I am sure there will always be a post for you in the diplomatic service or something like that. With our connections that would be no problem at all."

The world was spinning badly now and I felt quite uncomfortable. I must talk to Marita, I resolved. This was the only way. The contessa read my thoughts. "Go to her, and talk it over with her," she said soothingly. "Yes, go, go. But please be kind to my baby. She is so young, so vulnerable, remember!" "Yes – I'll remember," I repeated after her. "Promise?" asked the contessa, with her most innocent, pleading look. "Promise," I repeated weakly. I got up and left the room.

When I opened the door, Marita was standing there – in a flood of tears.

"You hate me now, I know.... How you must hate me... I heard most of it ... I couldn't help it... I should not have let Mamma talk to you this way... It's all finished... I know..." – she was speaking between sobs.

I looked at her. What I saw was a child in despair. Her face was all wet with tears. I had never seen anything like it, that expression of despair, of rejection. "Be kind to my baby," the Contessa's plea was still ringing in my ears. I had promised to be kind, not to hurt this poor, devastated creature, whose only crime was that she loved me. Nobody had loved me this way before. This must be something unique and precious – who was I to kill something so pure, so strong so spontaneous?

I said absolutely nothing. I was speechless, completely unable to think what to say. She looked at me like a whipped spaniel, ready to run away at smallest gesture of displeasure or rejection.

I don't quite know what happened. The next thing I knew, she was in my arms and she was kissing me with total, blind abandon. She was warm, she was soft, she was adorable.

\* \* \*

My return to the Regiment was a surprisingly painless and – for me – joyous occasion. My worries that after such a long absence I would have difficulty in fitting back into the military machine, that the unit's internal mechanism would have got used to functioning without me, that there would be some jealousy as a result of my Roman holidays – all these vanished, almost immediately, after my arrival.

Not only was I welcomed back with open arms by the Colonel and his staff, but also my colleagues greeted me with affection and joy. In addition to resuming the command of my old troop, I was offered a very interesting task, that of supervising the fitting of new artillery pieces to a number of the tanks and the re-training of the tank crews. The regimental technical officer, whose job this would normally have been, was already engaged on another urgent project and could not be spared. I still retained – it appeared – my old reputation of being able to get things done. This was largely undeserved but, as to date I had managed to avoid any major disasters, the accolade still remained with me.

I was delighted to be back and threw myself into my work with all the zest and enthusiasm which was natural to me. I was glad to be once again among my brother officers and with my own troop, with whom I had that special bond that only combat and shared danger can produce. None of it seemed to have been lost during my long absence in hospital and on leave. It all added up to that warm 'glad to be home' feeling.

The dramatic events of the last few days in Rome seemed remote now. I felt slightly uneasy whenever I thought about it but, as I had so much to do and was so far away, the whole thing felt unreal and less important. Deep down I knew, I think, that I had allowed things to drift too far that, if I wanted to end it all, I had missed the moment when this could logically have taken place. I was involved by default.

The fact that Marita's sudden revelations had bowled me over should not have stopped me from stating my own position clearly and unequivocally. The trouble was that I still could not make up my mind what my position actually was. Did I love her or not? I was not sure what love felt like or what it ought to feel like. Maybe this was love. The Italians were always telling me that I was a typical example of the Nordic race and consequently not as passionate as the fiery Latinos. Maybe this is what being possessed of a Nordic temperament implied. I hoped my doubts were unnecessary, but until such time as I could experience the 'real thing' how could I know? So, as often happens with me, when I didn't know, I didn't do anything about it.

Meanwhile I was receiving letters from Marita. They were very sweet letters.

She was much less sophisticated in writing than in conversation. Almost daily thick wads of lined copy paper would arrive in her rather immature handwriting. She would describe, in minute detail, what she had been doing every day, writing about her studies, about her family, her friends; and from time to time, without any apparent rhyme or reason, she would include a paragraph describing her feelings for me, her love, her devotion, her determination to make me happy in order to repay me, in some infinitely small way , the happiness which I had given her by not rejecting her out of hand.

All this I read with amazement. I felt unworthy of this kind of love. I did not understand it and it frightened me in a way. Was it possible that I could be the object of this kind of feeling? I could not work out why I was unable to feel the same sort of thing in return. I thought in confusion: was there some reason for this and if so was this reason to be found in me? Maybe I was not capable of such an emotion.

One day the Colonel sent for me. He said that I was to attend a course for officers responsible for the new 105mm howitzer gun project, the subject I was already working on. It was to be held in Bracciano, some 20 miles north of Rome and it was to last one week. I was to take a Jeep and leave in two days. "I am sure you will not be too unhappy, as it is only one hour's drive to where you would most likely want to be," he said. I smiled, but said nothing. I was not sure, but I had a feeling that fate was pushing me into the arms of Marita.

It turned out to be a very intensive week. The days were spent at the course, the evenings in Rome. Very little time remained for sleep. At the end of the week, while at the wheel of my Jeep on the return trip back to Osimo, I nearly ran the vehicle into a tree. I just could not keep my eyes open. My safe return was only achieved after a half-hour's nap under a bush.

Also during that week any doubts which I had had regarding my feelings towards Marita seemed to have vanished. I convinced myself that I loved her. I had a long talk with the Carpathian captain the day after my arrival, and he explained to me that my worries were largely imaginary, the product of my relative immaturity and lack of experience, that Marita's great love for me was bound to inspire me in due course. He knew several very successful marriages which had started that way and had proved to be exemplary in the end. He maintained that the enormous advantages of the eventual union between us would decisively outweigh nearly all the risks involved. The material security and the social advantages were, in his view, not to be sneezed at. Many a young man in my position would jump at this opportunity. Whether I was really convinced by him or whether it was just lack of determination on my part, I cannot tell, but I just let myself be carried by events, adopting a kind of fatalistic mode, not something which comes to me naturally.

Marita was sweetness personified. She was happy to see me, and that too was an important reason for my giving up my internal struggle. She knew that I liked social life and although she herself was not normally a social animal, she spent a lot of effort in planning and arranging very nice parties and dances for my benefit.

These gave me a further interesting insight into the life of Roman society, which despite the war was still pretty impressive. I also managed, during this short time, to acquire a brand new uniform, produced in record time by a Signor Mammini, the best military tailor in Rome. Fortunately I had enough money to pay for this luxury and could grandly refuse embarrassing offers of a loan. My already considerable narcissistic tendencies were being reinforced by Marita's ecstatic admiration, as a result of this sartorial improvement. "Mon Dieu, que tu es beau!" she would exclaim in front of everybody. My embarrassment, on hearing this was not entirely sincere, a bad sign in one who had hitherto regarded himself as being not conceited. At the end of that week we were considered by everybody to be a couple, awaiting the mere formality of an official engagement.

At heart, I felt myself fully committed. It was to be, I had no doubt, a brilliant match, which I was sure my parents, had they known, would have approved. This, to me, has always been a very important consideration.

* * *

But it was not how it ended. A further twist awaited me round the corner, as within a week after my return to the Regiment I was in love. Madly, passionately, idiotically, unexpectedly. I did not have to question or probe anything – I just knew. And the cruel twist was that her name was not Marita, but Antonia, the daughter of a doctor in Osimo.

It all started as a joke, or more accurately, as a bet. I was duty officer that day and had spent the preceding night in the office, by the telephone, as the job required. The following morning, early, I took a telephone call from the brigade HQ. It was a message for my Colonel to report to the Brigadier at 10am. The brigade duty officer, a good friend of mine, hinted strongly that this was to do with

224

our moving to new battle positions just south of Bologna. It meant that we were about to move to the front line. I was very excited. The moment we had been waiting for all winter had arrived.

My turn of duty ended at 6pm and I went in search of the Adjutant to hand him my report. I was told that he was in the mess, where a dance was in progress. Having been up all night, I did not feel like dancing. I was sleepy and hungry.

I found the Adjutant in the bar. He offered me a drink, which I refused. Having handed him my papers I was about to depart when he called me back: "Karol – before you go, do have a look into the ball room. There is a most fantastic bird there, who, we have decided, would suit you perfectly. She is with an Italian civilian chap and no one so far has succeeded in dancing with her. We thought you might have a go. Why don't you try, just for the hell of it?".

"Dancing is the last thing that I need, just now", I replied. "I am longing to have a bath, a quick bite and a good night's sleep. Besides, I am already spoken for, remember"... "He has lost his sense of fun already", said the Adjutant, "and he is not even engaged. What will marriage do to you, I dread to think. Let me make it more difficult for you now", he added with a smile, "If you succeed in getting one dance out of her, I will buy you dinner, either tonight or any other night, at your favourite Trattoria. So there..", he concluded. Well, that was different: a challenge and a possible dinner, I thought, not to be sneezed at. "All right, I'll have a look, nothing more", I conceded.

She was indeed a beauty. I spotted her in the crowd without difficulty. She was standing by the far door, as if ready to leave, with her escort, a tall good-looking Italian. "All right", I said to the Adjutant, "this will cost you a dinner. Just one dance. OK?" "OK", replied the Adjutant, highly amused.

I pushed my way, across the crowded dance floor, to where this ravishing creature stood. I felt bold and reckless. I felt like in a trance, not at all myself. She stopped talking and looked in my direction with, what seemed like, mild surprise. I was gripped by an insane determination to succeed and whilst aware that people were looking, something that normally would put me off, I pressed on regardless. My adrenaline was flowing freely, I didn't care if the whole world looked. However ridiculous it may have seemed to others – I just had to dance with this gorgeous stranger and it had to be now. Not tomorrow, or the next day – now!!

I addressed her in French and asked her to dance, at first in the normal, conventional way. She replied, in Italian, that she was on the point of leaving and that she couldn't. At this stage I allowed the force in me to take charge.

Words flowed like a torrent. Words which I wouldn't normally use, not in a thousand years. The fact that I knew she did not follow my French tirade, did not bother me in the least. It felt as if I had activated in me some hidden recording mechanism, which was playing back words, strange words, that were not mine. What I said was immaterial. It was the fluency of my delivery, that for me, was so unusual. I watched her lovely face as I spoke.

She looked at me – in disbelief, I thought, shaking her head, from time to time, and saying, to her companion "Ma non capisco. Che cosa dice?"– or "I don't follow. What is he saying?" – She looked amused and that, I reckoned, was already something. Encouraged by this I stepped up the effort. I was now making little jokes, utilising the few words of Italian that came to my mind, at random. This made her laugh and I felt even more hopeful.

"Un ballo solo, prego, prego, prego..." – I repeated in mock supplication, lifting one finger, to make sure that she understood that all I was asking was one dance, just one...

She turned to her escort, with a most charming smile and I understood that she was asking him if he minded. Then she turned to me, still smiling, lifted her long, lovely index finger and said, "Solo uno," and smoothly, beautifully draped herself into my arms. It was heaven, sheer undiluted heaven...

And so, dance followed dance, without resistance, without explanation, in defiance of time and convention – just as if it were all preordained.

* * *

"Buona notte, Karol," she said to me, opening the front door of the apartment house where she lived. "Buona notte, Antonia," I replied, "e grazie." She smiled at me and shut the door. I heard her hurrying up the stairs. It was a quarter to ten and she had promised her mother to be back at nine. I now stood facing a perfectly ordinary front door, to a perfectly ordinary apartment house, in an ordinary provincial town. It could have been any door in any town. To me it seemed palatial. Behind that door lived the object of my dreams and from now on this simple building seemed to be magical. In fact everything that evening seemed like magic.

As I was walking home to my billet, I plunged eagerly into my private world of reverie. I savoured the recollections of everything that had happened that night. Every dance we had danced, every word we had said. I delighted in playing back in my mind the images of her, of the way she looked, the way she danced . I made myself imagine that she was still with me and on my personal 'screen' I saw, quite clearly, how she walked by my side, tall, elegant, proud. A beautiful thoroughbred filly, I decided, that's what she reminded me of. It seemed that I had known her always. I tried to force myself into remembering how it had all started, and to my surprise I realised that just a few hours ago I had had no idea of her existence. Four hours, just four short hours ago my world was a different place. It was so different that then I had supposed that I was sleepy and hungry. When I remembered that, I laughed out loud. I wasn't hungry, I wasn't sleepy, but, Lord, I was happy, happy beyond belief. So this was what being in love felt like: amazing, quite amazing. My feet had wings, my thoughts had wings, my soul had wings.

When I returned to my billet, my landlady smiled at me in a mysterious way.

"Si ha divertito questa sera, Tenente?" she asked me enquiringly, had I enjoyed the evening? "Si grazie, Signora, molto," I assured her quite sincerely. She then told me that she had heard that I had been dancing all evening with the prettiest girl in Osimo or, probably, in the whole province of Ancona. I just smiled at her in reply. Life in Osimo held no secrets for Signora Giannini.

Preparations for our departure to the front started the following morning. We had only one week to get ready and although we had been expecting this for some time, it felt as if nothing was ready. I was rushed off my feet putting my troop into battle order, as well as supervising the final adjustments to the new armament, the installation of which had only just been completed. I had, literally, no time to eat.. The whole operation had to be kept secret from all civilians, so I could say nothing to Antonia. But Signora Giannini knew, immediately, and when she knew the whole town knew. Since the dance I had only seen Antonia once, for ten minutes, in the street. It was the following afternoon, when she was returning from her dressmaker. I asked if I could come and visit her at home. She looked embarrassed and said that it would be impossible. If I liked, we could meet the following afternoon, say, about six and if I had time, we could perhaps see a film together, she suggested. Six was too early for me, I told her. "So make it half past," she conceded.

On the third day after the dance a letter from Marita arrived. It was a shock. In my daze I had forgotten about her completely. I left it unopened for a long time. Suddenly, I became aware, that I had a huge problem on my hands.

For the remaining days I saw Antonia either in the street, or sometimes in the cinema. She had become very friendly, at times affectionate. Perhaps, I thought, she reciprocated my feelings. What I could not understand was why she would not allow me to come and see her at home. Each time I asked she said it was impossible.

She started to write to me, though. I was now receiving letters from two young women. Those in pale blue envelopes, with the initial A I opened eagerly, the others, in simple white ones, I tried to forget.

I knew that this could not go on, and that I had to resolve the situation. On the other hand, I concluded, nothing could be done now. Such matters could not be dealt with by correspondence, and under the circumstances, due to the final preparations for departure to the front, I could not even dream of getting permission to go to Rome. Besides, I told myself, the war may solve everything without any help from me. It was more than likely that I would be killed and there would be no need for me to do anything, or to cause pain to anybody. After some time I rather liked the idea of getting killed, as a noble way out of my predicament. I would have two young women mourning for me, I concluded . This seemed to soothe my troubled conscience, and having convinced myself that it was also the most romantic solution, I felt far less guilty.

I saw Antonia briefly the evening before our departure and she asked me if it was true that we were about to leave for the front. When I replied that I would rather not talk about it, she smiled a knowing smile. Italians have a healthy contempt for secrets and 'military' secrets are always the source of considerable mirth. "But you will try to come back to me, when all this is over?" I thought I saw a tear in her eye, when she said that. "Oh, yes I will," I replied truthfully, forgetting for the moment my firm determination to die.

On the morning of our departure a letter from Antonia was delivered to me by special messenger. I had simply no time to read it. It had to wait. I felt the thick monogrammed envelope safely stowed against my heart, emitting gentle whiffs of perfume, her perfume, every time I moved my left arm. When, eventually, I found an opportunity to be alone I opened the thick wad of writing. Her round, open, feminine hand beckoned me to savour the content. "Carissimo mio Karol," it started. That was lovely, but then what? I recognised individual words but the meaning of the sentences eluded me completely. She was writing without any allowances for my poor command of Italian. It had to wait until I could find someone who would help me to understand. All I was able to comprehend was "Carissimo mio Karol"...

When, days later, I found someone I could trust, I realised what a magnificent letter it was. It was written in a most unusual prose, in short, punchy sentences, often without verbs, a style reminiscent of Hemingway. No wonder I had found it difficult to follow. What I found very easy to follow, though, was that with her, as with me, it had been love at first sight. She thanked me for giving her life new meaning, fresh colour, a sense of excitement, a touch of chivalry and promise of romance. She had never imagined that such things existed in real life. She had, hitherto, been convinced that this kind of thing could only be found in films and books and it all was a fantasy of film directors and fiction writers. When I pushed my way across that dance floor, she said, and asked her to dance, that was, for her, the moment of revelation, it was then that she realised that life could be something else, something wonderful.

The old lady who translated it for me was moved to tears, she thought it was such a beautiful letter. "You are a very lucky young man," she said to me in French, "it is unusual for modern girls to write this well." So I showed her Antonia's photograph, which I had carried on me for some days now. "And she is such a beauty, too," she added after expert examination. What I did not tell this good lady was that ,due to my earlier mistakes, I would not be able to see this gorgeous creature again, that the only way left to me was to die on the battlefield and thus solve the unfortunate impasse, once and for all.

\* \* \*

"Man shoots – God guides the bullets," says an old Polish proverb. In the course of this campaign the bullets kept away from me. When, on 8th May 1945, after the few weeks of fighting,

Germany finally surrendered, I was very much alive, I felt well and despite numerous near misses I did not have a scratch on me.

I also felt pleased. I was glad to be alive and was thrilled that both my body and my mind had proved capable of withstanding the hardships of war. I had been warned beforehand, by my older colleagues, that often, after a prolonged spell in hospital, one felt less enthusiastic about taking risks. This, fortunately, had not seemed to be the case with me.

Most of all, I was looking forward to seeing Antonia again. I remembered, of course, that I had in front of me the daunting task of sorting things out with Marita. I could not forget that, but somehow even this did not seem quite as difficult, as before. I was more confident about everything. I felt sure that I would be able to do it gently, without making it too difficult for her. The sooner the better, though, I thought... With this in mind I asked my Colonel for two days' leave.

The plan was that I would take a Jeep, travel to Osimo first, see Antonia, and then go to Rome and see Marita and her parents. The Colonel was not very keen and said that he could only spare me for 36 hours and that was all. I calculated rapidly: I had some 200 kilometres to go from Bologna to Ancona, plus a few more to Osimo. This I could manage, in a Jeep, in some five hours. From Osimo to Rome it would be more like 280 kilometres, mainly over mountain roads and it was bound to take some ten hours of solid driving. Calculating optimistically , if I used 15 hours' driving each way, a total of 30 hours, I would have a grand total of six hours of visiting time and whatever sleep I could fit in. It was tight, very tight, but I accepted.

On the day I cheated a little. Instead of starting at 8 am from Bologna, the hour shown on my pass, I started at five. I arrived in Osimo at about 11 am. and saw Antonia for half an hour in a small cafe. She looked ravishing and was very happy to see me. I did not tell her anything about Rome. There would be plenty of time to tell her when all this was over, I reckoned.

My journey to Rome proved much longer than I had calculated. The mountain roads were badly congested with military traffic and many bridges were still down. It took me more than 12 hours, and when I arrived in Rome I was exhausted. It was nearly midnight when I finally made it to Marita's place.

She received me in the little morning room that I knew so well.

She looked tired and worried. After a few minutes, before I had time to say anything of consequence, she gave me a strange look: "You have come to break off our understanding," she said. When, I gasped, in search of words, she continued, "You see, a woman can feel these things. I could see it in your eyes the moment you came in." She seemed calm, and spoke with total self-control. "Presumably, you have met somebody else and fallen in love with her. So you have concluded that you never loved me – anyway ..." She tailed off, smiling a sad little smile.

Yes, I admitted unhappily, this was exactly what had happened. I was desperately sorry , I said, but it had all come as a great surprise to me, too. Under the circumstances, I felt, it had to be cleared up between us. Hence the untimely visit. I had come as soon as I could.

"Oh, I always knew that, for you, it was different to what it was for me. I loved you from the moment I saw you. As for you, who knows? You may have thought that after some time, you might learn to love me, but you were never quite sure, were you? You see," she looked at me again, and smiled the strange, painful little smile, that I had never seen until that night, "you see, I was fully prepared for our marriage to be a 'civilised arrangement', as so frequently occurs in Italy. You would have had your own life and your freedom, provided that you only maintained certain basic rules of discretion. Very much like the marriage of my parents, you know ..."

This was unbelievable. Could she really be saying such cynical things, Marita, who was not yet twenty? Immediately, sensing my surprise, she added, "I am afraid this probably shocks you, but in Italy girls are prepared for the realities of life at an early age."

I was confused. Confused and horrified. I had been preparing myself for this conversation for many days, of course, but had never anticipated anything like this. It seemed as if I was facing a 'scheming' woman, not an innocent girl. All this was truly shocking to my ears. I had better say what I had come here to say, see her mother and go, I said to myself.

So I told her what I had planned to tell her. She listened patiently, but when I came to the bit that I wanted to see her parents, she surprised me again. This, she said, was impossible, she would not allow it. The whole thing was between us and concerned nobody else. Could she explain why not, I asked, surely her parents had the right to know? To this she would not reply directly. She kept repeating what she had said before, assuring me that she would do it in her own time and in her own way. Certainly not now, though. I could not agree. I insisted that, as ours was an understanding which was made with the knowledge of her parents, it was only proper that I should tell them myself. She kept refusing, with surprising determination.

In the end I threatened to ask the servants to call her mother. She would have to see me. Marita changed her tack. She started pleading with me: why was I making things harder for her? she asked. I had come here to be released from whatever there was between us. She released me now. What else did I need? She released me, as she was the only person who could do it. It was her life, it was her right, nobody else's.

My arguments that parents had their rights too, fell on deaf ears. Not in this case, she said. It might have applied ,perhaps, if ours had been an official engagement, but no such engagement existed between us. She promised me that she would do it 'nicely' – but she had to do it in her own way. Could I not see that she was right, could I not give her this last chance of saving her face? I had, after all, someone new in my life, she had no-one any more... What had she done to me to deserve this additional torment? So it went on and on.

It was getting late, desperately late. We were getting nowhere. She was always at least one jump ahead of me. I felt defeated, lost and desperately tired. The idea of escaping all this was becoming irresistible.

My eyes felt like lead, her voice was ringing in my ears, but her words did not seem to mean anything to me any more.

I had to go. With difficulty, I got up. She looked anxious. Was I leaving? she asked. Yes, I replied, I had to drive all the way to Bologna to report back to my regiment by the morning. She looked at her watch. It was morning already, she observed. I forced a smile. I kissed her on the forehead, as one kisses children, and staggered out.

I had lost my argument, but gained my freedom. She had won her argument but gained nothing . There could be no winners in this sort of contest, could there?

\* \* \*

When I arrived at Bologna the following morning, I found, that the Regiment had already moved. They were on their way South-West and – I was told – if I hurried I could catch them easily. I decided, that I wasn't going to hurry anywhere. I located a nice little inn – and slept for 15 hours. No-one was going to miss me now, I concluded. I had a perfect alibi.

The memories of Rome kept returning. I couldn't shake them off. Even the thought of seeing Antonia did not seem so tempting any more. I kept remembering Marita's face and everything she had said during that ghastly visit.

Several weeks passed. The Regiment transferred back to Osimo. Happily, we were back in this charming little town. I returned to my old billet, with the Gianninis. I started seeing Antonia daily. Memories of Rome, whilst still there, gradually, began to fade away.

Some time in June or maybe even at the beginning of July two letters arrived for me. They were both from Rome. The first I opened was from the Carpathian Captain. He was writing in confidence, he said. He wanted me to know that he had seen the Contessa recently. She was, apparently, annoyed with me. She had a feeling that I was trying to break off my engagement with Marita and that I was doing it in an insensitive manner, which she had found surprising, since she had always taken me for a gentleman. He advised that I should come to Rome immediately and "sort it all out". He was sure it was a misunderstanding and that all would be well in the end. He concluded by placing himself at my disposal if I needed any help.

The second letter was from the Contessa. She had noticed, she said, for some time a change in her daughter. Marita looked sad and tired. When asked for reasons of her strange behaviour she had, at first, refused to answer, but "a mother's intuition" made the Contessa convinced that it had something to do with me. So, the other day, after some probing, Marita had admitted that there were problems between me and her. The Contessa was sure that it was just a "lovers' tiff", nothing serious and that with her help things could be resolved without difficulty. Could I come to Rome and see her, before I saw Marita? Marita's happiness was far too precious to the Contessa to be left in the hands of someone so young and innocent. The Contessa was awaiting my arrival with great impatience. She had always liked me, she said, and was sure she could trust me. She was equally sure that I knew I could trust her unreservedly.

I was not sure. Both these letters seemed to indicate that Marita had not done what she had assured me she would. She had not told her parents anything. It was the Contessa who had taken the initiative. She said she had had to do some probing, but what had it produced? Or, perhaps, Marita had told her after all. Perhaps it was the Contessa who was playing her little games. The bit in her letter where she asked me to see her first sounded suspiciously like that. How could I tell? For several days I struggled with these and other questions. I could not sleep.

A week or so later, the Colonel called me. He was just back from a meeting with General Anders, our Corps Commander, he said. The General had told him that the Polish Ambassador to the Vatican had come to see him about me. The Contessa was wheeling out her 'big guns' via her Vatican connections. The matter was getting "politically embarrassing". The Colonel did not want to influence me in any way, as it was clearly my personal affair, but if I could sort it out without a scandal he would be very pleased. This time he offered me a week's leave.

Rapidly and no doubt unreasonably, a sinister picture was beginning to build in my mind. It all looked like a conspiracy: They were after me, they wanted to force me into a marriage against my will. "They" meaning the Contessa, for to me she appeared as the principal villain in this Renaissance plot. It seemed that she was some sort of Lucrezia Borgia, who manipulated everybody: Marita, the Carpathian Captain, the Vatican and even General Anders. The fact that Marita's mind had been poisoned by her mother's 'realistic' visions of a 'civilised' marriage was the best proof of her perfidious ways. The Captain was just a messenger, a tool of the Contessa's. Even the Papal Curia appeared to be working under her influence. Sinister, sinister ... that's what it seemed to me the more I thought about it.

So what could I do to protect myself against this nightmare? Just ignore it – that was my only weapon. Not to see anybody, not to write to anybody, and above all not to go to Rome. Just sit tight and wait. Nobody could make me marry against my will, not even General Anders. He could send me to my death, if he wanted, in my military capacity, but to order me to marry – certainly not!

Having found this simplistic formula I stuck to it. I refused to reply to letters, I refused to accept leave, and I did not confide in anybody, for fear of being persuaded otherwise. Even Antonia didn't know of my problems.

But her mere presence was good for me. Unknowingly she was my best tonic. I knew she did not expect me to marry her. On the contrary, I discovered that the reason for not being invited into her home was just that her parents did not want to acknowledge my very existence. My presence in their house could, they believed, place me in the role of a potential suitor for their daughter's hand.

Whilst slightly pompous and antiquated, this suited me fine. Marriage was not on my agenda. Of course, I knew that as far as 'eligibility' was concerned I was absolutely nowhere. This was what I had been trying to tell the Contessa back in Rome and what she had refused to recognise. "Long live the middle classes," I concluded. They seemed to have more sense than the Roman aristocracy.

Garrison life, after the end of hostilities, was relaxed and peaceful. I had a lot of free time. The afternoons could be spent in the company of Antonia. We organised charming little picnics with her and her friends or went to the local cinema. The summer was glorious on the Adriatic coast and we made the best of it. Occasionally, my fellow officers and I were invited to delightful parties, held in the houses of the local nobility. As Antonia did not frequent those circles, she was sometimes a little annoyed but never seriously. Life, on the whole, was very pleasant.

I received two more letters from the Captain, still advising me to come to Rome and talk to the Contessa, but even he seemed to suspect that the Contessa had overplayed her hand. He tried to explain her diplomatic manoeuvres via the Vatican as "a mother's worry for her daughter's happiness."

A few more weeks passed – and my passive resistance seemed to be producing the desired effect. No-one was writing to me any more.

One evening, in the mess, the Colonel called me over. He said that "General Uncle" wanted to see me.

"General Uncle" was a code name which we used in my regiment for a real general who happened to be my uncle. He was, in fact, my mother's first cousin. I was very proud to have such an uncle as he was a very glamorous personality. He was very good-looking, young for a general, and enjoyed a reputation for being a brave and successful commander. It was he who had been responsible for the final manoeuvre which encircled Bologna and finished off the Wehrmacht on our sector of the front. Ever since I had joined the army, in Soviet Russia, I had made a point of seeing him at least a few times a year and he was always very kind to me. This invitation was, therefore, not entirely unexpected.

I was told to report to the General's HQ at 9 am the following morning. When I arrived I was shown straight in by his ADC, who was a good friend of mine. No time even to catch up on the latest gossip. I went in and stood to attention, awaiting the General's signal. "Uncle General" was sitting behind a very simple table signing some papers. He looked up and smiled his charismatic smile.

My goodness, he was a handsome man, I noted silently. The General got up to greet me. His movements were swift and youthful. Energetically, he extended his right hand to me. We shook hands. I watched his left arm swing limply, as if independent from his body. I knew this to be the consequence of an old war wound, which, gave him a unique, rather elegant, mannerism. His personality was enhanced by this old injury. "As a true showman," I thought, "even his defects work for him." He asked me to sit down.

We spoke about the recent campaign and the General asked for details of my role in it. He spoke in short, rather clipped, sentences. He had a knack of making everything sound simple and easy. Unlike the other high-ranking officers I knew, with him everything appeared logical. Well, nearly everything, as from time to time he was known to produce one of his, rather famous, metaphors which frequently surprised all concerned. They were meant to illustrate his point, but very often produced the opposite effect. When asked for clarification, the General would smile and say : "Work it out for yourself."

"Well, what is it I hear about your exploits in Rome?" he asked suddenly. I felt my face turning red. A deep breath did not seem to help much, so while I struggled, trying to control my circulation, the General went on, "You are aware, no doubt, that Roman society is buzzing with comment regarding your involvement with one of their debutantes. Not very flattering comment, from what I could gather. Would you care to give me your version of the story?"

I told him, as briefly, as I could, the bare facts. He asked a few questions. They were good, fair questions. "Do I take it that you have no intention of marrying this young lady?" he asked. "No," I replied, "I will not marry her."

"There are two kinds of young women," said the General, with a vague smile. The kind you marry and the kind you have fun with. They are easily recognisable. Unmistakable, if you like. The kind you marry, you must not have anything to do with, unless you intend to marry her. The other kind are much safer. You can get to know them better, you can be friends with them, or whatever else you may both decide. But never, on any account, have anything to do with the young lady of the 'marrying sort' – unless you do intend to marry her. Simple, isn't it?"

"Couldn't be simpler," I agreed. I said that I now understood that this was the error I had committed at the very beginning, when I thought, that I could be friends with Marita. Obviously I could not. I saw it now, I wished I could have seen it earlier.

"Your case is a bit, like giving a razor blade to a monkey," continued the General with a broad smile. Immediately, I recognised this to be one of his famous metaphors, so I said, "And – I suppose – I will have to work this one out for myself..." "Quite so, quite so," replied the General.

"Still, I wouldn't worry about it too much, if I were you. The main question is to decide who is responsible for the result: the monkey or the person who gives it the razor-blade ..." He looked at me keenly, as if to make sure that I was with him. I listened attentively. "So – try to be less of a monkey next time round. A first error can be put down to inexperience, a second one, invariably to stupidity".

The General got up. The interview was at an end. I snapped to attention.

The General came round the desk again. We shook hands, I turned about and left the room. Andrew, his ADC, was on the telephone, so I waved to him and left the building. For the first time in months, I felt a little less unhappy.

# Chapter 18

# MIRACLES TAKE A LITTLE LONGER

I can't think of anyone, even among the most moderately successful businessmen, who at the outset of their careers, were less qualified for their trade than I was. I seemed positively hopeless. In everyone's view I did not possess any of the attributes which are popularly considered essential for this pursuit: I was not good at figures, was rather shy, did not have the cunning, hard-nosed arrogance considered indispensable to make a successful 'man of affairs' and above all I did not like bargaining. I either bought things at the asking price or left them alone. Haggling was foreign to my nature. My colleagues always laughed at me: "Karol would never make any money at business, he is far too soft," they would say. Quite sincerely, I shared that view.

Then, towards the end of our stay in Italy, when it became clear that we would be sent to England and probably never return to Poland, I began to wonder what I would do when, eventually, the time came to leave the army. Going to university, at the age of 25 seemed most unattractive. I regarded myself as past that stage. I could not think of having to go back to books and endless exams. Not after all I had been through. Then, a couple of unrelated events took place which, in a strange way, made me think the unthinkable.

The first seed was sown in my mind by an amateur fortune-teller. Her name was Maria Grazia Gallo, the daughter of an Italian nobleman. Despite fairly reduced circumstances, the Gallos maintained a grand lifestyle and lived in a palatial residence, in the middle of Osimo. Maria Grazia was a sophisticated young woman, more attractive than pretty, possessed of fairly liberal ideas. I liked her and she liked me and we were good friends. Leading a fairly unrestricted life she would sometimes drop into our mess for a drink or a game of cards, something which would be unthinkable among the more conventional middle-class girls.

One afternoon, when I came into the mess, I saw Maria Grazia at the card table. On closer inspection I discovered that she was not playing cards but fortune-telling. A group of officers were standing around her, laughing and joking.

"Oh – Karol, you are just in time," she said, when she saw me, "Come over and let me read your fortune for you. I feel in particularly good form this afternoon."

"No thank you," I said, "I am not interested. I don't want to know what awaits me. I would rather leave it that way, if you don't mind."

"Oh, what a spoilsport you can be," she said in mock reproach. "Never mind. I will do it anyway, whether you like it or not. What do you say?" she turned to my colleagues for support. They all agreed and she started to shuffle a deck of cards.

I was watching from a distance. I really didn't want to know. I have an instinctive fear of tampering with the occult. There was nowhere for me to hide, though. Like it or not I had to hear everything. She began to lay the cards on the table. I heard her making little exclamations, as she went along, little cries of, "Oh... Ah... I say," which, I assumed, were meant to enhance our curiosity. From time to time she would look up, as if to make sure that I was still there.

"So what have we got here?" she began in an artificially mysterious voice. "Let us see... You will be married within the next two or three years. But not to your current girl-friend, someone else, someone you knew a long time ago. It will be a happy marriage, but you will have no children. Brown is her colour, she likes to wear brown... You will not return to Poland. You will live abroad... I see that you will be involved with money, lots of money, some sort of business, perhaps, or banking, or something like that. Money and a lot of travel... But the beginnings will be very hard. To start with you will be poor. But not unhappy. On the contrary, yours is a happy picture that I see here."

As she was talking , without wanting to, I started drifting nearer and nearer. She swept the cards off the table and looked up: "I didn't know you had financial inclinations," she said with a smile. "Neither did I," I replied, "and this, regrettably, undermines your credibility as a fortune-teller."

"I can only say what's in the cards," she replied. "In your case it seems very strong. I feel they are telling me the truth and, usually, the more improbable it sounds, the truer it proves to be. Miracles do happen, but often they take a little while."

"I can't imagine myself as a businessman, I have no flair for it, everyone knows that," I insisted. "Oh yes you do. And what's more it is your destiny. Don't fight destiny. It is stronger than you," she sounded unusually serious.

My 'destiny' sent me a further signal a few weeks later, this time in a more practical way. I was given a chance to participate in a business deal and thus, for the first time, get the feel of a real commercial transaction. Together with another officer, I was sent to Milan to negotiate the purchase of a quantity of cloth on behalf of the Regiment.

We were told to contact a White Russian businessman, of Armenian descent, well established in the textile trade in Milan, who was to facilitate the operation. It proved to be the simplest transaction imaginable, requiring from us the minimum amount of skill, but it contained several elements of a typical business deal. The gentleman in question, a Mr. Avaniesoff, was a seasoned businessman who enjoyed his work and did not seem to be put off by the fact that he was dealing with two complete novices. Wisely, he insisted on having everything from us in writing.

This, at first, proved a little awkward, as we did not know the terminology. Fortunately, we had in front of us his written quotation and we used it as a model for our side of the correspondence. He also insisted that, having selected the material, we should give him a written order, signed either by the Colonel or by the Regimental Quartermaster. I felt rather peeved at this apparent lack of trust, but he explained that this was a perfectly normal and correct way of conducting business. In the end we compromised and he accepted a telegram from our Adjutant, confirming that we were authorised to complete the purchase and that the money would be transmitted telegraphically within 7 days. While we were awaiting this communication we were able to sample true Armenian hospitality. We had a standing invitation for lunch and dinner at his home. His generosity was overwhelming. We consumed huge quantities of his food and drink, in the company of his wife and daughter, at his lavishly furnished apartment.

When the required confirmation arrived and the deal was completed I experienced, for the first time in my life, the thrill of a successful deal. I started to think that perhaps, after all, this could be something I would enjoy doing. In a very simplified form I had, I thought, the foretaste of the life of a businessman.

\* \* \*

It took only three years for the 'matrimonial' part of Maria Grazia's prophesy to materialise. In November 1948, in fact, I married a girl whom I had known well since childhood. The marriage proved to be a happy one; we never had any children and we lived in England. So everything, thus far, proved exactly as she had foretold. Even the detail of my wife's favourite colour proved to be true. Among the very few dresses which she then possessed, two were decidedly brown.

As far as my business career was concerned, the prophesy proved rather slower in coming true. It took many years before I could feel that I was making any headway, but then, when I finally discovered my 'winning formula' things began to develop at a considerably livelier pace.

But we must get back to the beginning, to the dark, distant days of post-war austerity, of rationing, of ruins. England, the victorious Ally, looked in comparison with the defeated Italy like a very poor relation. London was devastated. Only then did I realise at what cost victory had been won.

In Italy a Pole felt like a victorious Ally, like a conquering hero; In England, like a gatecrasher or, at best, a poor relation. We felt we were silently blamed for the painful consequences of the war. "After all," we would be told, "It was to defend Poland that we went to war." By innuendo most of the misery which had ensued was silently laid at our door. Arguments to the contrary usually fell on deaf ears. Everybody remembered how the war had started. It was difficult for the average person to comprehend why we refused to go home. Poland was now rid of the Germans, they would say. The fact that it now found itself under the Soviets instead was not considered an impediment. Russia was an ally and Uncle Joe, as Stalin was referred to in the popular press, had after all helped to beat Jerry, so he couldn't be so bad. There was an other element, too, an element which, reportedly, was not present while the fighting lasted and which crept slowly onto the English scene. The 'man in the street' had become distinctly xenophobic. Everything 'foreign' was suspect, foreign ex-allies included. The moment one opened one's mouth and uttered a few words with a foreign accent, a hitherto friendly individual would turn icily indifferent. This climate persisted, more or less, until the mass influx of the black and Indian immigrants years later, when we were 'upgraded' somewhat in our hosts' estimation.

It would be unfair, however, to suggest that my initial lack of success was solely caused by the British reluctance to associate with a Pole.

The main reason remained, clearly, with me. I was completely unprepared for what I was trying to do. My contacts were few and those I had were of the wrong kind. I knew one or two Englishmen from the Army, but they belonged to the upper classes. As a result, I soon discovered, they were more of a liability than an asset. They did not know anybody who could help, as they simply did not associate with 'that kind of person'. Their lifestyle was also unsuitable for me. To them, unless one had an income of £2,000 a year, one might as well shoot oneself. They offered me friendly loans but nothing that could help me in improving my ability to earn enough to repay them.

My financial reserves were minimal. I received a total demobilisation gratuity of £110 as a 'golden handshake' on leaving the forces, most of which I spent with Messrs. Hobson Bros. of Cork Street, bespoke tailors, investing in three good suits, which I firmly believed would help me in projecting the right image in the lofty boardrooms of the City of London. While the visual result was pleasing, the practical effect was negligible, as there was no way for me to penetrate these bastions of finance and commerce. I was reduced to writing an innumerable number of letters using mostly Kelly's Directory for guidance.

Predictably, I received no replies. The only invitations I did receive were to innumerable cocktail parties. I was not important enough to rank for a dinner invitation , so I practically lived on Cashew nuts, which, as I soon established, were in themselves a fairly good source of nourishment.

From my upper-class English friends I soon learned that, if one lived in London, one had to have a 'good address', to command the sort of credibility that I was after. With my extremely meagre resources this was pretty well impossible. By sheer coincidence, however, even this I managed to solve. I discovered that an aunt of mine lived in an up-market boarding house in Hans Road, SW1. It was she who told me that her landlady, a Miss Sewell, a paragon of urban respectability, had a tiny cubby-hole, in her attic, which she might consider letting to me if I played my cards right, for 30 shillings a week. My aunt engineered an introduction and I managed to impress Miss Sewell sufficiently to become her tenant at that desirable address.

So, I was wearing the right sort of clothes, I lived at a good address, I even possessed a battered old Underwood typewriter and a business accommodation address to which my correspondence could be sent. There was, regrettably, very little correspondence, not of the right kind, anyway.

I was getting tired of cashew nuts and the sight of the red and gold covers of Kelly's Directory filled me with aversion.

Then one day I received a letter. A very nice letter, written in remarkably friendly terms. It referred to my agency for Italian accordions and suggested a meeting at their offices. The company's name was Panex (London) Ltd., Import and Export Merchants, of 199, Harrow Road. The letter was signed by a director named V. Duschnitz and the list of directors consisted of three names: G.N. Greenfield, F.W. Duschnitz (Austrian) and V. Duschnitz (Austrian). Company Law in those days required the nationality of each non-British director to be displayed on the notepaper.

I was a little put off by the address. Harrow Road did not strike me as the most desirable location for the headquarters of a successful enterprise, but as this was my only positive reply to date, I decided to explore.

Now, I should perhaps explain about the accordions. Before leaving Italy I had secured, though friends, the sole agency for the British Isles of a firm called Serenelli of Castelfidardo, manufacturers of piano accordions. Italians, being classified as an enemy nation, had no possibility of travelling to England. The idea was that as I was going to England I might help them in establishing an export market there. That was the theory. In practice, however, all major importers, most of whom resided in Charing Cross Road, London, were only interested in Horner accordions, a famous German product, and Serenelli offered no interest to them at all.

On the appointed day I arrived at 199, Harrow Road, well before my interview. It was just as well that I had plenty of time in hand as I found it very difficult to locate the premises in question. A detailed search and some pretty smart detective work led me to the back of a garage, near a bombed site, where I located, discreetly displayed on the door "Panex (London) Ltd – Main

Office – Please ring and enter." My first inclination was to cut and run, but, on reflection I decided to obey the instruction. I rang and entered.

I was confronted by a typewriter, a telephone and a rather flimsy card table, behind which sat a rather handsome middle-aged woman, who was typing furiously. She smiled and got up. "You must be Mr. Czosnowski, you are very punctual, that's good. I am Vera Duschnitz. Please excuse the mess. We are about to move to a more suitable location. I hope you are not put off by all this." I was invited to sit down and offered a cup of tea.

Mrs. Duschnitz had a pleasant personality and a friendly manner. She spoke easily in what appeared, to me, very good English and explained, in some detail, what they were trying to do. The firm had been founded only a few months previously by a certain Gordon Greenfield, who was part-owner of a small chain of laundry shops. He was in her words "110 per cent English – if you know what I mean," but was not interested in this sort of business. His real interest was in cars. "He drives like a maniac," she said with admiration.

He was the son of a successful businessman and was not particularly given to hard work. ("All the donkey work rests with me – if you know what I mean"...)

Her husband was also a director, but had a "dicky heart" so the "buck stops here," and she put on a good imitation of president Truman's American voice. She carried on like this for quite some time. I learned that her husband was Jewish, while she was not. They had escaped from Austria in 1938, and were due to receive their naturalisation papers any day now, whereupon they would be known as Mr. and Mrs. Dee ("Very English, don't you think?") and that in itself should make business very much easier – "Us being English – if you follow my drift." I didn't, but let her get on with it.

"All these letters, you can see here, are to our agents abroad," she continued. "We have more than fifty, and each day I have 20 or more letters to write. They come from all the Colonies and they are mostly looking for English piece goods. At a penny a yard profit, not bad, don't you think?"

I didn't know what 'piece goods' were, but I gathered that she was referring to some sort of textiles. Accordions, so far, had not been mentioned. So I waited, somewhat confused.

After an hour or so a hazy picture started to emerge. Since its formation, some months ago, Panex had not as yet completed a single transaction, but several were in the pipeline. The company was being financed by Gordon Greenfield, who paid the Duschnitzes a small retainer. Vera, as she asked me to call her, suggested that I might like to come and work with them on similar terms, receiving say £3 per week plus commission on deals completed, use their office and telephone and visit clients when required. It did not matter if I dealt in accordions, piece goods, or any other products, provided there was a profit in it. I asked for some time to think it over. She felt that the following day should be plenty and on this we parted company.

* * *

The next morning I returned to Harrow Road. After consider-able meditation, and very little sleep, I had decided to override my doubts and accept the offer, but for a trial period only. I thought that one month would give me a chance to assess the genuineness of this strange set-up. When I arrived, Gordon Greenfield was sitting in the visitor's chair. After formal intro-ductions there was a brief moment of confusion as there seemed no way of accommodating a third person. A third chair, even when available, could not be placed anywhere, for lack of floor space. There were files everywhere, principally on the floor. The problem was solved when Greenfield offered me his chair and he himself elected to sit on the window sill. Despite my objections, this formation was maintained for the duration of the meeting.

I took a good look at Greenfield. In his late thirties, on the lower side of medium height, with a fleshy, but young-looking face and surprisingly bushy eyebrows, he gave me a neutral impression. I could not make up my mind if I liked him or not. His dark brown, well-groomed hair gave him an appearance of neat-ness, while his dark eyes looked tired and indecisive from behind massive, black-framed glasses. "Not someone I would like to have with me in my tank, in action," I thought, rather unkindly.

We discussed our proposed co-operation. The formula I now submitted, the product of that one sleepless night, proved so simple and easy to administer that, in the years to come, I was to make many similar arrangements with other people when, even-tually, I took charge of the business. In its substance it consisted of a 75%/25% division of the gross profit, Panex taking the lion's share, in return for paying all normal expenses such as telephones, postage and other overheads and also paying me £3 per week on account of commission.

Without a word the package was accepted, including my request for a trial. period. I was not sure if I should be pleased or not, but both Gordon and Vera welcomed me 'on the team' with great enthusiasm. Gordon even offered me a lift home in his motor car, which was, he announced proudly, a Talbot drop-head. As I had never heard of the make and did not appear to be sufficiently impressed, he explained to me the proud history of this marque. The journey to Hans Road proved a hair-raising experience. Vera was right; he did drive like a maniac. Fortunately there was very little traffic so we did not hit any other vehicles, but instead missed many objects by the narrowest of margins. I climbed out of the Talbot drop-head in front of Harrods a happy man, grateful to the Almighty that having spared my life through the dangers of the Taiga and the fire-power of the Third Reich, He had delivered me safely to Miss Sewell's boarding house, shaken but otherwise unharmed. Gordon beamed at me from behind his steering wheel: "Driving is my main hobby. I feel that one should do things well, or not at all," he explained. "Not at all, as far as I was concerned," I thought to myself, still breathing heavily.

\* \* \*

Within five weeks of my arrival at Harrow Road I completed my first deal. It wasn't much, but it was something. While Vera was still struggling with her first order for 'piece goods', I earned my first £5.10s profit. The goods involved were not accordions, however, nor piece goods, but watches. Yes, watches. It all started something like this: I had, all my life, had a distinct aversion to handling textiles. I was looking one day through an Italian trade paper which Serenelli used to send me from time to time.

One of the advertisements, I found, was for "Italian Watches for Export, made by Swiss Technicians, in Como, Italy." Now this could be something, I thought. Swiss watches were only available against payment in hard currency, and consequently strictly rationed and available only through established channels. Italian watches, made to Swiss standards, would not be subject to the same restrictions and could presumably be purchased freely. On the spur of the moment I telephoned the firm in Como.

Vera was rather shocked by this reckless move. Telephoning Italy in answer to an advertisement, she said , seemed rather extravagant, to say the least. As I spoke fluent Italian, and announced proudly that I was calling from London, I was immediately connected with the boss, a Signor Voigt. His name indicated Swiss ancestry, which in itself was proof of a Swiss connection.

What I established was that they manufactured cheap watches, maybe not suitable for England, but eminently suitable for the British Colonies. The cheapest model was about 8 shillings and the most expensive, gold-plated, 22 shillings. Even I knew that this was a bargain. At the end of my call Signor Voigt promised to send me his catalogue and complete price list, and a long and fruitful co-operation was born.

Our markets were mostly in West Africa. I decided to price the cheapest model at 10s.6d. plus postage, and devised a method of using a firm called Danzas, in Como, international forwarding agents, to organise the postage, thus ensuring the secrecy of the valuable source of my supplies. This formula worked for several years, until the day when Swiss currency became more plentiful and consequently Swiss watches easier to acquire.

\* \* \*

With my improved financial status, my social life moved up a gear. I made several new friends, this time mainly in the City. They were not of the kind who could help me in my business, as yet, working mostly at Lloyds and on the Stock Exchange, but were a considerable improvement on the younger sons of peers, as they actually worked for their living. I felt more comfortable in their company.

Among them was a young man called Jimmy Glen, a Scot who had spent the war with the Scots Guards, but had had to leave the service as a result of some health problem and had taken a job with a company called British Eastern Merchants, commodity dealers, specialising in Asian markets. An old Etonian, he was my 'guru' on matters of protocol and related problems. He was a great expert on London clubs, and could give me interesting historical facts on each of them.

He also guided me in my choice of socks and ties and what to wear for any given occasion. He was not an intellectual, as one could easily ascertain, but a loyal friend and a 'good sort' in the most ample meaning of the term.

I always made a point of dropping in on him at his smart offices in Threadneedle Street, secretly hoping that one day I might also qualify for such grand surroundings. His secretary, a Miss Oliver, always gave me a cup of coffee and from time to time I would go out with Jimmy for a drink and a sandwich to one of the charming City pubs. Jimmy, being Scottish, was careful with money and although, by my standards he was rich, earning over £500 a year, he considered himself on the poor side.

"You must invite me to your offices one day," he would say. "Nothing as grand as yours," I said truthfully, knowing full well that I would never subject him to such a ghastly experience. He didn't even know where my office was, so I felt secure behind the smoke-screen of secrecy.

But no secret can ever remain a secret for long. Jimmy must have seen my visiting card somewhere and the unthinkable happened. As he was seeing an Eastern potentate who was residing in the Cumberland Hotel (a hostelry, which Jimmy preferred to avoid, as it was not "his sort of hotel") he decided to drop in on me at my place for a coffee and a chat. I was not there at the time.

As luck would have it, while staggering in a state of shock in the area of 199, Harrow Road, convinced that he was mistaken, he happened to bump into Vera, who was out in the street to buy cigarettes. He chose to ask her if she could direct him to the headquarters of Panex and received an enthusiastic confirmation that he should follow her and she would guide him personally, as she was a director of that famous institution.

Jimmy was still convinced that it was the wrong Panex, that it could not possibly be me, but Vera dispelled his doubts. "Of course, Karol," she exclaimed, "a most charming and gifted young man. Do I know him? you ask. Of course, he is like a son to me. I taught him everything he knows." She dragged Jimmy into the office, where the usual artistic disorder reigned, sat him down and force-fed him a cup of tea, despite his protestations that he did not want any. I did not know anything about this until much later, of course.

I was visiting a client, that afternoon, near Liverpool Street. The meeting ended late and rather than get into the evening crush on the tube, I decided to have a bite to eat in a pub in Threadneedle Street. Just as I was about to demolish my cheese and pickle sandwich, Jimmy walked in with another man whom I didn't know. When our eyes met I made a discreet little gesture of recognition and instead of the usual friendly smile Jimmy turned pale, as if he had seen a ghost.

He excused himself from his companion and approached me with a most extraordinary expression on his handsome face. He grabbed me by the elbow, almost brutally, and hissed, "Wait for me, will you, I must talk to you..." These ominous words were accompanied by an even more tragic face. I could not make it out. What could have happened? I watched him from where I stood while he was trying to finish his conversation, giving me from time to time an anxious look, as if to make sure that I would not vanish. Most unlike Jimmy, I thought now anticipating the worst, , something terrible must have happened.

"Oh Karol, Oh Karol," he kept on repeating when he finally joined me. "Oh Karol, how dreadful, how horrible, you poor, poor man. You don't have to pretend any more, I know everything, oh how dreadful... I am so sorry."

I looked at him with total dismay. "Jimmy, for Pete's sake calm down and tell me what is bothering you, what has happened?" "I am all right," cried Jimmy, "it is you, you fool, why didn't you tell me? Anything would be better than this. I know everything. This dreadful woman told me your secret, your ghastly secret. Why didn't you confide in me, why didn't you trust me? Am I not your friend?"

At long last I extracted the whole story. Now that he knew, I felt relieved. I had never enjoyed concealing the truth, I just wanted to spare Jimmy the obvious discomfort of knowing that I was working in such an inelegant environment. Now I was sure he would understand. But he didn't. To him it seemed a sin, a betrayal of the most sacred values, without which life had no meaning. A gentleman should die, rather than work with such people in such conditions.

What he could not understand was that I seemed perfectly relaxed about it all and that I was not trying to escape this 'fate worse than death'. My argument that a gentleman remained a gentleman irrespective of where he found himself and with whom he associated, provided he behaved honourably, did not meet with any understanding with him. "How can you behave honourably in those conditions, dealing with that kind of person, Karol, I ask you, how?"

We argued like this until closing time, by which stage Jimmy was fairly drunk and I took him home, to his modest, but tasteful single-bedroom flat in Chelsea.

Things never returned to where they had been before his shocking discovery. Even years later, when I was safely established in my elegant offices in Bruton Street and we saw each other in elegant places, the old Jimmy never returned. Something had died in him that fateful afternoon when he was being entertained in the Harrow Road by Vera Duschnitz.

\* \* \*

In the spring of 1948 we moved to new offices at 42, Bolsover Street, W1, near Great Portland Street tube station. The place was not palatial, but represented a considerable improvement over our previous domain in the Harrow Road and, briefly, in Westbourne Grove, which we had just vacated. The whole block at Harrow Road having been condemned by the War Damage Department, we moved in a hurry to the Duschnitz flat in Westbourne Grove, where conditions were even worse than before. Apart from having to suffer from lack of space we also had to inhale the smells of Vera's cooking, which was rich in garlic ("on account of Fred's heart problem – if you know what I mean") and the sight of an impressive array of garments, mostly rather personal, of Vera's and Fred's, strung on lines in truly unexpected places. Despite being in the basement of the most humble of buildings, number 42, Bolsover Street was, in comparison, sheer heaven. To add to my delight I managed to secure a whole room to myself, where I installed a heavy mahogany desk, newly acquired for 30 shillings at a nearby junk shop, my personal Olivetti typewriter and all my files.

I delighted in this glorious solitude, and work became a real pleasure.

In fact work and pleasure seemed one and the same thing to me. When I was asked, Was this work or pleasure? I was tempted to reply that, surely, there was no difference.

We occupied a space of some 700 square feet which was divided into three rooms. Gordon and Vera sat in one, Miss Walton, the new secretary and Fred in the next and I in the third. I was by now the chief source of the firm's income and enjoyed considerable independence. Watches were selling well and each one of them now bore the brand of "Panex", boldly visible on its dial.

1948 saw another important milestone in my life, as towards the end of it I got married. I bumped into Marysia Heydel by chance in the lobby of a Polish hotel in the Cromwell Road, where I had spent the previous night while my room at Miss Sewell's was being repainted. She had just arrived in London from the Middle East and had checked into the hotel for one night, before taking on a new job in Surrey, as nanny to some Polish Naval Commander's children. We recognised each other instantly, since I had seen her in the spring of 1944, in Jerusalem, just before being shipped to Italy. We had known each other, of course, as children and later had even attended the same dancing classes together.

I invited her to dinner to the nearest Lyons Corner House and we spent a pleasant evening together, reminiscing about Poland and the war. I lost sight of her for a while after this as she was working in Chiddingfold, on the borders of Surrey and West Sussex, and seldom came to London.

She did not enjoy being a nanny and soon returned to London having found a good job at Hachettes, the French book shop, where her command of foreign languages was an asset.

From then on I saw a lot of her. She liked walking, in those days, and we walked together for hours, occasionally stopping for a cup of tea and a sandwich at some convenient spot. She was a total contrast with my Italian girl friends. I did not have to explain anything to her, she always knew what I meant. One word would be enough, or even just a smile. It was like finding oneself back in an old familiar, welcoming place, having been previously lost in the wilderness. She looked at me with her blue-green, very expressive eyes, and her glance conveyed peace and tranquillity, which I needed desperately.

For the whole summer we just walked and talked. We never spoke of our feelings for each other and she never displayed, even remotely, that well-known anxiety which some young women suffer from, concerning the nature of a young man's 'intentions'. I used to sing for her a lot, which she liked.

One evening, I remember, we were sitting on a bench in Hyde Park, and I was humming a tune from "Annie Get Your Gun," a popular musical just then. There was one song in particular that she liked. Frank Sinatra, later made it his own, called "The girl that I marry". While I sang it for her I observed that she looked incredibly gorgeous. She was adorable, so I kissed her, for the first time ever. She responded beautifully. We both knew that a bond was born just then, a bond which was to last for the rest of our lives.

I made no proposal and received no acceptance, we both just knew. She looked at me in her special way. "Oh! I think you are wonderful," she said in a slightly husky voice. "You are not so bad yourself," I replied, rather unromantically. She looked surprised, just for a split second. Then she squeezed my arm affectionately and said in English, "And you are terrible naughty, as well." She pronounced the word 'naughty' like 'notty' and from then on she kept referring to me as Notty.

Our wedding took place on 6th November 1948 at the Brompton Oratory, in Kensington. Neither her parents nor mine could attend, for many reasons, including a total lack of money. I was going through a rather lean patch financially just then, having spent all my reserves on furnishing my new office, so we had a grand total of £3.10s.0d. between us. There was no reception, of course and we all just had a cup of tea and a sandwich at Marysia's aunt's place, and thus embarked on our long married life together, which was to last for over 48 years. As Maria Grazia had predicted, back in Osimo, ours was a happy union, purpose-made in heaven.

\* \* \*

I now started selling to London confirming houses. A confirming house, in those days, was the by-product of the Colonial system. All countries which belonged to the Sterling Area, mostly those that were part of the British Empire, had great advantages, in duty and taxes, when making any purchases in England. As they themselves did not have much money, they would usually place their orders through British confirming houses, located either in London, Manchester or other major industrial and commercial centres.

Thus a small shopkeeper, say in Nairobi, would go to the representative of a British confirming house there and enquire for prices of cotton materials or machinery or, in my case, watches. This would eventually result in an order which the London confirming house would place with me, assuring me that payment would be made by them within 7 days after dispatch. This was an excellent system, but to use it I had to secure, first, the services of a bank to finance me for the period between paying the Italians and receiving the cash. I simply had no bank willing to undertake such a simple operation. The usual clearing banks, like Barclays, Lloyds and Westminster wouldn't hear of it. They were busy enough handling Mrs. Brown's shopping money and ICI's overdraft. Panex did not qualify.

So I went to work with maximum despatch. I was often invited to cocktail parties at the Italian Embassy, whose Cinzano and cashew nuts I had grown rather fond of, and 'attacked' their commercial counsellor, a decent man whose limited diplomatic skills prevented him from aspiring to any higher appointment, and put him to work. He soon suggested that I should speak to a Mr. Schweizer, the London representative of the Banco di Roma.

He made the appointment for me and I went to see him, in a rather dingy office in the City. Mr. Schweizer, a Swiss with Italian connections, listened to my problem and thought that, whilst his bank could not help as it did not, as yet, have a branch in London, he could possibly introduce me to some merchant banker, who could. His question was what I proposed to pay him for the introduction. I was at a loss as to what to suggest, so I played for time, and pretended that I had an urgent matter to attend to and that, if he didn't mind I would come back within the hour. He agreed. I was not good at figures, it will be remembered, and there were no pocket calculators in those days, so it took me the whole hour to figure out, in longhand so to speak, the price for my 'entry ticket' to London banking.

I came to the following conclusion: I proposed a quarter of one percent on the amount of money the bank would lend me over the first three months of our association. My offer was accepted, and that is how my co-operation with Messrs. P.P. Rodocanachi & Co., of 65, London Wall started, which was to be the backbone of my business for at least a dozen subsequent years.

My arrangement with Rodo, as we used to call them, was also based on my formula, this one also the result of several sleepless nights. I am sure there was nothing new there, and presumably such formulae had been used by others before me, but as I was totally without guidance and had no-one to advise me, I had to 're-invent' anew things which were probably used by the ancient Egyptians five thousand years before. My proposal was agreed to and worked like this: I would submit to Rodo a copy of the order and deposit, in cash, 25% of the value of my sale. If they liked the client and the terms of the transaction they would provide the remaining 75% with which to pay my supplier. I was particularly fond, it would appear, of the combination of 25/75 or 75/25, both in my commission arrangements and in my banking.

As a result of my securing the co-operation of Rodo, I was able to take advantage of the services of Confirming Houses, thus enlarging substantially the scope of my business.

* * *

It was a few months later that I concluded my first transaction involving steel.

Steel had always appealed to me, as a product. It sounded good, masculine. To be a steel magnate or even a steel baron, would have suited me well.

I knew vaguely a Pole called Marian Krosnowski, who traded in steel in Belgium. I must have met him at one of the early cocktail parties and we probably exchanged cards. Anyway Krosnowski rang me one day and said that he had heard from one of his friends in the steel world that the Indians were currently looking for large diameter steel pipe, which was generally scarce, but which he could get through his contacts with Cockrill. Could I see if I could find anyone among the London houses who might be interested? He promised to send me full details in the post. (I did not have a Telex, in those days). When I received the details, which I only half understood, I copied them faithfully onto a stencil with my Gestetner copying machine and sent a circular, by penny post, to all those names in the book who sounded remotely connected with India. Among them, I remember distinctly, was the name of Tata Ltd. Now 'tata' in Polish means 'daddy'. I wasn't sure if it had anything to do with India, but I liked the name so I stuck another penny onto a manila envelope and sent it to 'daddy'.

The following day I received a call from the secretary of a

director at Tata, stating that a Mr. Saklatvala would like to see me at their offices at 18, Grosvenor Place at my convenience. She said that 3 pm the next day would suit Mr. Saklatvala, so he would be most obliged if I could make it. The whole thing sounded almost farcical. One had the impression of a Royal command and not an ordinary business appointment.

I mentioned this to Gordon, who was a great expert on India ("Being 110% English – if you know what I mean," to quote Vera's favourite expression). He explained to me that Tata owned half of India's industry, including steel works, textile mills and even aircraft factories, and that the Saklatvalas were members of the Indian aristocracy, of ancient Parsee lineage, closely associated with the Tata family. By now I was convinced that I had taken on something beyond my capabilities, but having agreed to the appointment I decided to keep it, repeating to myself Capt. Rędziejowski's old dictum that "A Polish officer fears no-one but God".

On the morning in question I donned my best Hobson Bros. suit and a tie, personally chosen for me by Jimmy Glen, and at the appropriate hour repaired to Grosvenor Place to face my ordeal. The offices of Tata (which are still there to this day) were appointed in the best of taste. I was received by a beauty queen, discreetly smelling of Chanel No. 5, and was asked to wait in an exquisitely furnished little salon. Very good English hunting prints decorated the walls and the furniture was, unquestionably, genuine Georgian.

Mr. Saklatvala had manners obtainable only through the best English schooling. He was small, but very elegant and spoke excellent English.

We sat in another little salon. I commented on the sporting prints and asked if they were by Henry Alken, to which he said that, yes, they were and that he had a nicer collection upstairs, in his own office, but could not show them to me just now, as there was a delegation from India waiting for him and he was, therefore, rather pressed for time.

After these elegant generalities we got down to business. He said that he would like to buy some tube from us but, as he had not heard of Panex before, he would want to know a little more about my company. I decided to tell him the truth. No point in bluffing it out, I thought. I told him that the company was relatively new, that

255

I had some connections, though friends, in the Belgian steel industry, and that I was confident of my source of supply.

"Judging by your name, you are not English," he said. I told him I was a Pole. "Do you know Prince Radziwill?" he asked. "Which one?" I enquired. "Oh, is there more than one?" he sounded surprised. "Well yes, I can think of a dozen," I replied, "Poland, is well supplied with Princes," I smiled at my own joke. He didn't. Instead he gave me a long, shrewd look.

"We need this tube rather quickly," he continued. "Yes I understand. How soon can you open your letter of credit?* I enquired, "I can't think of any reason why we should not be able to ship within, say, four weeks after we get one." I thought this sounded pretty professional, so I waited confidently for his reply. "Tata would never open a letter of credit," there was a pompous tone in his voice. "Our standing is good, you know. It is recognised as such in every civilised country."

"But I have to open a letter of credit to my suppliers, otherwise they will not take my order," I pleaded. "That's your problem," he said curtly. "What I can promise you is that we shall pay you within 30 days from the date of shipment. Who are your bankers, anyway?" I now felt that this was the end of the interview. My chances of completing this deal were evaporating rapidly. "Goodbye to my dreams," I thought mournfully. "My bankers are probably not known to you," I said bashfully, "they are a small private bank in the City called Rodocanachi & Co." I was now waiting to be dismissed. Instead of which Saklatvala smiled, his thin, elegant smile: "Oh, I know them well," he said, "Do you know Alfred Loria, their senior partner?" "Of course," I replied "He handles my account." "Would you mind if I were to have a word with him on the telephone?" he said, "this might help me to get some information about you, and it could actually help you to get your finances sorted out. We must do that, I should think. Don't you?" "Yes, of course," I said weakly, "if you like". I could visualise in my mind the grim scenario: Loria would probably tell him that I was trading in watches and that I knew nothing about steel. 1000 tons, in those days, was worth some 100,000 dollars, which was way above my means.

---

* A letter of credit is a form of bank guarantee, commonly used in international transactions.

Even if all went well and I actually landed this order, where could I get 25,000 dollars for the margin which Rodo would require to finance this deal, following our 25/75% formula?

I returned to the office very much depressed. On my arrival Gordon rushed to me with the news that Loria, from Rodocanachi had phoned, and would like me to call him back forthwith. I started dialling his number in very low spirits. When I was put through Loria sounded most cheerful. "So congratulations, you are about to book an order with mighty Tata. Well done," he sounded most amused. I couldn't make this out. What on earth was happening?

I asked him to elaborate. Saklatvala, it emerged, was an old acquaintance of Loria's when he had been with another Italian bank. Loria was very keen to get closer to Tata and felt that this deal could help him to achieve his objective. "Yes," I said, "but there is a small problem. Tata refused to open a letter of credit. They want me to agree to 30 days. How can we solve that?" "Oh, I know," said Loria calmly, "these Indian princes are very touchy. 30 days, for them, is very generous, they normally like to pay in 90. I rather think they need these tubes badly." "Not badly enough to help me out of this impasse. I simply could not raise 25,000 dollars for the margin for this transaction, so this is, probably, good-bye Mr. Saklatvala..." "Not necessarily," said Loria to my surprise. "In this particular case I am prepared to make an exception. If you can find 10% or 10,000 dollars I would be prepared to give you the green light." I was amazed. He was keen. So I asked him to leave it with me and I would see how much I could find. I knew that it was still too much. I could raise maybe 5,000 dollars but certainly not ten. So I decided to phone Marian in Brussels. I suggested that if he could trust me with a  5,000 dollars loan I would put up the other five and we would have a deal. He asked me to tell him openly how much I was making on this transaction. I said that I was adding a good margin of 5%. As it turned out he also had a 5% profit on his side. "So why don't we do it in joint account, play it as partners? We put in 5000 dollars each and let Rodo finance it all."

And that is how my first 'big deal' came to pass. Apart from earning the princely sum of 5000 dollars I also learned several valuable lessons. Among these was that if you have a really good deal there is always a way to finance it.

The fact that Loria must have given the Indian a good reference on me was another aspect which gave me a lot of satisfaction.

My first big deal worked beautifully. We delivered everything on time and got paid on time, but I never received another order from Tata. They must have had a temporary 'hiccup' just then, from which I benefited. Good old 'Daddy'. So that was how I got into steel.

* * *

During the next decade I worked a lot with Krosnowski. He was a good few years older than me and had been in business before the war. His elder brother Zygmunt and he had formed Belexim S.A., in Brussels, immediately after the war and, having lots of good contacts in Belgium, he made a good deal of money within a relatively short space of time. Marian and Zygmunt then fell out and divided the business, Marian keeping the Belgian firm, while Zygmunt emigrated to America. In the process they closed down their London operation and as Marian was rather keen to have a presence in Britain he used me for some years as his London office. This was formalised some time later when we registered a joint company, called Panex (Overseas) Ltd. and moved offices to 40/44, George Street, just off Baker Street. In the process I bought out the Duschnitzes and got rid of various other hangers-on like Ronald Polliitt and Victor Bazowski, who had briefly worked with us on a commission basis. Gordon Greenfield stayed on as my only co-director.

Marian was a flamboyant personality, a good mixer and incurable extrovert. He liked high living and tried to make me follow his lead. "This is how you win friends and influence people," he used to say, "No-one will buy from you unless you earn their friendship, by giving them a good time." I was not, by nature, a big spender and it took me some years before I evolved my own philosophy in this respect.

Marian had many friends, a number of whom have also provided us with lucrative business. There was one man in particular whom I shall always remember. His name was Saeed Chifchi, a Turk from Ankara, head of a successful family business. He had the concession for Turkey of Dodge Bros., the motor manufacturers from Detroit, USA. Turkey was, at that time, going through a particularly bad crisis involving their balance of payments and consequently imports were almost at a standstill for lack of foreign currency. There was, however, a way of overcoming this, by getting long- term loans.. Such loans could not be obtained without a British Government guarantee.

There was, and still is, a Government Agency called ECGD (Export Credits Guarantee Department) and selected transactions could be considered if they were also beneficial to the British export drive.

Chifchi persuaded the British authorities that his business qualified for their support and as Dodge had a British operation, in Kew in London, several orders were placed with them under this scheme. In this connection, however, Saeed Chifchi needed the services of a trusted British exporter and Marian suggested that I would be suitable for the purpose. The business provided a good profit for both Marian and me, so it was all very satisfactory. That is how I met Chifchi, and he and I became good friends.

He was a very interesting man. His grandfather, of peasant stock and originally from Eastern Turkey, had settled in Ankara around the turn of the century and opened a little garage, repairing cars and other machinery. His son, Saeed's father, made all the money, being a keen supporter of and adviser to Kemal Ataturk, and Saeed, with his brothers, had consolidated the business.

Saeed was an oriental who, while feeling quite at ease in the West, never allowed Western ways to dilute or weaken his oriental philosophy.

He felt that his roots were nearer to the cradle of humanity and that thus his doctrine was nearer to the absolute truth. He treated Europeans with benevolence, but with a hint of condescension, rather as an older, more experienced person treats the fumbling experiments of the young. In a very gentle and charming manner he would try to suggest and persuade. In this he displayed infinite patience. I always felt the he was conducting a personal 'crusade' and was trying to re-educate the erring Westerners to the correct ways of the East, often at considerable discomfort to himself. At least this was how it seemed to me. He rejected certain Western conventions.

He would never, for example, book his hotel. He would arrive at the Savoy, unannounced, with or without one of his wives, with a huge quantity of luggage. The hotel manager was immediately summoned, but would invariably say that the hotel was full and that, as he had not booked, he could not be accommodated. Hotel managers, as every one knows, are past masters in turning people away when the necessity arises. It is an unequal contest which the unwanted client invariably loses.

Not Chifchi. He would calmly install himself in the lounge, open a Turkish newspaper and remain like this for hours, all his luggage blocking up the passageways. At meal times he would go to the restaurant and order the most expensive and elaborate dishes and the best wines, leaving gigantic tips to the head waiter and proportionately smaller ones to all the restaurant staff. He would then resume his place in the lounge and continue the study of his paper. Meanwhile, the hotel manager would be going crazy. All his approaches to this difficult but obviously important and generous potential guest having been dismissed with a beaming smile and most sympathetic words: "Oh, please don't worry, Mr. Manager, I am perfectly all right where I am. Believe me, I sympathise with your problem, but I cannot help you. The problem is yours not mine, but you can easily solve it by showing me to my usual suite."

In the end he always won. The poor manager, in utter despair, somehow always managed to dispose of another guest and escorted Chifchi to his favourite suite, thus qualifying for a most enormous tip. His patience and charm and his fabulous generosity melted even the most determined hotel manager's heart. When I asked him why he would not let me book his hotel for him a few days in advance, he would say, "There is no need, mon ami, the manager is a good friend of mine. He always gives me the room I like."

Chifchi was a practising follower of Mohammed. He rose at dawn and said his prayers, strictly in accordance with the dictates of the Koran. He also had more than one wife. In actual fact he had just two. They were referred to as "La grande Madame" and "La petite Madame".

With this there was a small problem, as the Republic of Turkey, following the reforms introduced by Ataturk in the early twenties, had abolished polygamy, so that under the current Turkish law his second marriage was invalid. But in this, as in anything else, Saeed Chifchi was able to display his moral fortitude and manifest his opposition to Western influences. He ignored the secular law, maintaining that in the matter of morals the Prophet could never

260

be wrong. "I am very modest," he would say, "I have only two." Everybody knew that he was perfectly entitled to have four.

He used to bring his wives to the West frequently, in strict rotation. He was, in this, as in anything else, meticulously fair. When his senior wife was with him, we all knew that he would be bored and mildly depressed. She was a pretty depressing person. Although only in her middle forties and still relatively good-looking she would only talk about her health, or more precisely, the lack of it. She also spent most of her time in Harley Street, in the waiting rooms of top consultants. Chifchi, good husband that he was, went with her and as neither of them could speak sufficiently good English I was dragged along as an interpreter. The most irksome thing was that I was required to participate in the actual consultations, and to add even further to my discomfiture, most of these centred on the gynaecological aspects of Mrs. Chifchi's heath. I recall vividly, when, half-way through a particularly gruesome session, the consultant in question turned to me and asked, "You are, I take it, a member of the medical profession?" When I assured him I was not, he observed, "This must be jolly embarrassing for you!" It certainly was.

But when I pleaded with Saeed to excuse me from the more intimate aspects of this procedure, he would put his arm around me, in a truly fatherly gesture and say, "Oh, I know, but what can I do? You are my friend and she is my wife. I assure you solemnly that I would do the same for you, if the necessity arose." I am sure he would, too, but I never discovered what my wife's reaction would have been to such a generous offer. Fortunately the necessity never arose.

When the Petite Madame's turn came to accompany her husband life took an altogether happier aspect. She was delightful and he was delighted.

He must have been in his early fifties, at the time, while she couldn't have been more than 22, or perhaps even younger. Extremely pretty, vivacious and innocent-looking, she spoke very few words of anything other than Turkish, but this did not deter her from chattering and laughing and joking. Her vocabulary was limited to some five or six basic expressions such as "Good" or "Bad" and "I like" or "I not like" and "Nice" or "Not nice". He or she, as applied to men or women, had no meaning to her. Everything to her was "He". She would ask for example when speaking about my wife's opinion: "He like – Yes?" to which one would reply "He like – yes" or "he like – no." More complex matters had to be explained via her husband. What she lacked in vocabulary she made up in expressiveness. Her lovely face told one everything. If she liked something a lot, she would roll her eyes and say with an angelic expression: "N i c e.... Yes?" to which one was expected to reply, "Yes please."

In the presence of his senior wife Chifchi did not touch alcohol. When the young one was with him he drank quite a lot. "La petite," as he called her, would smile delightedly and pointing to him would say, "B a d ... Yes?" and make a little gesture indicating that she was referring to his drinking.

We discovered a little bar-restaurant in Soho which they liked a lot. It was tiny and was equipped with a long bar and just a few simple tables. There was a minute dance floor and a piano which provided the music. She loved dancing and as Chifchi was a little clumsy on this small dance floor he would encourage me to dance with La Petite. We soon discovered that the pianist could also play the accordion and was most skilled with the Tango. "La Comparsita" was his piece de resistance. La Petite loved that tune which she called "La Parasita" and frequently asked her husband if she could dance with me the Parasita. He would smile benevolently and agree. I was not at all keen, knowing how jealous oriental husbands can get. "Go, go," he would say, "she is young and you are young, you dance, I watch. But remember you are my friend. Like this, not like this," and here he would indicate that there was to be no 'cheek to cheek', or any other nonsense. We both adhered to his rules, conscious of his benevolent gaze. From time to time, though, when she saw he was in a particularly good frame of mind she would turn to me and say "Valentino – yes?" Valentino was her code word for a flamboyant way of dancing the tango, which I once demonstrated to her and which involved considerable amount of throwing her about the floor, with faked brutality, as Rudolf Valentino used to do in the old silent films. In this she was remarkably agile and enjoyed it greatly. Chifchi was delighted and laughed and clapped, but when things got a little bit out of hand and we both enjoyed it too much he would say, "Come young Karol, sit now – old Saeed now dance cheek to cheek," and she would immediately and enthusiastically throw herself into his arms, giggling spontaneously, like a child.

Saeed simply delighted in buying her presents. But he would never do it unless the senior wife received a slightly better present first. While La Petite was incredibly sweet and always showed ecstatic enthusiasm. Whatever the senior one got from him, she would look unimpressed and even, on the face of it, rather annoyed. But despite it all Saeed, undeterred by all this, continued in his personal practice of fairness.

Once a year each of them would receive from him a new fur coat. The Grande Madame would get hers first and it would be at least one stage more expensive than the one he would give to La Petite. Thus, if La Grande Madame reached the stage of a full length mink coat, for instance, La Petite would qualify for an Ocelot. He made his purchases in Paris, Brussels, sometimes even New York and once, to my knowledge, in London. Like everything else with him, it was an experience which I shall not easily forget.

One year, at about the end of February, he arrived with La Petite and announced that this time he would buy her a fur coat in London. By that time she had reached the stage of qualifying for a short Chinchilla coat, the senior lady having received a full length one some time earlier. He was planning to stay in London for some three weeks, so I was hoping that their going shopping would relieve me of some pressure during the daytime,

It proved to be so only for the first two days, while they were looking around, but on the third day Chifchi appeared in my office with La Petite, obviously requiring my undivided attention. They had, I was told, located the right garment at Harrods. It was priced at £3,900. I commented that it sounded to me about right, to which he said, "This, of course, is their asking price. I want your advice as to the level of my counter-proposal. Should I start at £1000 or maybe a little less?" I couldn't believe my ears. I asked him to confirm that we were talking about the Harrods in Knightsbridge. When he assured me that we were, it was my turn to assume a benevolent, if slightly condescending, attitude towards this kind but misguided individual and explained at great length, with what I felt was the right degree of emphasis, that there were certain places in England where one simply did not bargain. Harrods happened to be one of them. "Why," he enquired innocently, "they are in business, aren't they?

Nothing could shift him from his opinion. If someone was in

business and was not a complete fool he knew he had to bargain, whoever he was and wherever he was located. Bargaining, or compromising or horse-trading, whatever name one would use, was going on in all walks of life, politics or business alike. "If you do not bargain, or compromise you go bust," he concluded. "I will prove to you, that in two weeks, I shall buy this coat for under £2000. You will see." I was about to witness the test of his philosophy.

The manager of the fur department was a Mr. Gross, and when Saeed first indicated to him, that he could consider buying his garment at £1000, his reaction was exactly as I had anticipated. He turned icily indignant and appeared to control himself only with the greatest difficulty. He asked me to convey to "this gentleman" that he was dealing with the best department house in England and that he regretted very much, but he had other, more pressing, matters to attend to; that the price was clearly marked on the ticket, and that it was not negotiable. On this he bowed with exaggerated stiffness and retired. Chifchi turned to me and said in quite a loud voice, beaming with goodwill, "He is good. Very good. I shall enjoy this..."

Chifchi's methods were similar to those he had used in his dealings with the hotel managers. His weapons were, as always, kindness, good humour and an infinite amount of patience. He would make a point of visiting "my friend, Mr. Manager Gross" every morning, at about nine-thirty, just after Harrods had opened its doors, and would enquire with the most touching solicitude if he had slept well, if he wasn't worried about all this unsold stock etc. He would observe, with concern that "my friend" did look a little pale. He was sure that the unsold Chinchilla was but a minor additional worry, but one he could easily get rid of if he would only listen to his friendly advice.

He would point out that even though he, Chifchi, was not in this trade, he realised that we were way past the fur buying season and that if he were him he would want to sell the stock quickly, before it became worthless.. Mr. Gross, who had started by obviously despising Saeed, began, within about a week, visibly enjoying his calls. After ten days he turned to me and remarked, "One must admire Mr. Chifchi's tenacity. I wish we had a little more of it in this country." When I translated this to Saeed, he grabbed him by his arm and gave him a most brotherly hug. At this we all burst out laughing. Very shortly afterwards the deal was concluded. The price agreed was £1,750.

Characteristically, Chifchi did not gloat, or brag about his victory. He was delighted but in a very genuine way. One could imagine that his attitude was not unlike that of the biblical father, who had just welcomed home his prodigal son.

I sighed a big sigh of relief, and as I was about to write out a cheque, on his account, to pay for his valuable acquisition, he laid his big hand on the cheque-book to stop me writing. "Now Mr. Manager Gross," he turned to his victim "five per cent commission for my friend Karol here, he has worked so hard...". I was stunned, at first, but then, collapsed in hoots of laughter. "No, no," I pleaded, "enough, enough..." Chifchi looked only mildly amused. "Why are you laughing, he is a good man. He would have paid it to you, I am sure." Finally even Chifchi gave up, and let me write out the cheque for the figure originally agreed.

He looked satisfied. Unbelievably, so did Mr. Gross.

* * *

Meanwhile, my business was developing well. So well, in fact, that towards the end of the fifties I was confident enough to move my offices once more. This time it was a real improvement, for we moved to 11, Bruton Street, in the heart of Mayfair. I hired a good architect, who planned out everything with professional perfectionism, with fitted carpets, sound insulation, special lighting, the lot, and for my own office I allowed myself the ultimate luxury, a real touch of class: a set of six hunting prints by Henry Alken, at the cost of £600, in honour of my first steel deal with Mr. Saklatvala of Tata Ltd.

As I reclined nonchalantly in my new executive swivel-chair behind my six-foot teak desk, I quietly assessed the harvest of the recent years: in the outer offices, apart from Gordon there was now Mrs. Tillett, my new personal secretary, in addition to a telephone operator and two junior girls doing general typing; I had just engaged Jindra Fleishner, who brought with him excellent Yugoslav contacts and his secretary, Mrs. Wenyon. There was also Reg Briggs and his assistant, who were dealing with my shipping, and a nice man called Leon Kryj, a Pole, who had good relations with steel stockholders.

The company owned two ships and kept another one on time

charter, several motor cars, including my personal Humber Supersnipe. Marysia and I were now living in our own brand-new 'desirable bungalow' in a good part of Wimbledon, and I was considering opening my own office in Spain, to handle the increasing volume of business in that promising market.

"I know," I said to myself, "this miracle did take a little longer, thirteen years to be precise, but I would be an insensitive fool if I were not satisfied."

And at that precise moment I permitted myself to think the most dangerous of thoughts: that, at long last, I had arrived, that from now on things were bound to continue to improve, that the indicator was going to climb up and up and that only the sky was going to be my limit.

\* \* \*

I was wrong. I had not arrived. Not by a long way. In fact it was to take me a further dozen years to reach that delectable state.

The decade that followed my move to Bruton Street was not an auspicious period for me. It felt like being on a rollercoaster. Steady spells of ascent were followed by sudden, nauseating dives. If times of adversity are meant to forge one's character, mine was being forged with a vengeance. There were moments when I was seriously tempted to give up.

My first set-back took place shortly after I moved into Mayfair. In January 1959, in fact, my good friend Walter Marais and I jointly bought an old ship, which we subsequently sold to Japan, complete with a cargo of steel scrap. The contract provided that we should deliver the ship and its cargo to Japan at our own risk and expense. It was a big deal, the biggest that I had handled thus far. The idea had been tried by several people before us with considerable success, so Walter and I pooled our resources, and put this transaction together with remarkable ease. We named the ship the Pamaru

The deal started going wrong almost at once. It was as if there was a curse on the boat. Each individual element of the transaction which we had put together with considerable care and under constant professional advice went catastrophically wrong. The ship's engine broke down several times en route to Japan. She docked for repairs in Gibraltar, had to be towed to Suez, spent nearly three weeks in dock in Colombo and eventually broke

266

down completely outside Manila, from where it had to be towed all the way to Japan. Because of the delays our original buyers cancelled the contract. We had to find a new buyer in a hurry, inevitably at a considerably lower price. Meanwhile, the market was falling and the buyers grew progressively more nervous.

The biggest drama, however, took place in Tokyo Bay. While the ship was being unloaded outside the port of Yokohama an extraordinary storm broke out. It lasted three days. The force of the wind was such that the Pamaru dragged her anchor and collided with another vessel moored some distance away. The cost of the damage was insured, the delay was not. It took some days to sort it all out. Meanwhile we ran out of time. The contract expired and the buyers would not hear of a further extensions. Our joint loss was £120,000, a huge sum in those days.

My share of the loss, £60,000 was well beyond my means. I had to look for a different solution.

By sheer luck, another friend of mine, who was a director of a trading company in the City of London told me that his company was being re-organised. They had in their group a semi-dormant firm called Bishopsgate Steels and the new chairman was looking for someone who would re-activate their steel trading business. I applied. My negotiations proved successful and as a result I incorporated my business with theirs and in the process managed to cover all my Pamaru losses in full. I also became a main board member of the Cookson Group of companies, with a very respectable salary and, what would be considered then, 'good prospects.'

For the next six years everything went well. My association with Cooksons was a success and my own affairs seemed to have settled into a very satisfactory routine. Until 1967, when everything went wrong again.

The bank which owned the Cookson group decided to close down their trading activities. As a result I had to arrange, at very short notice, a 'management buy-out' of my company, borrowing £100,000 for the purpose. At the same time I became involved in a lawsuit, which I lost at the cost of £100,000. As if that was not enough, I had to contend with further two adversities, the bankruptcy of a German associate and the closure of our Spanish mining activities, accounting for yet another £100,000 deficit. Within a few months my hitherto prosperous business found itself owing £300,000. (several millions in today's money).

It seemed to me then that I was finished, totally destroyed. But, as sometimes happens in life, a faint glimmer of hope appeared, apparently from nowhere. A friend of mine who was an important executive in United States Steels Corporation, at that time the biggest steelmaker in the world, owed me a favour. I called on him to help me secure their representation for one of the main European markets. Unfortunately, he said, all good the markets were already allocated. There was only Roumania. We were both aware that trying to sell American steel to a communist dictatorship was a waste of time. Still I took it on and, unbelievably, by the sheerest good luck, various unrelated political and economic factors coincided and it ended up being an extremely lucrative market. Almost at once I was selling steel to Roumania by the shipload. I was soon able to repay my debts with a speed that amazed and delighted my creditors. By the end of the 60's I was back on course.

The 1970's were for me a time of considerable fulfilment. I invited Walter Marais, the man who had shared the Pamaru adventure with me, to become my partner. This gave me a little more free time to dedicate myself to other pursuits. I took up riding again and soon bought my first horse.

At the back of my mind I had a thought, a kind of promise which I had given to my father, before I left Poland that, if at all possible, I would to try to ride to hounds in England. It had been his great ambition that, as he had never been able to sample the delights of English hunting himself, I would do it 'for both of us', as he used to say. Several of his older 'horsey friends', Tadeusz Dachowski or Joseph Gizycki to name but two had, towards the end of the last century, hunted a few seasons with the Quorn when the fabulous Lord Lonsdale was master and Tom Firr, the renowned huntsman, was carrying the horn. From my earliest childhood I had been made familiar with their thrills and spills and, somehow, I never doubted that, one day, I would be able to do the same. My time has now arrived, I thought, as I was in England and, at long last, had a little money to spare. I decided to give it a try. If I waited much longer, it might be too late.

The renewed contact with horses seemed to change me. I felt more confident, more complete, more balanced within myself. It was as if the proximity of these wonderful animals released in me forces which were hitherto lying dormant. It also seemed to

268

improve my performance in business. Although I was devoting less time to my office, as I spent daily many hours in the saddle, I became stronger and more convincing. In some peculiar way my equestrian pursuits adjusted in me the vital balance between boldness and prudence. Marysia noticed it too. Although I spent more time away from home, she did not grow jealous of my sporting pursuits. She followed them with benevolent interest. .

To begin with I kept my horses at livery, first in Wimbledon and later in Surrey. This arrangement was satisfactory, but not perfect. Ideally, I felt, I should have a small yard of my own. I started looking for a suitable property.

It wasn't until 1973 that I found something which, in my view, had promise. and was not prohibitively expensive. The farm in question, called Saddlecombe Stables, near Epsom in Surrey, had two great advantages. It was close to London and it was cheap. Its disadvantages, however, were endless, the principal snag being that it was sold to me with a five year lease still running and, if I wanted to move in at once, the tenant would have to be persuaded to move out first. In addition, the place was very badly run down. In fact, several people, who saw it then, believed that nothing could be made of it, that it was beyond redemption. But I liked it. I thought that with a little imagination and a certain amount of expenditure it could be turned into something useful. I was also confident that I would be able to persuade the sitting tenant to leave before the termination of his lease.

I bought the farm for £33,000. It consisted of a coach house, some semi-derelict stables and a small indoor manege, all in about 15 acres of very neglected parkland. The rent which I was getting was reasonable, though, and I reckoned that if the worst came to the worse I could treat the purchase as a sort of investment.

Contrary to my expectations, my tenant wouldn't hear of moving. It wasn't until July 1979, when the lease ran out, that I took possession of my property, and not before a session in court, as the tenant would not move even though his tenancy had expired.

The years that followed proved to be the most interesting and fulfilling of my life. My business was doing very well. I was really busy. I was either doing deals or sitting in the saddle hunting, or supervising the rebuilding of my new farm. My days would start at the crack of dawn and, often ended well after midnight as, in order to keep my business going I would invite my customers out to dinner and conduct my negotiations in restaurants. Was I under pressure? Yes, I suppose I was but, if so, it did not seem to affect me adversely. In fact, I loved it.

My newly found activity, that of transforming a 'complete disaster', as my friends called it, into a habitable and viable property, fired my imagination completely. I was constantly planning, drawing, negotiating, dreaming. I suddenly realised what an enormous joy it was to build, to see flat, two-dimensional drawings take their three-dimensional shapes before my eyes. On my small scale I experienced the thrills of creation. In my own humble way, I understood the feelings of the great patrons of architecture of past ages, the popes, the kings, the princes, the fathers of our civilisation. Although I was not building a palace or a basilica, I felt that the process was basically the same. The scale was much smaller, of course. But that seemed the sole difference.

To help me in this I had the luck to have the assistance of Ann Galley, a good architect, who had been our neighbour in Wimbledon. She understood my crazy ideas and patiently and tactfully translated them into working drawings and supervised the contractors, while I was elsewhere, travelling 'to make enough money to pay for all this', as we called it, or riding my horses in the hunting field.

At the end of five years Saddlecombe was more or less complete. It now consisted of some 40 acres of much improved pasture (the result of a number of additional acquisitions) a perfectly habitable house, two staff cottages, two stable yards totalling 19 large loose boxes, a full-size indoor riding manege and an even bigger outdoor one, plus tack rooms, hay stores and all the normal auxiliary facilities. I also divided the park into twenty sizeable paddocks and planted over 1000 trees and shrubs. Finally, I had tremendous fun buying furniture, carpets, pictures, curtains, pots and pans and all the little things for every day living. In July 1984, Marysia, her cousin Hania, 'Uncle General' and I had a little celebration on, what the general called, "the fifth anniversary of the victory at Saddlecombe".

Thirty-six years, somehow, did not seem such a long time at all. The victory, such as it was, the 'miracle' if you like, had at last taken place. But this time round I was mature enough to recognise the transitory nature of this gift . What had been given to me, what had been achieved was not mine. It was lent to me for an unspecified period, on terms which I did not and could not understand. It could be taken away from me, I knew, at any time, irrespective of any logic or merit, as had so often happened in the past.

I decided to enjoy what I had and not ask any questions; to live from day to day, without making any claims on the future. My 'script' was still hidden from me and I knew it would be improper to try and break the seal that guarded it from my gaze.

Meanwhile, my destiny was smiling at me, her slow, benevolent smile...

# Chapter 19

# FOXHUNTING

Horses have played a big role in my life. It was probably hereditary. Like his father before him, my father, in his youth, was a keen horseman. His best friends were horsemen too, some of them riders of great distinction.

I started riding in my childhood but, as was customary in those days, had little formal equestrian education and apart from a few lessons, which my grandfather arranged for me with a proper trainer, I was taught by my father's stud groom. I picked up a lot later, though, when we moved permanently to the country, principally from cavalry officers who were based on a part of our estate, so that for a good deal of my holidays I was able to ride not only my own horse, but other peoples', and to take part in some equestrian events and small competitions. It wasn't until well after the war that I became interested in the more academic side of equitation.

I always dreamed that I would, one day, resume riding and take up hunting with a good English pack. For a long time my financial circumstances prevented me from doing this. Subsequent complications and set-backs delayed it further. I did not buy my first horse in England until 1970, when I was 49. But I made up for it soon afterwards. From then on, horses took up a great deal of my time.

My reminiscences would be incomplete, therefore, without devoting at least one chapter to this side of my life, particularly to hunting.

As everything else in this world, equestrian sport has its delights and disasters. Dreams often turn into nightmares, delights are followed by setbacks. Those who are seriously devoted to the sport learn to accept that one cannot exist without the other. I have had a fair share of both.

Now that I have had to give up hunting, I like to reminisce. I like to evoke from the album of my memory scenes, events, sometimes even sequences covering entire days.

Most vivid in my memory is my first season with the Quorn. This coincided with the introduction to big-time hunting of a new horse. He was not exactly new, as I had had him for four years by then, but I had had problems with his health, with his training and particularly with his temperament, with the result that at the age of eight he was still a novice hunter. His name was Dandino, or Dino for short. He was a big chestnut thoroughbred gelding. His body was superb, it was his temperament which was in doubt. Many experts told me that he would not be suited for hunting, but I always hoped that somewhere in that beautiful head of his was a key which, if I were able to locate it, would make him into a splendid cross-country ride. I used to say that I felt like a fiddler who had been given a Stradivarius violin. He knew that the instrument was capable of producing a most heavenly sound. The problem was how to get to it.

On that particular December morning we met at a pub, the 'Black Boy', if I remember correctly. It was a Friday, a fashionable day, and the field was well up to the maximum, at least 150 riders. I was a bit nervous. The Quorn, after all, was the best hunt in the land and here was I, a new boy, mounted on a novice horse. Michael Farrin, the huntsman, had the bitch pack out, in anticipation of a fast, galloping day.

The winter sun was struggling through the morning mist and there was a nip of frost in the air. The space in front of the pub was packed; hounds, the hunt servants and the masters occupying the centre stage, the rest of the mounted field standing or milling around in the remaining area, many spilling onto the road. Despite my slight nerves, I had to admire the beauty of the scene. The colours, the elegance and particularly the quality of the horses. This was the most visible difference between a 'Shire pack' and a 'provincial hunt'. Blood horses were the most suited to the open galloping country, and the big natural fences.

And the country itself was something special. Sculptured by foxhunters for foxhunters, it was simply breathtaking. Little clumps of trees, planted generations ago, provided an ideal environment for foxes; and the hedges, those strong rows of blackthorn, formed good barriers for grazing cattle and gave the foxhunter a chance to keep up with hounds, if his nerve and his horse were up to jumping them.

We moved off, as usual, shortly after eleven. Dandino was quite worked up by then and I was trying to relax him. I slotted him in at a discreet distance from the head of the hunt and we started trotting on the road towards the first draw. I could see a long line of bobbing hats before me and knew that an even longer line was behind me. The other horses were also excited, some of them even cantering on the tarmac. I managed so far to maintain the trot, but only just.

About half a mile down the road we turned into a field. The covert was a few hundred yards in front of us. Michael Farrin put the pack in and started to draw. I knew it could be a long wait or a short one, depending on scenting condition, that unpredictable ingredient of hunting, much discussed, but totally incomprehensible, even to the expert.

I had been hunting regularly for some eight seasons now. I started modestly with a 'provincial' pack near London, the Surrey Union Hunt. I smiled with benevolent condescension, remembering my zealous efforts to learn the rules, be accepted among the elite, my joy at being invited to wear their button and the yellow collar and be acknowledged as 'one of the boys'. I had only two hunters then and a trailer, which I towed myself behind my normal business car. What a delight it was at the end of the day when my horse had jumped everything, maybe even given 'a lead' to somebody less experienced.

After that I graduated to a better hunt, the Warwickshire, where I spent a full season. I had a groom of my own, a girl called Judy, and my horses, four of them by then, were stabled in a small yard which I hired for the season. The Warwickshire considered itself to be a very smart pack and a rather difficult country to cross, so it proved to be a valuable experience. Next was the Grafton.

A friend of mine, a man called Tom Coombs who lived in Sulgrave, found me a nice little yard there. I already had a small establishment in Surrey, where Liz Mead was my full-time groom. At Sulgrave the livery was very good and the two young men who were running it did it mostly for the benefit of Tommy and myself, while Liz would come sometimes, just for a day.

The people in the Grafton were very kind to me. The then senior Master, Col. Neil Foster, told Tommy, in fact, that he was thinking of asking me to join him as master. I was invited to preside over some meetings, as a preliminary procedure to the actual formal proposal. I was really flattered by this suggestion, but I could not consider it. I had a mission to fulfil. I knew that before I was too old, I had to get to the Quorn.

So I moved on. My next step took me to Leicestershire, almost there but not quite, next door, in fact, to the Fernie. I took an old Victorian stable block at Illstone-on-the-Hill, where I installed Liz, Debbie her assistant, and my eight hunters. I put my name down on the waiting list for the Quorn and took to hunting over the green expanses of the foxhunters' favourite lands. The following season I moved my yard again, to East Langton, by which time I was invited to join the Quorn.

So this brings us back to our story and to the stretch of pasture land, as we were waiting outside the covert for hounds to find and move off. At the back of my mind I remembered that, despite my eight seasons of solid hunting, I was now trying something new, that my previous experiences were not quite sufficient to guide me safely over this country. Up to now I had always been following someone, either the master, or a fellow subscriber. The jumps were usually 'hunt jumps', places built into the enclosures for the purpose of hunting and made mostly of wood, or 'timber' as the hunting people would call them, well marked and safe. In contrast, the Quorn was largely natural. One jumped some timber, but the real Quorn follower liked to jump hedges. On occasions one was even able to 'take one's own line', something unthinkable in lesser hunts.

A beautiful chorus of hound music suddenly interrupted my reminiscences, and brought me back into the present. Hounds seemed to be on to a line. Did I hear the huntsman blow the 'gone away', the rousing sound of the horn, which makes the old hunters prick their ears and their riders' hearts miss a beat? Dandino was sitting right down with excitement and definitely giving signs that he was ready to go. James Teacher, the field master, was still waiting.

Then suddenly he turned his horse and aimed him at a nice big hedge. This was it. The riders in front of me were now shaking up their horses and spreading to take the first obstacle. Dandino was boiling over and I was having trouble in holding him. I suddenly saw that there was a gap. Somebody's horse had refused, giving me just enough room. I released my 'handbrake' and put Dandino into a slowish canter. The big engine under me was throbbing nicely as we approached, a huge heave and we were over. What joy. First jumps can be tricky.

We jumped a couple more fences and then we stopped. Hounds were right in front of us. They had lost the line already and were running round with their noses down, trying to figure out where to go. How disappointing.

The huntsman lifted the pack and took it along a hedge, while we followed, still bunched together, still hoping that another burst would soon ensue. No such luck. Grudgingly I had to admit that scent was poor and that this would probably mean a disappointing morning.

So we were wandering from covert to covert, but it seemed to be the same story everywhere. We even jumped a few fences, but had to pull up sharply after each one, so as not override hounds. Dandino had switched off by now. We were slipping further and further down the line. There seemed no need to stay in front in a 'stop-go' type of ride. Horses soon get bored with it, just as humans do.

At about 1 o'clock we were still at it. We were now on a road, not far from Lowesby and I was walking at the end of a long line of riders and horses. I looked at my watch, thinking that Liz was probably waiting for me in the box, at Barsby Back Lane, with my second horse. It would be time to change soon.

As I was walking along at the very end of this cavalcade, I saw a man with a familiar face. He was standing by the road with his arm in a sling. It was the 'Friendly Farmer' from the Fernie, a man I nicknamed FF for short. I never knew his name, but he was always very kind to me. His land was right on the border of the Fernie and the Quorn, so he could hunt with both packs. I knew that he had had a bad fall a couple of weeks ago and so had joined the foot followers. I stopped to greet him. As we were chatting away I could hear a commotion half a mile ahead of us, right at the top of this endless column. "Sounds as if they're off," said FF after listening for a while.

"Blast," I said, regretting that I had let myself drift so far behind, "I shall never get anywhere near that one, not in a thousand years". "Tell you what I would do in your place," said FF, "I would just canter down this lane, quiet as a mouse. There should be a couple of gates there in the woods and a stream, but they shouldn't be too difficult to open this early in the season. If not, you will not have much trouble jumping them. Your chap would be well up to it." "Right, thanks a lot," I waved to him and slipped discreetly down a grassy ride, lined by leafless beech trees.

I followed FF's directions. I found the gates, could open the first one but had to jump the other as it was fairly jammed into the ground, and had a bit trouble finding a place to jump the stream as it had barbed wire strung along it. Eventually, I managed to find a spot where a tree had fallen onto the wire. So I jumped it there. With great relief we emerged from the woods.

As we turned the corner the sight took my breath away. Not only were we out of the wood, literally, but we had in front of us the most glorious sea of grass and on it, right in front us, disappearing into the slight mist, Michael Farrin and the bitch pack galloping at full speed. They were flying. The undulating land was sliced by big blackthorn hedges and there was nobody else in sight. This was the stuff that dreams were made of, this was a foxhunter's heaven.

Dandino knew that serious business was about to begin. This was no gymkhana, this was the real thing. It would be now that we should discover if he was as good as he looked. I put him into a gallop, a fair hunting pace. We had in front of us the best that Leicestershire could offer. Could we live with the best?

There were two fields dividing us from the pack and still no-one else in sight. We were really motoring when we met the first fence, a strong blackthorn hedge. A lovely big jump, just right for the speed. The next came, it seemed, a few strides away. Yes, he was jumping well. The cold wind was cutting into my nostrils, my eyes were beginning to water, I felt the powerful engine revving under me, and saw the hedges coming towards me one after the other. After a while it felt as if we were standing still and the landscape was gliding under us noiselessly, except for the rush of wind in my ears and the rhythmical breathing of my horse. A sense of suspension, as if in a dream.

I lifted my eyes, looking for Michael and the hounds. We were certainly nearer. Dandino was obviously fast as well as a good jumper. I started steering him slightly to my left to remain down wind in case hounds should lose the line and should have to stop. But this was a good line, they would not lose it. I could now hear quite clearly the glorious music of the pack in full cry. They were closely bunched together, just as they should be. This was copy book stuff!

We were now coming to a road. It looked like the one leading to where our boxes should be with the change of horses, what luck!. It seemed that Michael was stopping the hounds. The fox had obviously got away. Good for him, I wished him well. I looked at my watch, it was nearly two, high time to change. The morning had started so badly, – but look at us now...

As we walked out onto the road I took a good look at Dandino. No cuts, all shoes on, his breathing was nearly back to normal. He seemed fine, in fact he seemed positively delighted. I patted him affectionately.

As I walked, still slightly dazed by the exhilarating ride, on a loose rein, my horse steaming in the cold air, it suddenly came to me: despite all the predictions to the contrary, Dino was going to be the superb hunter that I always thought he would be, against all the pessimistic predictions of the experts. During these last 30 minutes, during this heavenly dash across Lowesby Park, we had found, by sheer luck, the missing key to my Stradivarius. We had made it at last!

I found Liz exactly where I expected her. The ramp of the box was down and I could see the head of my other horse, Union Jack, over the partition. The rest of the mounted field were now arriving in a rush. They had got delayed in a farmyard on the way and had had to go round on the roads for miles. I didn't say anything to anybody about my dream ride, except to Liz. I told her very briefly, while dismounting, that we had had a super gallop, that Dino was jumping well, and that as far as I could see he hadn't touched a thing. We pulled Jack out and put Dino in. Once mounted on my fresh horse I re-joined the hounds at the very top of the long line of boxes. The sun was gone, it was beginning to drizzle and it was getting colder.

The day finished at 4 o'clock, in the dark and in pouring rain. It had been a good day, a wonderful day. Both horses had gone well. What pleased me more than anything was that something had 'clicked' between me and Dandino, something that I felt was going to be quite unique and that thrilled me beyond measure.

\* \* \*

There were, of course, other less happy days. I took my share of falls and was involved in accidents. On the whole, though, when in Leicestershire, I managed to avoid serious injury, mainly thanks to having good horses and probably also by avoiding the more obvious risks, which in my earlier years I would have been tempted to take. After some ten seasons I was, on the whole, in reasonably good shape.

During the 1980s I had to alter my method of hunting. I gave up my yard in East Langton. Liz got married and started a family. Without her it was not quite the same. She still remained in my employ but was now based at Saddlecombe and only occasionally found time to visit the old battlefields. I tried to carry on with the Quorn while keeping my horses at livery, but it did not work out. I was spoilt. Having got used to perfection I could not adapt to second best. Besides, I was getting older, and found commuting three or four times a week a considerable bore. That was just a contributory factor however, the main reason was that my horses were not being looked after as well as under Liz's supervision. Reluctantly I decided to move all my hunters back to Saddle-combe, which by then was fully re-built, and take up hunting with the Chiddingfold, Leconfield and Cowdray, in West Sussex.

It is a much slower country and one only needed one horse a day, so Liz or perhaps another member of my staff could come out with me too. We all felt that it was a bit of a comedown but in many respects it was much easier.

I had fewer hunters by then. Union Jack and Dominic were dead. Bitter Ellen and Pharaoh were retired. I still had Windmill, Tapster and a newcomer called Barnaby. John of Gaunt and Raffles were not very well and went out infrequently.

But Dandino, despite his nineteen summers, was still in good enough health to be hunting regularly. He was positively 'hooked' on hunting. When being plaited in the morning on a hunting day he would shake like jelly with anticipatory excitement. On the days when it was not his turn and he saw other horses going, he was furious with jealousy. It was with him a true obsession. In deference to his old age I never kept him out very long. After about three hours we would invariably go back to the box. It all worked out rather well, but at the back of my mind I was dreading the thought that one day we would have to retire him altogether.

On New Year's day in 1988 I took him out alone. I drove him

myself to the meet, which was to be in the park of Petworth House. Liz came by car to help me get going and took a few photographs. Dandino looked and felt at his best and was much admired. When we moved off after the meet, he started by pulling quite hard. In a few bounds he regained his customary place at the head of the field and stayed there all day. It was a moderate day but Dino was very pleased with himself. We returned home happy and by five in the evening he was standing in his box munching his hay, as usual.

His turn came again on Saturday, 9th January. We met at Littleton Farm and I had with me three other horses: Liz on Windmill Boy, Lisa on Gossip and Jackie on Harry. The meet was not a particularly promising one and we all went so as to give the horses a day out.

Dandino was going beautifully. There was not much jumping in that part of the country, but we were galloping across some lovely meadows, just loping along in a leisurely way. Dino was very relaxed, soft and happy. We stopped at the top of a hill, having jumped a small rail on the way. Most of the field headed downhill, towards a wood. I decided to wait with my party where I was for a while. I did not want to get bogged down in the woods, which were often tricky in that part of the country. When I noticed, however, that the field had got through the woods and had emerged into the open, on the far side, I decided to follow them at a leisurely pace.

We cantered slowly down a grass verge. Just as we were nearing the end of that field Dino stumbled badly and pulled up sharply in a couple of strides.

He stopped on three legs holding his near fore limply in the air. I jumped off immediately. It was dreadful. His fetlock joint was touching the ground and his hoof was pointing away at a ghastly angle. I knew at once this was serious..

From then on it was a nightmare. We were miles from any-where. One of the hunt secretaries, a Mrs. Hare, came to us and at my request went immediately in search of the terrier man. The idea was for him to go in his Land Rover and 'phone the vet. We knew it would be ages. Poor Dino was standing shivering in the cold. It must have happened just before 1 pm. A foot follower, a Mrs. Wilson, came and offered her coat, with which we covered his back. Mrs. Hare came back again, to say that she had found the terrier man and he was on his way to the nearest telephone. I sent Liz and the girls back to the box to wait for me there. There was nothing she, or anybody else could do, until the vet arrived. I was determined to remain with my horse. Stan Mays, a local farmer, arrived with a blanket. With Mrs. Wilson's coat and Stan's blanket on, he stopped shivering, but he was beginning to feel the pain. At about 1.30 a Mrs. Perrin, the wife of a local farmer, arrived with some bandages.

We managed to improvise a form of support for the fetlock joint and Dino seemed happier. He could put some weight on the injured foreleg with less pain.

It was not until about 1.40 that the vet finally arrived. He gave Dino a massive pain-killing injection. His preliminary diagnosis was bad. He confirmed that the injury was very serious. Some 20 minutes later another hunt supporter, a Mr. David Tupper, arrived with a Land Rover and trailer. The vet re-bandaged Dino's leg again for the journey and with great apprehension we initiated the tricky loading operation. To my surprise and relief, Dino was very eager to get in. He hopped on three legs with extraordinary agility into the trailer, without much assistance from us. He seemed better.

We had to cross a considerable stretch of very rough ground. I knew that the trailer was bound to rock violently from side to side, which would make it very difficult for the patient to keep his balance. Against all advice I decided to ride with Dino in the trailer. I armed myself with a long stick with which I could tap the top of the roof of the towing car, as a signal for him to stop, in case Dino was showing signs of falling over. We went very slowly and stopped frequently. Dino was anxious but managed to balance himself surprisingly well despite the jerky rocking movements. He looked at me all the time. He needed re-assurance. I knew these would probably be my last moments with him alone. I tried not to think of what I felt was inevitable. My job now was not to allow myself to get sloppy or sentimental. I had to remain cheerful. So I talked to him all the time, patting him gently and affectionately pulling his ears. He was so very brave and trusting. When we emerged eventually onto a proper road and the trailer stopped rocking, the vehicle accelerated gradually and Dandino relaxed a little. He just pressed himself gently against my shoulder to feel my presence and seemed to be dozing off. The pain-killer was taking effect.

We arrived a Stan Mayes's yard and slowly led Dino to a lovely big box, all ready with a huge bed of fresh-smelling straw. I asked the vet to give him another strong injection of morphine, before he started examining him more thoroughly. While all this was going on, somebody gave me a lift to where Liz and my box were parked.

On my return, some 30 minutes later, I went to see Dandino. The vet had just finished his examination. The news was bad: the main tendon was severed, quite hopelessly, probably on a flint. One of those freak accidents, one chance in a million. He confirmed that there was no way he could be saved.

As I watched in agony the vet led out Dandino slowly into the forecourt of Stan Mayes's yard. Although limping dreadfully he was still beautiful. I shut my eyes. One sharp crack of the gun and my favourite hunter crashed to the ground. In a split second he was dead.

There were many people standing around when it happened. All hunting people, all horse lovers. As I was about to turn round to get to the safety of my own horse box, one of the ladies, a Mrs. Douglas, ran to me sobbing openly. She embraced me in a charming gesture of compassion. "I am so sorry, I am so sorry," she kept repeating, between sobs. "Such a lovely horse, such a magnificent horse..." I squeezed her hand in gratitude, my own grief making me speechless. I turned round and went.

As we were driving away I ventured a last look. The body of my favourite horse was lying where he had fallen, now covered with a horse blanket.

Dandino may not have been my best horse. There were some which were probably better, but he was always special. There was this unique bond between us, which I have never found with any of my other horses, and I have had thirty-six of them in all. I bought him when he was four years old and he died at the age of 19.

I was heartbroken at the loss of my dearest horse. But, on the other hand I tried to remember that he had died as a result of an accident and that he fell doing what he most loved. Retirement would have been difficult for him. He died on the battlefield like the good soldier that he was.

He was a typical 'one man horse' and I happened to be that one man.

* * *

282

In a vague, imprecise sort of way I believe in destiny. I would not be able to describe, with any precision, how our destiny operates. All I have is this rather nebulous feeling that things have been written somewhere for each one of us and 'that which has been written' cannot be changed.

I have a cousin, however, who is very specific on the subject. He seems to be able to explain exactly how it works. In his view we are governed by a sort of celestial control tower, manned by a highly qualified group of angels. Like in a busy airport they regulate all take-offs and landings and allocate to each one of us one or more 'slots' or 'windows' just as the flight controllers do. When the appropriate slot appears we either die or are born, whatever is laid down in our timetable. Sometimes these slots may be cancelled or postponed.

Almost three years after Dandino's death, on 24th November 1990, I had a definite feeling that my own slot for take-off was being offered to me. There had, no doubt, been other similar situations in my earlier life, when this had also taken place, but if so I was not conscious of it. But on this one occasion I was so keenly aware of it that the memory of the feeling is still very vivid in my mind.

On the day in question I was riding Barnaby, a good hunter, whom I had ridden for three complete seasons. We met at Elkham Farm, West Sussex, near Balls Cross and spent the morning pottering around the woods. Liz was out too, riding Windmill Boy. The air felt cool, but the ground was muddy and slippery. At about one o'clock we jumped out of the woods onto an open field. I remember that Barnaby did not take that fence very well, he fiddled it, as we say. The next fence in the open was a small hedge. Barnaby was never very keen on hedges, he would much rather jump timber, so I chose what appeared to me a good spot and rode him towards it with some energy.

A couple of strides before he seemed to hesitate, backed off as we say, so I kicked him on. He did not stop, in a way he did obey, but instead of jumping proceeded to 'climb' the hedge instead, a most peculiar manoeuvre.

There was, as it turned out later, a strand of barbed wire in the hedge, into which his front legs got entangled. We could neither go forwards nor backwards. I felt that Barnaby was losing his balance and that very slowly we were keeling over, onto the hedge and over it.

As I sat in the saddle, totally helpless, I watched like on a film in slow motion, as Barnaby, with me on top, fell first onto the hedge and then, equally slowly, into the ditch on the far side of it. As the muddy ground was coming closer, an inch a minute, I was still sitting firmly in the saddle, not having moved at all. I did not seem to be able to move in any way. I felt I was riveted in the plate.

Without any feeling of fear, I observed that Barnaby's neck embedded itself into the mud first, then his shoulders, then my own face and then I felt the weight of the horse right on top of me. My heart did not miss a beat, I did not try to do anything to protect myself from my predicament, I just lay there, totally immobilised, pinned down by half a ton of horse. As a result I was fully submerged into the mud, at the bottom of the ditch feeling the warm body of Barnaby on top of me. It seemed we spent hours in this strange immobility.

I then felt that Barnaby was struggling. I became aware that more weight was being placed onto my shoulders. He was apparently trying to get up.

Then came the moment I shall never forget. The moment when I was sure my slot had actually opened. I felt the cold of the steel of Barnaby's shoe being tentatively placed against my right cheek. It wobbled somewhat, went higher onto my temple, then lower, nearer my jaw. It was a very gentle pressure, as if testing the footing. In that very moment I felt distinctly that my time had come. No fear, no feeling of any sort, I just waited.

I remember that the pressure gradually increased, until it got very strong. It was then that I felt that the side of my face was being crushed and in that split second I remember thinking, "Please God – no!" It was not due to panic, or any form of fear, just a simple request.

The next thing I felt was that the bones of my face collapsed under the pressure. I felt that something in my head cracked; or more accurately, gave way. My head was then embedded even deeper into the mud. Barnaby was standing now, shaking himself, like a dog. He then galloped off, while I was lying in the ditch, wondering if I was dead. I remember thinking that I might as well remain where I was. There was no point in attempting to get up, since at the slightest move my head would fall off.

The next thing that happened was that somebody, a rider still mounted, was standing over me shouting, "Are you all right? Are you all right?" – a silly sort of question, under the circumstances, but understandable. I decided to risk it and tried to move, just to see what would happen. Nothing did. Surprisingly I was able to get up.

Very carefully I touched my face with my muddy glove. It was still there, how strange, there was even no blood. I tried to move my jaw and it moved, not very well but it did. I asked someone if I had a wound, or a cut. The answer was that there was nothing to see, it seemed all right.

By that time Liz had come back, having jumped the hedge, at the head of the field. She took a good look at me and pronounced that she couldn't see anything catastrophic. Nothing dramatic, as she put it.

Simon Reece, who was a regular Chidd and Lec follower and who also happened to be a doctor of medicine, came to me soon, while Liz caught Barnaby and led him back to me. He had a look at my head and jaw and said that, as far as he could see, there was nothing wrong, but he felt I should go back home immediately.

All this happened, of course, miles from anywhere, so I remounted Barnaby with considerable difficulty. Once in the saddle I felt surprisingly well, so we decided to hurry back to the box, as I was beginning to feel quite considerable pain and my face was beginning to swell. So we set off to Balls Cross at a gallop.

When I reached the cab of my lorry, my face looked bad. It was very swollen and very painful. But I was definitely alive and for that I was very grateful.

While Liz was driving me in my horsebox towards the stables I said a little prayer of thanks. I directed a special passage to the angelic controller who, from his seat in the heavenly control tower, was in charge of allocating take-off slots for names starting with "C".

As it turned out my jaw was broken in three places, rather badly, but as the surgeon said, it could have been a lot worse.

\* \* \*

So perhaps before I finish these few short glimpses into my sporting past I could be allowed to return for one more moment to Leicestershire and re-live just one scene, which for some reason has remained in my memory.

It must have been towards the end of a season, February most likely, in the year 1981 or '82. It was well after 4 p.m. and getting dark. Michael Farrin, the Quorn huntsman, had just stopped hounds, as visibility was getting dangerously poor. I was sitting on a great horse, John of Gaunt, the retired British Horse Trials champion, and the best cross-country ride imaginable. He was sweating on the neck and around his ears but otherwise felt fresh. I was much hotter than him, but felt that, for the last hour, I had been in heaven. We had just finished a fabulous run and must have jumped thirty fences that afternoon, one after the other, all big Leicestershire hedges.

The field was dispersing now, most of the locals cutting across country to their respective residences or farms. I was trying to orientate myself and work out which way would be best for me to find Liz and my horsebox, before it got completely dark. As I was passing Fred Barker, the master, I took off my muddy top hat: "Good night master," I said. "Good night Karol," he replied, "don't get lost in the dark." I wasn't worried so much about that. I was trying to avoid the main roads, since I knew that John, my mount, despite being the best ride across any country, was the worst possible ride in traffic, and at night, with car headlights blinding him, he would be murder.

Suddenly I heard someone trotting behind me. He too, when passing the master, said his "Goodnight master". I recognised the unmistakable, husky voice of Lord Paget, one of the great hunting characters of Leicestershire, mounted on one of his greys. I heard him remark, "Apart from a few sticky patches, a jolly good run. Goodnight." Lord Paget of Northampton, QC, a Labour peer, who according to gossip had only joined the labour party to spite his father, was not a typical socialist. He owned Lubenham Lodge, a few thousand acres of excellent grazing in the Fernie country and, despite his age, was a pretty difficult man to follow in a good hunt. He was also a great authority on the sport.

When eventually I found Liz, waiting for me in pitch darkness, when we had boxed up John and I had poured myself a hot cup of tea, Reggie Paget's words came back to me and I repeated them out loud: "Apart from a few sticky patches, a jolly good run."

Liz turned to me and asked, "Is that your description of the day?"

"Yes," I replied "It is. Come to think of it," I added, "it could also be a pretty accurate description of my life."

286